MONSTROUS OPERA

PRINCETON STUDIES IN OPERA
CAROLYN ABBATE AND ROGER PARKER
SERIES EDITORS

MONSTROUS OPERA

RAMEAU AND THE
TRAGIC TRADITION

Charles Dill

PRINCETON UNIVERSITY PRESS   PRINCETON, NEW JERSEY

Copyright © 1998 by Princeton University Press
Published by Princeton University Press, 41 William Street,
Princeton, New Jersey 08540
In the United Kingdom: Princeton University Press, Chichester,
West Sussex
All Rights Reserved

Library of Congress Cataloging-in-Publication Data
Dill, Charles William.
Monstrous opera : Rameau and the tragic tradition / Charles Dill.
p.   cm.
Includes bibliographical references (p.   ) and index.
ISBN 0-691-04443-0 (alk. paper)
1. Rameau, Jean Philippe, 1683–1764. Operas.
2. Opera—France—18th century.   3. Tragedy in music.   I. Title.
ML410.R2M66   1998
782.1′092—dc21   97-31073   CIP

This book has been composed in Galliard

Princeton University Press books are printed on acid-free paper and
meet the guidelines for permanence and durability of the Committee
on Production Guidelines for Book Longevity of the Council on
Library Resources

http://pup.princeton.edu

Printed in the United States of America

1 3 5 7 9 10 8 6 4 2

For My Parents

Contents

JEAN-PHILIPPE RAMEAU is by most measures a remarkable historical sub-ject. In making this assertion, I do not mean to belabor the notion that he is a subject *of* history: that he lived and worked 250 years ago, was an im-portant figure for the history of Western music, or is subject to attention from music historians. These observations we can take as self-evident re-flections of historiographic and musicological practice. Rather, I mean to call attention to Rameau's role as an agent *in* history. Few eighteenth-cen-tury composers worked with as much difficulty under the yoke of such a tradition as the Lullian *tragédie en musique*; few speculated as extensively about music theory; and few were written about, disparaged, praised, and argued over as was Rameau, certainly not by the likes of Voltaire and Rousseau. Carl Dahlhaus captures something of this distinction when he points out that historical subjects are more than the figures whom histori-ans observe: "The subject does not simply 'have' a history; it must produce one, and only in so doing does it become a subject at all."[1] This construc-tion, with its overtones of invention or performance, renders the historical subject less an interest for our detached perusal and more what he or she actually was: an active participant in the events we study. Adopting Dahlhaus's view, we could say that Rameau worked within French society and culture and in doing so constructed from them a historical subject.

Yet what I have in mind eludes Dahlhaus's model as well, since his for-mulation grants the historical agent a degree of authority that Rameau's case undermines: for the aristocrats, functionaries, and journalists who made up his audiences, Rameau was sometimes a hero and sometimes a vil-lain, sometimes a great composer and sometimes a hack, sometimes an im-portant thinker and sometimes an enigmatic joke. Rameau undoubtedly wanted to control his public image, as his unceasing polemics attest, but his success rate varied wildly, and his strategies can appear strange, even senseless, today. The historical subject produced in this manner cannot be congruent in every respect with the persona he intended, and this makes the historian's task doubly difficult. The historical subject is effectively twice removed from the historical scene: first by the familiar sense of in-tervening historical receptions, which the historian would ideally like to re-move, and second by the composer's lack of a coherent personage even in his own time. If we hold with Dahlhaus's formulation, then we should place more emphasis on its auxiliary verb. The historical subject *must* pro-duce itself, *must have* produced itself, as a consequence of performing the activities we deem significant—but what he or she produced is at best contingent.

I would argue that the issues Rameau contended with in his career made him a truly remarkable historical subject, albeit a contradictory and refractory one. We may choose not to relish the poststructuralist resonances of this situation, but they remain a necessary condition for our knowing him nevertheless. Along with his music, they constitute what we know best about someone Louis Laloy described as essentially unknowable: "Jean-Philippe Rameau was not disposed to confidences: aside from his works, brilliant in their freshness and audacity, he knew to keep his life secret, obscure, solitary, impenetrable. Thus, when he died, his panegyrists found themselves sorely hampered. All that one knew of him was reducible practically to the dates of the first performances of his operas, ballets, divertissements, and pastorales."[2] To borrow a distinction from Michel Foucault, we know a great deal about Rameau as an *author*—as someone who has been written about and discussed—but very little about him as a *writer*—as someone who actively wrote, composed, and participated in operatic debates, someone who in Dahlhaus's sense produced his historical subjectivity.[3] Surely some of the pleasure one derives from studying Rameau resides in the irony that an individual who dedicated so much of his career to reasoning about music could, in the end, remain so unreasonable with regard to himself.

This is not to say that Rameau fails to achieve a useful subjectivity for the historian, only that one observes him by what are at best indirect means. In this context it is worth recalling why at least some music critics and historians invoke historical subjects in the first place: we do so, as Dahlhaus liked to point out, to learn more about musical works. This being the case, it is not so important that we track down Rameau the composer-writer, the private individual who set notes down on paper, in order to have him "confide" in us, as Roland Barthes put it.[4] What Rameau intended to do is ultimately less important, because it is unknowable, than what contemporaries, critics, and historians believed his intentions to be. His historical agency has been transmitted to us not through his acts as a *writer,* but rather through the things others have written about him as Rameau, the *author.* Alexander Nehamas's rather more generous definition of *author* captures this notion of the historical subject as a nexus for interpretations. It has the added advantage of returning our attention to the artworks that led many of us to inquire in the first place: "In interpretation strictly conceived we account for the features of an object by appealing to the features of an unusual, original agent whose action we take it to be and who is manifested in it."[5] In the sense represented by Nehamas's model, we will always look for a "Rameau" to hold together our changing knowledge of eighteenth-century French opera and its repertories, styles, genres, and developments, but this figure will be no more synonymous with the composer-writer Rameau than the simulacrums imagined by his contemporaries. He will instead always be a manufactured entity, a composer-author, pieced together from observations, who allows us to discuss a group of related compositions.

Such ruminations may seem an indirect route to the discussion of Rameau's tragedies, but they are important precisely because previous treatments have tended to equate the composer-author with the composer-writer. Accounts of Rameau in the twentieth century, with a notable exception to be discussed momentarily, have treated him according to a life-and-works model: the composer's life and historical position have served as the basis for musical discussions, on the grounds that they will eventually yield up his musical secrets. In the case of a composer about whom we have so little personal information, the temptation necessarily follows to chase down still more information, in the hope that the combined mass will eventually provide the confidences that the composer himself withheld. Laloy, who despaired ever knowing the composer-writer Rameau, stated his intention nevertheless to pursue this elusive figure at no uncertain cost to propriety or dignity: "We have, since such is the need of posterity, forced the doors of [Rameau's] house and violated his sepulchre."[6] The need of posterity must be great indeed if the ostensible goal of understanding the composer, the better to understand his music, leads us even to violence. Yet in the end, we are left with little to justify this imagery; biography and composition in Laloy's hands remain mutually exclusive fields of inquiry. Instead, the compounding of historical detail—that knowledge, beyond the mere dates of compositions, to be wrested from the composer—allowed Laloy to evade musical observation altogether by the details' becoming a concern in their own right. Control over the historical subject does not necessarily result in control over the works.

    In early writings of the present century, such as those by Laloy and Lionel de La Laurencie, the tension between life and works was great enough to create a fundamental bifurcation.[7] Books were divided into discrete considerations first of the life and then of the works. In the category *life* writers discussed certain aspects of Rameau's career: the years prior to his arrival in Paris, the most important people around him, critical reactions to his works, critical reactions to his theoretical writings, the chronology of his compositions, and the peculiarities of his personality. In the category *works,* they reviewed the composer's most admired techniques: handling of choruses, airs, and dances; orchestration; and especially harmonic language. Laloy treated Rameau's theoretical writings as a third, equally hermetic, category; La Laurencie's combination of music theory and compositions within the category works, however, more accurately indicates that

Rameau's theoretical writings were a second sort of *work* to be distinguished from his life.

This split reappears without critical question in some of the most important recent studies of Rameau. One sees it in the articles for *The New Grove Dictionary of Music and Musicians,* where it rules by editorial default, and traces of this subjective dichotomy remain in Sylvie Bouissou's admirable study of *Les Boréades,* where an extended compositional history introduces, but remains sealed off from, discussions of *livret* and music.[8] What began as a strategic necessity has become a formula, and, as a result, the goals of the life-and-works format have been inverted: Rameau's works serve to confirm the known, established features of his life. That is, his music was indeed fresh and audacious, as admirers claimed; its effects were calculated, as critics suggested; and its excellence has made the composer himself worthy of study. Thus, Rameau remains a subject of history, but not a subject in history.

Paul-Marie Masson's *L'Opéra de Rameau* provides the most extensive and original critique of this problem. His book, which is the single most important model for discussing Rameau's music, rearranges the priorities of the life-and-works format to suggest that historical commentary can serve musical exegesis. Describing his 595-page monument to Rameau's operas as "a critical essay," he situates it over and against historical inquiries: "It is a question here of *criticism* and not history properly speaking. One will not find in what follows a detailed narrative of Rameau's dramatic career or the circumstances that accompanied the elaboration, creation, and reprises of each of his operas."[9] He suggests that he has deliberately set aside the historical data that ordinarily constitute the *life,* yet this data was hardly absent from his book.

What did this consummate music historian hope to gain by claiming to avoid history in general and *life* in particular? What Masson appears to have been seeking was less a removal of the life category from the familiar approach than a redistribution of priorities in which works would become the focal point of study. In his preface, Masson suggested that he found the state of historical data inadequate for a truly historical treatment, whereas the recent appearance of Rameau's *Oeuvres complètes* made a treatment of the music not only a pressing task but also an exciting prospect. This led him to hint at a more ambitious program. Projecting a form of hermeneutic circle onto his present and future work, Masson announced that he would use historical data only to obtain better readings of Rameau's music. Subsequent research, including a briefly entertained biographical companion to *L'Opéra de Rameau,* would draw on what was learned in this manner to develop better histories of French opera in general and Rameau in particular. By focusing on music, the critical essay would bind together disparate strands of historical knowledge. Though Masson's projected two-part project remained uncompleted, his synthesizing Hegelian vision set *L'Opéra de Rameau* apart from other writings on Rameau by treating the historical subject as open to development while imagining a future point when a truer, or at least stabler, history of Rameau would obtain. Masson's project thus at times sounds deceptively modern in its critical goals, as, for example, when he claims that "[o]ne of the principal tasks of the critic is to reconstruct the work in some manner alongside the author himself."[10] Rather than claiming to have known Rameau's intentions, to have received the composer's confidences, or to have pillaged them from the composer's sepulchre, Masson placed himself in a complex, dialectical relationship with the historical subject, imagining what it was like to be an active historical agent (much as in Dahlhaus's sense).

Yet in the end, as we see in the book's organization, Masson accomplished something rather different from what he promised. In his use of ostensibly neutral categories to divide and subdivide Rameau's music— livret, recitative, airs, vocal ensembles, dramatic symphonies, dance pieces, dramatic expression—*L'Opéra de Rameau* does not so much reconstruct the music alongside the composer as wrest the works from him in order to plot them on a conceptual grid. The particular form of criticism Masson practiced resembles less our own criticism at the end of the twentieth century than the scientistic style criticism popularized by Guido Adler at the beginning of this century.[11] His method accomplishes its goals through a process of radical homogenization, reducing different repertory to its lowest common denominator with procrustean confidence. Far from actively reimagining the moment of creation, which would mark a reasonably honest approach to critical activity, Masson instead subjected Rameau's works to a form of pigeonholing. What he accomplished, then, is not so different from the life-and-works model as it first appears. He may deflect attention from the composer-writer to the written work, but this is no more than what most life-and-works writers would have considered the goal of their methodology. The tools may differ as well, but this has less to do with criticism, in the modern sense, than with the shift in topic he attends to. The goals are the same: to pry loose those secrets that the composer refused to give up, to render him and his works manageable, and to avoid potentially misleading information offered up in the name of the composer-author. As in the life-and-works model, then, Masson's efforts result principally in acts of confirmation, proving tautologically that Rameau's operas manifest a compositional style identifiable with Rameau and with the most significant features of various popular genres, the properties of French music in general, or the kind of music written in the middle decades of the eighteenth century. Both the life-and-works and the style-critical approaches ultimately treat music as the product of historical agents— whether composer, genre, nation, or period—without necessarily treating the works themselves as historical artifacts.[12] They reiterate the priority of the composer-as-author even as they take pains to locate the composer-as-writer.

My point here is not to challenge traditional musicological approaches to Rameau but to explore how one might proceed with the task of better understanding the intricate relationship between composer and music. It is my contention that to develop our understanding of Rameau, we cannot continue collecting facts in the time-honored hope that their combined mass will reveal the composer-writer or otherwise provide us with his confidences. Rather, we must recognize that for any given notion of Rameau we entertain, there are always other historical versions of Rameau awaiting study, residing in the vast and heterogeneous body of criticism—polemical, political, historical, style-critical—brought to bear on the composer. Treating the works as artifacts leads us to relinquish the task of discovering the composer-writer and forces us instead to concentrate on the only figure available, the composer-author.

In what follows, then, I propose to give up a line of inquiry I perceive to be largely futile. By no means do I refer to the interesting and profitable task of collecting historical data, whose value through the course of the twentieth century has become obvious, but rather to the more questionable one of claiming that this historical data in some way reveals the music's inner workings. The promise may still exist, but in much the same way as the thorny question concerning the value that Beethoven's sketchbooks have for understanding his completed works, the value of this historical documentation in its own right remains unproven. Instead, I propose to let the tragedies take on the central role and to push historical data into a peripheral, dependent relationship with them. This sounds much like the promises Masson offered up at the outset of *L'Opéra de Rameau,* and the similarity is intentional. Studying how the works created possibilities for critical responses, and hence the potential for historical subjectivities, still strikes me as a useful methodology. I am not, however, asserting one of the standard methodologies of modern musicology, whether style criticism, source criticism, analysis, or whatever. For example, although I will employ analysis, my goals are not analytic ones. In the case of Rameau, whereas analysis can almost always turn up something of interest, it threatens under extensive application to diminish the complex relationship between works, composer, and audience that initially provided the works with historical significance. These are the very meanings that allowed Rameau to assume such a complex role as a composer-author. Similarly, although source criticism will be of considerable importance at several points in this study, the goals I have in mind are not source-critical. A catalogue of source information ultimately can no more stand in for the actual work than a score or recording can.

What makes Rameau's operas significant is at least in part that they serve as a ground upon which the composer and his audiences contested the issues related to authorship: the properties that marked a good *tragédie en musique,* the properties that made a composer a good composer of tragedies, the place of musical craft within French operatic music, the role of the French public in shaping the composer's career, the roles a composer assumed in society, and the marks culture left on musical composition. We know of these works (in a way that we do not, for example, know those of François Francoeur and François Rebel), precisely because of the public attention they have received. This historical process does not separate life from work or work from life, but instead it forces the two categories into a richer dialectical relationship by acknowledging the work's status as a signifier in French culture. Accordingly, music is no longer the product of a single, easily designated historical agent or of various historicist entities; rather it exists in history, having a being-in-history. Because of this, it is dynamic, its status changing in response to the heterogeneous interpretations imposed upon it. Because audiences do not agree on what made a work good, a composer gifted, and so on, any given tragedy by Rameau becomes a kind of palimpsest. And among the hands reinscribing these documents, the composer's must be counted. Rameau was not satisfied to present a work in its ideal state, leaving it to fate: he revised and recomposed his works, in the early weeks of production and especially for subsequent revivals; he responded to sometimes brutal criticism with theoretical justifications of his ideas and he argued publicly over the opera's content. If we are in some sense to understand his works, then we must understand how they were transfixed by competing, semiotic interests.

Patchwork composer and patchwork opera—our inability to obtain a whole and conclusive view of either is fascinating to no small extent because it mirrors a similar inability among eighteenth-century commentators. They, however, had a means for dealing with individuals and creations of this kind. They called them "monstrous," and in so naming they found them easier to deal with.

This wide-ranging reconsideration of the relationships between composer, work, and audience has led me to reconsider as well a number of different sources. As a result, the transcriptions of eighteenth-century texts, including livrets and scores, have retained the original orthography, and the translations are mine unless otherwise noted. This same concern has also led me to a greater appreciation of the eighteenth-century printed scores, which employed reduced orchestration, because in most instances these were the most widely circulated versions of the music. These scores have, unless I have indicated otherwise, served as the basis for my musical examples. I have made some small alterations to the musical texts for the sake of clarity and consistency, but in general I have tried to conform to the original orthography and layout wherever possible.

The list of friends and colleagues who have contributed information, ideas, criticism, and encouragement is large indeed. In a brief list I must include Bruce Alan Brown, Scott Burnham, Thomas Christensen, Susan Cook, David Crook, Julie D'Acci, Lawrence Earp, Cynthia M. Gessele, Thomas Green, Brian Hyer, Wolfgang Kemp, Pamela Potter, Elizabeth Powers, Ron Radano, Lois Rosow, Milt Sleeter, Ellen Sleeter, Jennifer Strauss, and Marina Warner. The original manuscript benefited greatly from a careful reading by Anne Heiles for Princeton University Press. Some of the ideas presented here grew out of an invaluable year as a Dissertation Fellow at the Getty Center for the History of Art and the Humanities. Portions were completed with assistance from the Wisconsin Alumni Research Fund and a contribution to the University of Wisconsin Foundation by the family of Charles Rogan. Finally, I must express my gratitude to Sarah and Kevin Dill for their forbearance and support.

Portions of chapters 2 and 3 have been reprinted from "Rameau Reading Lully: Meaning and System in Rameau's Recitative Tradition," *Cambridge Opera Journal* 6 (March 1994): 1–17, with the permission of Cambridge University Press. Portions of chapter 4 are reprinted from "Creative Process in Rameau's *Castor et Pollux,*" in *The Creative Process,* Studies in the History of Music, no. 3 (New York: Broude Brothers, 1992), 93–106, with the permission of Broude Brothers Limited (copyright 1993 by Broude Brothers Limited). I am grateful to Roger Parker, Ronald Broude, and Ellen Beebe for their careful reading of these essays.

C livret 1737   CASTOR/ET / POLLUX, / *TRAGEDIE* / *Représen-*
tée pour la prémiere fois, / PAR L'ACADEMIE
ROYALE / DE MUSIQUE; / *Le vingt-quatriéme*
jour d'Octobre 1737. / DE L'IMPRIMERIE / De
Jean-Baptiste-Christophe Ballard, / Seul Imprimeur du Roy, & de l'Académie Royale de Musique
/ M. D CCXXXVII. / *AVEC PRIVILEGE DU ROY.*

C livret 1754   *CASTOR / ET / POLLUX, / TRAGÉDIE, /*
REPRÉSENTÉE / *POUR LA PREMIERE FOIS,* /
PAR L'ACADÉMIE ROYALE / *DE MUSIQUE,* / *Le*
24 *Octobre* 1737. / Et Remise au Théâtre le huit Jan-
vier 1754. / *PRIX XXX SOLS.* / *AUX DÉPENS DE*
L'ACADÉMIE. / A PARIS, Chez la V. Delormel &
Fils, Imprimeur de ladite / Académie, rue du Foin, à
l'Image Ste. Geneviéve. / *On trouvera des Livres de*
Paroles à la Salle de l'Opéra. / M. DCC. LIV. / *AVEC*
APPROBATION ET PRIVILEGE DU ROY.

C score 1737   CASTOR ET POLLUX, / TRAGEDIE / MISE EN
MUSIQUE / *Par Monsieur* Rameau, / Représentée
pour la premiere fois, par l'Académie Royale / de
Musique, le 24 Octobre 1737. / *Prix en blanc douze*
livres. / SE VEND A PARIS, / Chez{ / PRAULT fils,
Quay de Conty, vis-à-vis la descente du Pont-neuf, à la
Charité, / la veuve BOIVIN, rue Saint Honoré, à la
Regle d'or, / M. LECLAIR, rue de Roule, à la Croix
d'or, / M. DUVAL, Marchand Papetier, proche l'O-
pera, / &chez l'AUTEUR, rue des Bons-Enfans. /
Avec Approbation & Privilege du Roy.

C score 1754   CASTOR / ET POLLUX. / TRAGÉDIE. / *Mise en*
Musique / PAR Mᴿ. RAMEAU. / *Représentée pour la*
premiere fois par L'Academie Royale de Musique Le 24.
/ *Octobre 1737. Refondu, Et remis au Théâtre au Mois*
de Decembre 1754. / Prix en blanc 15ᵗʰ. / *Gravée par*
Le Sʳ. Hue. / SE VEND A PARIS / Chez { / *L'Auteur*
Rue des bons Enfans. / *Et aux adresses ordinaires.* / *A*
la Porte de l'Opera. / *Avec approbation Et privilege du*
Roy. / *Imprimée par Monthulay.*

CTW   Rameau, Jean-Philippe. *Complete Theoretical Writings.* 6 vols. Edited by Erwin R. Jacobi. N.p.: American Institute of Musicology, 1967–1972.

CWV   Voltaire [François-Marie Arouet]. *The Complete Works of Voltaire.* Edited by Theodore Besterman et al. 135 vols. Oxford: The Voltaire Foundation, 1968– .

D livret 1739 DARDANUS, / *TRAGEDIE* / REPRÉSENTÉE POUR LA PREMIERE FOIS, / PAR L'ACADEMIE ROYALE / DE MUSIQUE, / *Le Jeudy dix-neuf Novembre* 1739. / DE L'IMPRIMERIE / DE JEAN-BAPTISTE-CHRISTOPHE BALLARD, / Seul Imprimeur du Roy, et de l'Academie Royale de Musique. / A Paris, au Mont-Parnasse, ruë Saint-Jean-de-Beauvais. / M. D CCXXXIX. / *AVEC PRIVILEGE DU ROY.* / LE PRIX EST DE XXX. SOLS.

D livret 1744 DARDANUS, / *TRAGEDIE* / REPRÉSENTÉE POUR LA PREMIERE FOIS, / PAR L'ACADEMIE ROYALE / DE MUSIQUE, / *Le Jeudy dix-neuf Novembre* 1739. / NOUVELLE EDITION, / *Remise au théâtre, le mardi* 21 *Avril* 1744. / DE L'IMPRIMERIE / DE JEAN-BAPTISTE-CHRISTOPHE BALLARD, / Doyen des imprimeurs du Roy, seul pour la musique, / et pour l'Academie royale de musique. / A Paris, au Mont-Parnasse, ruë saint-Jean-de-Beauvais. / M. DCC XLIV. / *AVEC PRIVILEGE DU ROY.* / LE PRIX EST DE XXX SOLS.

D score 1739 DARDANUS, / *TRAGEDIE*, / MISE EN MUSIQUE / PAR M. RAMEAU, / ET REPRESENTÉE POUR LA PREMIERE FOIS, / PAR L'ACADÉMIE ROYALE DE MUSIQUE, / Le dix-neuf Octobre 1739. / *Le Prix, en blanc,* 13. liv. *Et relié,* 15 liv. / A PARIS, / CHEZ { / L'AUTEUR, RUE DES BONS-ENFANS, A L'HOTEL D'EFFIAT. / LA VEUVE BOIVIN, RUE S. HONORE', A LA REGLE D'OR. / M. LE CLAIR, RUE DU ROULE, A LA CROIX D'OR. / Mᶜ MONET, GRANDE PLACE DE L'HOSTEL DE SOISSONS, A LA LYRE D'OR. / *AVEC APPROBATION ET PRIVILEGE DU ROY.*

D score 1744 DARDANUS, / *NOUVELLE TRAGÉDIE,* / MISE EN MUSIQUE / PAR M. RAMEAU, / ET RÉPRÉSENTÉE POUR LA PREMIERE FOIS, / *PAR L'ACADÉMIE ROYALE DE MUSIQUE,* / LE 7. AVRIL 1744. / *Le prix, en blanc,* 13. liv. *Et relié,* 15. liv. / A

	PARIS, / CHEZ { / L'AUTEUR, RUE S. HONORE', A LA REGLE D'OR, / M. LE CLAIR, RUE DU ROULE, A LA CROIX D'OR. / *AVEC APPROBATION ET PRIVILEGE DU ROY.*
F-Pn	Paris, Bibliothèque nationale.
H livret 1733	HIPPOLYTE / ET / ARICIE, / *TRAGEDIE,* / REPRÉSENTÉE POUR LA PREMIERE FOIS, / PAR L'ACADEMIE ROYALE / DE MUSIQUE; / *Le Jeudy premier Octobre* 1733. / DE L'IMPRIMERIE / De JEAN-BAPTISTE-CHRISTOPHE BALLARD, / Seul Imprimeur du Roy, & de l'Académie Royale de Musique. / M. D CCXXXIII. / *AVECU PRIVILEGE DU ROY.* / LE PRIX EST DE XXX. SOLS.
H livret 1742	HIPPOLYTE / ET / ARICIE, / *TRAGEDIE,* / REPRÉSENTÉE / PAR L'ACADEMIE ROYALE / DE MUSIQUE; / Pour la premiere fois, le jeudi premier octobre 1733. / *Remise au théâtre le mardy 11 septembre* 1742. / DE L'IMPRIMERIE / DE J-B-CHRISTOPHE BALLARD, seul imprimeur / du Roi, et de l'academie royale de musique; / Paris, au Mont-Parnasse, rue saint Jean-de-Beauvais. / M. DCC. XLII. / *Avec Privilége de Sa Majesté.* / LE PRIX EST DE XXX. SOLS.
H score 1733	HIPPOLITE / *ET* / ARICIE / *Tragedie Mise en Musique* / *PAR* / M^R. RAMEAU / *Représentée par l'Academie* / *Royale de Musique* / *Le Jeudy Premier Octobre 1733.* / PARTITION IN FOLIO / Gravé par De Gland / *Prix en blanc 18th.* / *et 21th. Reliée.* / A PARIS / Chez { / *L'Hauteur Rue du Chantre* / *Le S^r.* *Boivin M^d. Rüe S^t. Honoré à la Regle d'Or.* / *Le S^r. Le Clerc M^d. Rüe du Roule à la Croix d'Or.* / *Avec Privilegé du Roy* / *Imprimé par Montulé.*
LIG	LES INDES GALANTES, / *BALLET,* / RÉDUIT A QUATRE GRANDS CONCERTS: / AVEC UNE NOUVELLE ENTRE'E COMPLETTE. / *Par Monsieur RAMEAU.* / Le Prix en blanc douze livres. / SE VEND A PARIS, / Chez { / M. BOIVIN, rüe Saint Honoré, à la Regle d'Or. / M. LECLAIR, rue du Roulle, à la Croix d'Or. / L'AUTEUR, rüe des Bons Enfans, à l'Hôtel d'Effiat. / *AVEC PRIVILEGE DU ROI.*
JPR	*Jean-Philippe Rameau. Colloque International organisé par la société Rameau. Dijon—21–24 septembre 1983.* Edited by Jérôme de La Gorce. Paris: Champion, 1987.

LSL	Rousseau, Jean-Jacques. *Lettre sur la musique françoise.* 1753.
NS	Rameau, Jean-Philippe. *Nouveau système de musique theorique, où l'on découvre le principe de toutes les regles necessaires à la pratique.* Paris: Jean-Baptiste-Christophe Ballard, 1726.
OC	Rameau, Jean-Philippe. *Oeuvres complètes.* 18 vols. Edited by Camille Saint-Saëns et al. Paris: A. Durand et fils, 1895–1924. Reprint, New York: Broude Brothers, 1968.
OCV	Voltaire [François-Marie Arouet]. *Oeuvres complètes de Voltaire.* 52 vols. Edited by Louis Moland. Paris: Garnier Frères, 1883–85.
OSN	Rameau, Jean-Philippe. *Observations sur notre instinct pour la musique, et son principe.* Paris: Prault fils, Lambert, Duchesne, 1754.
QDB	Launay, Denise, editor. *La Querelle des bouffons.* 3 vols. Geneva: Minkoff, 1973.
RG	*Recueil general des opera representez par l'Académie royale de musique, depuis son etablissement.* 16 vols. Paris: Ballard, 1703–1746. Facsimile ed. in 3 vols., Geneva: Slatkine, 1971.
Z livret 1749	*ZOROASTRE, / TRAGEDIE. / REPRESENTÉE / PAR L'ACADEMIE ROYALE / DE MUSIQUE, / POUR LA PREMIERE FOIS, / Le Vendredy cinq Décembre 1749. / PRIX XXX SOLS. / AUX DEPENS DE L'ACADEMIE.* / On trouvera les Livres de Paroles à la Salle de l'Opera & à l'Académie Royale / de Musique, rue S. Nicaise. / M. D.C.C. XLIX. / *AVEC APPROBATION ET PRIVILEGE DU ROY.*
Z livret 1756	*ZOROASTRE, / OPÉRA, / REPRÉSENTÉ / POUR LA PREMIERE FOIS / PAR L'ACADÉMIE ROYALE / DE MUSIQUE, / Le 5. Décembre 1749. / ET REMIS AU THÉATRE / Le Mardi 20 Janvier 1756. / PRIX XXX SOLS. / AUX DÉPENS DE L'A-CADÉMIE.* / A PARIS, Chez la V. Delormel & Fils, Imprimeur de / ladite Académie, rue du Foin à l'Image St. Geneviéve. / *On trouvera des Livres de Paroles à la Salle de l'Opéra.* / M. DCC. LVI. / *AVEC APPRO-BATION ET PRIVILEGE DU ROI.*

MONSTROUS OPERA

CHAPTER 1

Monstrous Opera

I BEGIN not with tragedy but with Jean-Philippe Rameau's earliest foray into the lighter genre now referred to as *opéra-ballet,* and I begin not with the 1735 work itself but with its engraved edition, first published in the following year. The preface to the 1736 edition, or print, of *Les Indes galantes* opens with a surprising admission:

> The public having appeared less satisfied with the scenes of [*Les*] *Indes galantes* than with the rest of the work, I believed I ought not question its judgment, and for this reason I present it here with only the symphonies, interspersed with some short songs, *ariettes,* measured recitatives, duos, trios, quartets, and choruses from the prologue and first three entrées, which in all form more than eighty detached pieces from which I have formed four large *concerts* in different keys. These symphonies have been ordered as *pièces de clavecin,* and their ornaments conform to those in my other *pièces de clavecin,* without this preventing them from being played by other instruments, since this would only entail taking the highest notes for the *dessus* and the lowest notes for the bass. Whatever in the score is too high for the cello can be transposed an octave lower.[1]

These remarks characterize the print first by its omission of the opera's scenes. The public had expressed dissatisfaction with them, and in response the composer or the publisher removed them. The word *scène* implied various things in eighteenth-century France, but since the composer went on to list what remained after removing them, what he meant in this instance is clear. What was missing was recitative. The public did not approve of the plot-bearing passages in this opera, and so the music appeared in print deprived of its stories. Yet this abbreviation only hints at the transformation the work underwent. With its unusually late appearance, the print bears witness to extensive reinterpretation. Someone—apparently the composer himself, given the wording of the preface—reordered the contents of the prologue and three entrées in an attempt to make sense of what was left once the recitative scenes had been removed.[2] In this preface, marked by hesitations, blandishments, and pains taken to inform of the print's utility, we encounter the issues that characterize Rameau's later attempts at composing tragic opera: concerns with genre; a willingness, even an eagerness, to revise and recast; and a belief in a public, real or imagined, that observed, criticized, and in some sense determined the value of the composer's work.

Understanding something of this relationship between composer and audience will take us far toward understanding Rameau and his tragedies.

Such a print might at first seem to be of minor significance. After all, scores published in abbreviated format were common by 1736. Publishers balanced the expenses of publication against the public's desire for current, popular music, and title pages announced the scores' incomplete state with little compunction. A print of an opéra-ballet by Thomas la Doué Bertin, for example, contained an *Extrait de l'opéra des Plaisirs de la Campagne, contenant les airs à chanter, les récits qui se peuvent détacher, quelques scènes, et tous les airs à jouer*. A title page of a work by André Campra shows that even the prestigious *tragédie en musique* was not exempt from this treatment: *Extrait de l'opéra d'Iphigénie, contenant les airs à chanter & récits qui se peuvent détacher: la fureur d'Oreste, la première & la seconde scène du cinquième acte, et tous les airs à jouer*.[3] Publishers took what could be "detached" from these operas and made it available for performance in salons. Prospective buyers would not have assumed a published score was useful for much more than this; printers commonly published even unabridged scores with reduced orchestration, designed for performance at the keyboard rather than by an orchestra. In light of this publishing practice, Rameau's preface appears to be little more than an explanation or a guide to the contents of this particular edition; as a result, several scholars have not regarded the print as noteworthy. Louis Laloy concluded that Rameau did not mind arranging the work for concerts, and Graham Sadler's revised list of Rameau's works for *The New Grove French Baroque Masters* states that the print is a keyboard arrangement, pure and simple.[4]

The ease with which we register this as historical fact belies the serious consequences the print must have had for its composer. At pains in the preface to be polite, even solicitous, toward public opinion, Rameau may have felt he was fighting for his career with this, his second opera. His judgment as a composer—at least as a composer of recitative—had been challenged, and he responded with a version different from the one he might first have wished to publish. Using part entrepreneurship and part confession, in his preface Rameau undertook contradictory tasks: to convince the reader of the print's utility while nevertheless directing attention to the print's incomplete state. In a gesture foreign to its time and place, the composer challenged the logical motive of selling copies out of some more basic need he had to explain what this particular score was. The singling out of recitative, which was taken seriously in eighteenth-century France was especially damaging for him.[5] In a society that granted little intrinsic value to music apart from poetry, opera became insignificant without its plots. Thus Rameau exhibited his greatest concern for repositioning the original work in this altered, print version: to dismiss the original would have devalued his own newly won status as an opera composer. As we will see, this forced him to struggle with the problem of genre as reflected in the print. If some historians regard the print as unremarkable, others have found it strange and outlandish. Charles Malherbe wrote, "A single edition appears, and yet in a form so incomplete, so bizarre even, that one would have difficulty establishing in the history of the Opéra another instance of the same act. Parallel examples would be rare indeed, and it is perhaps unique in its genre."[6]

Rameau showed himself eager to salvage *Les Indes galantes* as opera wherever possible, as we see even on the title page. If the labeling of printed scores as *extraits* or *changements* was common, the title page of *Les Indes galantes* indicates a rather different procedure. It begins conventionally by proclaiming the work an opéra-ballet—"LES INDES GALANTES, / BALLET" (or, in some copies, "ballet-héroïque")—but undercuts this assertion with a different one in smaller typeface: "RÉDUIT A QUATRE GRANDS CONCERTS." Avoided are the implications of extraction, alteration, or other commercially acceptable forms of abbreviation, in favor of a reassertion of wholeness, made possible by recasting the genre of the print: *Les Indes galantes* was formerly a ballet, but now it is something else; an act has been performed upon it. Perhaps the purpose of the title page was to state, "This *was* the opéra-ballet *Les Indes galantes,* but it has been reduced to something else" or "This is music from the ballet *Les Indes galantes,* now presented in a different context," but either way a move or shift between genres takes place. Indeed, the categories *ballet* and *concert* may be less important than the verb connecting them, *réduire,* which could mean abbreviation but which also carries interesting overtones of compulsion (as in the statement, "I have been reduced to these circumstances"). The print, Rameau tells us, is not at all the ballet heard at the Opéra; he takes care to point out that it includes, in addition to the four concerts, a new entrée, music as yet unheard by the public. He feels justified here in reasserting the work's operatic status: "Since the new entrée *Les Sauvages,* which I add to the first three entrées, has not yet been heard, I have risked presenting it complete, happy if success responds to my concerns."[7] If we view the print simply as a keyboard arrangement, this inclusion appears to be a mistake, and yet for Rameau it clearly was not.[8] He stated that the presence of *Les Sauvages* was intentional, and he thereby created a truly unique print that swerves between impossible categorizations: an opéra-ballet without recitative, an opéra-ballet conceived as instrumental suites, or a set of concerts to which an entrée has been added.

We may conclude that the decision to omit recitatives from the 1736 print was not the composer's preference and that he went along with it under duress. If this is so, then the public pressure brought to bear on *Les Indes galantes* makes the print quite different from the *extraits* cited previously, its lack of recitatives implying that censure, censorship, suppression, prohibition, control, constraint, or containment had occurred. Such

duress, or pressure, would have been a significant, even a defining, moment
in the career of any composer. The composer who found himself in such a
position would have been well aware of how the opera-going public sa-
vored such incidents, talking about who ordered them, who enforced
them, and what the composer's privately vented feelings were. Assuming
that the events leading to the transformation of the opéra-ballet were real
and not imagined—sternly worded public rejection and not merely epigramatic rumors designed to hurt or ridicule—the physical state of the
score presented a reminder for all to see. Thus, the omission of recitative
from *Les Indes,* its absence, was paradoxically a noisy one resounding with
implications that we can only begin to imagine, implications that lead us
to question the role of genre in French opera.

If the 1736 print of *Les Indes galantes* is, as Malherbe observed, "bizarre
and unique," this is because among prints of its time it was chimerical, a
monstrous concoction of parts that ultimately amounted to neither opera
nor keyboard suite. The score purported to be everything to its audiences
and yet, in the end, was recognizable as no single entity. It is useless now
for most of the tasks that attract modern scholarship; no source could contribute less to a critical edition. Thus categorizing the print as a historical
event is not enough. Stating that Rameau did not mind arranging this edition or calling it a collection of keyboard suites serves no purpose other
than to simplify it for present-day consumption while failing to register its
complexity either as a cultural artifact or as a document from Rameau's career. Jonathan Culler, writing of the Swiss linguist Ferdinand de Saussure,
has observed that unusual incidents have meaning because they are indi-
cators of social and cultural activity: "When studying human behavior the
investigator cannot simply dismiss as subjective impressions the meaning
behavior has for members of a society. If people see an action as impolite,
that is a crucial fact, a social fact. To ignore the meanings actions and objects have in a society would be to study mere physical events. Anyone an-
alyzing human behavior is concerned not with events themselves but with
events that have meaning." Svetlana Alpers similarly suggests that documents of this kind call attention to the artwork as more than an emblem of
style or part of an *oeuvre,* pointing to it as a historical object in its own right.
The work participates in history.[9] The print of *Les Indes* is thus a magnet
for the critical concerns about Rameau during the first decade of his career
as an opera composer. If it resists our efforts to place it among other scores
of the time, it reminds us nevertheless of the intractability of Rameau and
his works for his audiences. It exemplifies how little we know of the composer's motivations and how surprising some of his actions were (and are)
to observers. To get at the importance of this document, we must devote
our attention less to *what* it means than to *how* it means, to how the opéra-

ballet *Les Indes galantes* drew together composer, supporters, and critics to redefine opera at a given historical moment.

The abbreviation of the original *Les Indes* in print is of course a widely recognized event in Rameau's career, cited most frequently as evidence of the antagonism Rameau experienced in the 1730s. Pierre-François Desfontaines's journal *Observations sur les écrits modernes* provides the principal document among critical responses to the opera, the observations appearing in the form of an anonymous letter to its editor:

> Yesterday I went to the Opéra. Ignoring the words [of *Les Indes galantes*] is not difficult. The music is perpetual magic in which nature plays no role. Nothing is so scabrous and rough: it is a path upon which one unceasingly jolts. The composer dispenses with buying the abbé de Saint-Pierre's ["joggling"] chair, such an excellent one is this opera, whose airs would be very proper for jarring the benumbed nerves of a paralytic![10] How different this jerking about is from the sweet disturbances that Campra, Destouches, Montéclair, Mouret, etc., knew to bring about. Unintelligibility, gibberish, neologism wishes to pass for discourse in music. There is too much of it. I am pulled about, flayed, dislocated by this diabolical sonata, *Les Indes galantes*.[11]

The vehemence of these remarks is a familiar theme in Rameau research, though the example is relatively early: *Castor et Pollux* (1737) and *Dardanus* (1739) would attract still more commentary in this vein, whereas earlier critics had limited their remarks to rumor and epigram.[12]

What is most striking, for our purposes, is the distance between such historical perceptions of Rameau's works as this one and our own perceptions. We now see in his operas a difference in degree from earlier works by other composers. Rameau's works were larger, more heavily orchestrated, and employed more complex harmonic writing, but in these respects they continued and extended trends reaching back to the very works by Destouches and Campra that Desfontaines's correspondent so evidently admired.[13] Where we see a difference in degree, the journal correspondent saw a difference in kind, a musical force so potent it threw the status of the work *qua* opera into question. Did earlier observers hear with ears more sensitive than ours? Some audience members of that time, Desfontaines's correspondent among them, still regarded Italian instrumental sonatas with suspicion, whereas we casually listen to the likes of Schönberg. Rameau's contemporaries must have been sensitive to the vicissitudes of their musical fashion in a way we cannot be. Still, we have brought a considerable research technology to bear on this repertory—editions, archives, source criticism, and analysis—and accordingly we should be able to observe this difference even if we cannot experience it firsthand.

We must measure the distance between perceptions of Rameau's works in his day and ours in cultural terms, as Culler and Alpers advocated:

Rameau's contemporaries unpacked different semiotic baggage than we do. Desfontaines's anonymous letter, for example, does not focus on the relationship between poetry and music, as a modern scholar might, but instead dismisses altogether the poetry of *Les Indes*. We must remember that, for many French music lovers, music *was* the issue.[14] Fontenelle's exasperated cry "Sonate, que me veux-tu?" remained a valid one for many audience members, and it is no coincidence that Desfontaines's correspondent used the word *sonata* to describe *Les Indes*. The word appears often in Rameau criticism. Yet we must remember too that the status of music was changing. Fontenelle, who was seventy-eight years old when *Les Indes* premiered, belonged to an earlier generation, and extensive changes in the status of music had occurred since he uttered that statement in his youth. Opéra-ballet had not only been introduced to the repertory of the Académie royale de musique, but had even undergone several stylistic transformations by this time. Instrumental music, and especially Italianate sonatas, had grown in popularity.[15] As Desfontaines made clear in responding to the correspondent's letter, by no means did everyone agree with its negative assessments: "The bad humor of the letter's author does not prevent the public from regarding Monsieur Rameau as one of the great musicians of our century. The most solid reproach one can make of his music is that the French ear is not enough accustomed to it. But how many people today still cannot enjoy the sonatas of Corelli and Vivaldi, for whom all connoisseurs nevertheless make such a great case?"[16] Even members of the same audience came to this music with differently attuned ears, and so it would appear that, whatever the state of their aural abilities, some of their interpretive strategies were far more sensitive than our own.

There is much to learn from the tension between the anonymous writer's and Desfontaines's responses. Desfontaines does not defend Rameau, as a modern writer would, by suggesting that the link between poetry and music was strong in *Les Indes galantes;* rather, he agrees with the critic. The substance of his defense is that by the mid-1730s the correspondent should have become accustomed to this kind of music. He should have familiarized himself with it because other people knowledgeable in music, its connoisseurs, had already done so. There was a strong generational element in the opposing opinions that existed independently of Rameau; the quarrel between *Lullistes* and *Ramistes* implicitly carried in its juxtaposition an echo of the seventeenth-century quarrel between ancients and moderns.[17] We might even argue that, from our perspective, Rameau invited disagreement without doing anything particularly extreme. He was certainly not the first composer accused of science, mathematics, and learning because his music presented difficulties; he was not the first about whom epigrams were written.[18] Rameau had by this time established his credentials as a *musician*—and the word critics used to describe opera composers is surely significant—

through his three sets of keyboard music, six cantatas, and five theoretical treatises. His first opera, *Hippolyte et Aricie* (1733), had contained surprising musical events, including an infamous exploration of enharmonic writing in the much-discussed second *Trio des parques*, whose wrenching enharmonic modulations had proven too difficult to perform. Even before hearing a single note audiences may have assumed *Les Indes galantes* was difficult, or at least problematic.

Les Indes galantes did present its listeners with problems. Writing on the topic of "expression" for the *Encyclopédie*, Louis de Cahusac mentioned them in terms of the generational conflict noted by Desfontaines: "*Les Indes galantes* appeared in 1735 to be an insurmountable difficulty. The majority of spectators departed [from the theater] declaiming against a music supercharged with sixteenth-notes, from which nothing could be retained. Six months later, all of the airs, from the overture to the last gavotte, were parodied and known to everyone. By the 1751 revival, our parterre sang "Brillant Soleil," etc., with as much facility as our fathers 'psalmized' *Armide est encore plus aimable*, etc."[19] Like Desfontaines and other commentators, Cahusac saw the problem as one of becoming familiar with Rameau's music. Familiarity bred, if not outright pleasure, at least a benign contempt.

Nevertheless, the *Les Indes galantes* print does not allow us to escape so easily, for there is still more to it than meets eye or ear. What, for example, had made "Brillant Soleil" seem such a good example of the problems created by Rameau's music? It contains examples of melismatic singing that might have seemed routine by the mid-1730s, short modulations to the submediant and supertonic keys, and a rather noisy (scabrous and rough?) accompaniment, but it is no *Trio des parques*. To the extent that the piece differs from earlier music, the difference is in degree, yet Rameau's supporters and detractors alike heard it as different in kind. Nor do our questions end here. However difficult "Brillant Soleil" proved to be, the print included the piece, and the composer should have omitted it if problematic pieces were the issue. Why was recitative omitted from the opéra-ballet instead? Cahusac, Desfontaines, and Desfontaines's correspondent ignored the recitative of *Les Indes galantes*, treating it as irrelevant to the discussion of Rameau. Whatever may have been distasteful about Rameau's recitative (and surely it possessed no single, ongoing feature so offensive as to force the removal) does not seem sufficient to justify the strange shape of the 1736 print.

Without diminishing the historical importance of Rameau's innovative compositional style, we must consider the possibility that something more than sixteenth-notes or unusual harmonies led to criticism of his operas. Here again Desfontaines's correspondent offers some clues when he raises the question of intelligibility by comparing *Les Indes galantes* to a sonata. Many observers believed that whereas textless music was describable, it could not be intelligible because it lacked semantic content: music could never signify meanings in the same way words did. The remarks of the abbé Jean-Baptiste Dubos were typical. The only instrumental music he admired was the mimetic music used in opera to depict dramatic events, and his remarks establish a clear hierarchy between music that possessed semantic content through imitation and music that did not:

> These symphonies that seem to us so beautiful when they are employed to imitate certain sounds would appear insipid to us—they would appear downright bad to us—if employed to imitate other sounds. The symphony from the opera *Issé* . . . would seem ridiculous if it were placed in the tomb scene of *Amadis*. These pieces of music, which move us so sensibly when they form part of a dramatic action, give rather mediocre pleasure when heard as sonatas or detached symphonies by someone who has never heard them at the Opéra and consequently cannot judge them without knowing their greatest merit, that is, the connection they have with the action, where they play a role, so to speak.[20]

By calling *Les Indes* a sonata, Desfontaines's correspondent claimed the opera was unintelligible in the same way that instrumental music was unintelligible.[21] That this term is more than simple metaphor is evident; *Les Indes* did indeed possess a livret, which should have provided its music with the necessary intelligibility. By dismissing the livret, the correspondent performed the same willful distortion found in the print, cutting away the opera's plot in order to make a point about it. With acts such as these, Rameau's critics conveyed fundamental information about their responses to his operas, and the terms that ring loudest are not those of musical style but those of communication: unintelligibility, gibberish, neologism.

It is, I think, relevant that Jeffrey Kallberg has reformulated notions of musical genre along the lines of intelligibility. Criticizing musicological treatments of genre that emphasize shared stylistic attributes, Kallberg argues instead that the importance of genre rests within its community of artists and listeners. He displaces musicology's traditional, scientistic concern with isolating, ranking, and providing stylistic attributes with a taxonomy, because such activities wrench the work out of its social setting. They assume that modern observers understand which attributes were most significant to a historical audience and that those attributes remained stable over substantial periods of time. Genre, for Kallberg, functions rather as a socially contingent agreement allowing members of the community to communicate; it is a form of contract between composer and audience.[22] For this reason, Kallberg describes genre as rhetorical. Composers select generic traits in order to make their creations comprehensible and to guide and assist audiences in their responses, much as a rhetorician chooses tropes and figures of speech in order to render ideas convincingly. A work's generic features provide an audience with a means for understanding it, a framework for judging its merit. The community refers to its shared horizon of generic characteristics, locating the artwork among similar works and attributing a work's success or failure to the presentation of generic traits, precisely because genre provides the means for making assumptions about artists' intentions. A composition such as *Les Indes galantes* was the site of a negotiation between composer and audience: a gambit by the composer to which audiences responded with acceptance and rejection.

This contextual notion of genre is especially important for understanding seventeenth- and eighteenth-century French culture. Among our strongest impressions of this period are the ideas that genre played a public role in the appreciation of artworks and that the public in turn sharply delimited the rhetorical play of genre. Genre transcended tacit agreement between artist and audience, becoming instead a means of governing artistic behaviors and ensuring conformity to tradition. Nicolas Boileau's injunctions to writers of poetic idylls capture this quality: ". . . follow Theocritus and Virgil: do not let those tender writings, dictated by the Graces, leave your hands; turn their pages day and night. Their wise verses alone will teach you by what art an author can descend without vulgarity. . . ."[23] For Boileau, each poetic genre had its model and its ideal poets, and it was a younger poet's responsibility to emulate them and to avoid letting innovations obscure the tradition. In this way genre was the channel through which artists and audiences communicated, but it was also the mark of authority, allowing new artists to claim merit while also allowing audiences to judge those claims. Writers spoke of *les règles* governing art, confident that readers understood them. Even in music the earliest formulations of aesthetic beauty took this rationalistic model of public expectation for granted.[24] The comments of the abbé Noël-Antoine Pluche illustrate the tendency:

> There is no one who is not permitted to have taste [for music], and just as one can, without being a poet, feel very well the difference between Virgil, who paints nature, and Lucan, who depicts the intellect, one can also feel the true beauties of music and wisely judge the merits of musicians without being a musician. But let us not risk either assigning any scorn to [musicians] or wishing to give preference to one over the other without the aid of an enlightening rule, avowed by musicians themselves, that decides the just value of their method.[25]

Critical thought of the kind Boileau made paradigmatic exerted a patriarchal force over subsequent generations, a force that the literary theorist Sima Godfrey has referred to as "l'effet Boileau."[26] So it was that Lullian opera, as strong musical precursor, came to embody an authoritative tradition, despite its disparagement of his colleague: Boileau's critical *model,* rather than his actual opinions about opera, had influenced subsequent discourse. Indeed, in his 1727 design for a French Parnassus, Évrard Titon du Tillet would place Boileau and Lully together among the nine French muses, the latter wearing a medallion bearing the likeness of his librettist Philippe Quinault.[27] The Lullian tradition, along with accretions like opéra-ballet, remained present for young composers and audience members through criticism and continual revivals.[28]

We can locate the obverse of this generic ideal in a concurrent fascination with monsters. Far from the phantasms of the post-Freudian subconscious, the monster of seventeenth- and eighteenth-century European culture was the deformed birth. Pierre Richelet's *Dictionnaire françois* defines a monster as "an animal born with parts much larger or smaller than it naturally ought to have" or as "an animal born with more parts than nature asks of it," whereas *Le Dictionnaire de l'Académie françoise* of 1694 describes it as an "animal that has a conformation contrary to the order of nature."[29] The *Encyclopédie* extends the description:

> [An] animal that is born with a conformation contrary to the order of nature, that is to say, with a structure of parts very different from those that characterize the species of animal from which it departs. There are even several kinds of monsters, according to the arrangement of their structures. . . .
>
> One would not give the name monster to an animal if there were only a light and superficial difference, if the object did not astonish.[30]

The tradition invoked here was a long and distinguished one. The members of a culture haunted by the intellectual achievements of antiquity would have been well versed in the logic that underlay Aristotle's discussion in the *Generation of Animals:* "Some [offspring] take after none of their kindred, although they take after some human being at any rate; others do not take after a human being at all in their appearance, but have gone so far that they resemble a monstrosity, and, for the matter of that, anyone who does not take after his parents is really in a way a monstrosity, since in these cases Nature has in a way strayed from the generic type."[31]

The distance was short from these kinds of statements to the observation that violations of genre were monstrous. Horace had elevated Aristotle's principle to an aesthetic ideal in *Ars poetica,* a treatise well-known in France through a translation by the conservative writer André Dacier. The opening words of the treatise suggest how easily the transition could be made:

> Suppose a painter wished to couple a horse's neck with a man's head, and to lay feathers of every hue on limbs gathered here and there, so that a woman,

lovely above, foully ended in an ugly fish below; would you restrain your laughter, my friends, if admitted to a private view? Believe me . . . a book will appear uncommonly like that picture, if impossible figures are wrought into it—like a sick man's dreams—with the result that neither head nor foot is ascribed to a single shape, and unity is lost.[32]

The point was not lost on French writers. René Rapin, in his *Les Reflexions sur la poetique de ce temps* (1675), used it to argue for the Aristotelian unity of action:

> Diversity has a vast foundation in heroic poetry: the enterprises of war, peace treaties, embassies, negotiations, voyages, embarcations, councils, deliberations, the buildings of palaces and cities, passions, unexpected recognitions, surprising and unlooked-for revolutions, and the different images of all that happens in the lives of the great can be employed, provided that they proceed to the same goal. Without this order, the most beautiful figures become monstrous and similar to the extravagances Horace ridiculed at the beginning of his *Ars poetica*.[33]

Monsters represented the failure of sense and logic. As Michel Foucault observed, such confabulations "desiccate speech, stop words in their tracks, contest the very possibility of grammar at its source."[34] They made meaning, and hence communication, impossible. In a post-Cartesian world where sense, grammar, and understanding were preeminent values, monsters were the ultimate offense to reason. They represented unintelligibility, gibberish, neologism.

It should come as no surprise then that monsters populated conservative opera criticism through the first half of the eighteenth century. A poem by Pierre de Villiers states that "operas are only a monstrous jumble." The poet bemoans its "monstrous heroes," and observes that if spoken theater introduced operatic features, the results would be "monstrous" as well. Another poem by Jean de Serré de Rieux, published in 1734, uses the monster image to criticize Italian opera, "Capriciously immolated, the rules of the scene find themselves violated by monstrous traits," and goes on to exhort, "Flee far from us, monsters of Italy." A reviewer in *Le Pour et contre*, who appears to have seen Serré's manuscript prior to publication, singled out this metaphor as an important theme of the poem: "It follows that a beautiful opera is never more than a beautiful monster." In Gabriel Bonnot de Mably's 1741 *Lettres a madame la marquise de P . . . sur l'opéra*, a character observes that "Opera was treated as a monster, an Italian folly; it was scarcely permitted the role of a pleasant concert," and another comments that "Opera is a monster which has neither proportion nor *vraisemblance*." In the same year, Toussaint Rémond de Saint-Mard observed, "that opera is a monstrous spectacle," and asked, "What kind of monster is a tragedy set

to music from one end to the other?" When, in 1742, Fontenelle acknowledged that unity of place was not missed in opera, a reviewer seized upon it
to launch a monstrous diatribe against opera: "M. [Fontenelle] states that
things happen without difficulty in opera, but that conclusions ought not
be drawn from this regarding tragedy. An opera is always a bad poem, and
the most beautiful work in this genre is only a monster." Even Voltaire had
something to say on the matter. In *Candide,* published in 1759, the noble
Pococurante explains to the title character, "I would perhaps like opera better if the secret had not been found of making it a monster that revolts
me."[35] In an especially cruel bit of popular doggerel appearing shortly after
the publication of the *Les Indes* print (and probably referring to the tragedy
Castor et Pollux), Rameau himself was subjected to the same treatment, depicted as the deformed offspring of Envy and the silenus Marsyas, famous
for having challenged Apollo to a musical contest: "There will be born to
you a boy. He will live to avenge his father, to thwart reason, to make a double outrage to the muses, because in addition to writing his raucous song
he will put rage into it. I hear, I see the cannibal: neck of an ostrich, wrin-
kled eyes, jaundiced, spiky-haired, crooked nose—the true mask of satire—
mouth for murdering and not for laughing, pointed head and lying heart,
dry legs. . . ."[36] Marginalia in the Chansonnier Maurepas identifies the
"cannibal" as Rameau, but what is most striking here is the monstrous imagery, compounded by references to Ericthonius, the snake-footed son of
Kekrops, and to the mask of satire, the ultimate mixed genre.[37] Because
genre was a prized quality, to be bestowed and withheld from operas with
equal rigor, the fear of unintelligibility was great, and critical discourse fairly
bristles with metaphors of incomprehensibility: bursts of sheer noise ("ca-
cophonie extraordinaire," "un grêle ou un orage, un charivari ou un sabat")
and animal cries ("miaulement").[38]

It seems likely that the issues embodied in the *Les Indes* print have less
to do with recitative or difficult music as stylistic matters than with the way
in which they combined to communicate with audiences. This would explain how recitative could be an issue without being noticeably extravagant
and why music like "Brillant Soleil" was thought of as difficult even after
it was performed by the parterre. For an audience with a strong sense of
generic tradition, the music in *Les Indes galantes* (and, as I will be arguing,
Rameau's tragedies in general) overwhelmed recitative, obliterating the
important narrative function of opera. The print of *Les Indes* was misshapen
in the same way the opera itself was misshapen.

For these same reasons, Rameau's attempts to recover validity for the
print followed exactly the wrong course. The public, finding *Les Indes
galantes* fascinating but also troublesome, exerted some kind of pressure
to have it printed in a generically stable form. Stripped of the pretense of
operatic narrative, the print as *extrait* allowed the work to conform to pre-

vailing impressions that it was singularly about music. Nevertheless, the composer, apparently eager to reclaim the prestige associated with full-blown opera, frittered away this generic stability. This process began on the title page, where the term *concert* appears instead of *extrait*. Writers such as Sebastien de Brossard and Michel Corette identify *concert* with the Italian word "concerto," taking it to refer to instrumental performances in the manner of the famed *concerts royaux*.[39] The word did not necessarily convey a sense of opus in the way we would be inclined to understand it today; in fact, the chronicler François de La Baume Le Blanc La Vallière used it to refer to pastiches or occasional works. He mentions a "Concert en forme de Fêtes, en cinq suites ou entrées, donné au Roi sur la cour de marbre à Versailles . . . à l'occasion de la Naissance de Monseigneur le Dauphin," which was an arrangement of numbers from popular operas by the composer François Colin de Blamont.[40] If *concert* on the title page of *Les Indes* implies this rather loose association, then we are being asked to see the print not simply as a collection of instrumental works but rather as four sets of pieces concocted from an opera. The opera itself remains untouched. The emphasis is on remaking the work, allowing its original form to stand more or less unchallenged in readers' minds. This odd gambit becomes more evident in the preface, where Rameau fails to hold with *concert* as a description of the print's content and instead pushes the already fragile sense of genre ever further in the direction of light entertainment, away from opera and toward pure music. He encourages his audience to treat the untexted music in the print as *pièces de clavecin*, removing its center of gravity from the public venue of the concert to the private salon.

To make this final move, Rameau had to conceptually trim away what remained of opera within the print, its "*airs chantants, ariettes,* measured recitatives, duos, trios, quartets, and choruses." To be sure, such translations of music occurred frequently in practice. What is at issue here is less the pure and abstract content of the print than Rameau's discomfort with what remained. The elaborate literal and figurative rearranging of the print's contents paradoxically obfuscates and underscores the distance between the print and the staged work. This rearrangement may have had the desired effect of moving the opera away from the opprobrium represented by the print, but it also points up the unique qualities of the print in an unsatisfactory way, making it an "impossible figure" of the monstrous kind that so vexed Horace, and this of course had been the problem with the opera itself. One is reminded of Godfrey's assertion that generic expectations in eighteenth-century France were a source not merely of guidance, as Boileau suggests, but of creative anxiety.[41]

Les Indes galantes thus becomes a form of palimpsest, upon which competing meanings and representations were written and rewritten. The opera public, wishing to convey the idea that Rameau's opéra-ballet was problematic, effected the removal of its recitatives. While it is a remarkable response to a composer's work, no one at the time would have questioned the public's right to adjudication, and Rameau openly deferred to it in his preface. But in actuality he only appeared to do so. In a typically convoluted response to public opinion, he rejected the notion that the opera was flawed, implying that once recitative was removed, the print no longer represented opera at all but rather any of several socially inferior genres. The print is a vanishing point into which the perspective afforded by a particular genre disappears altogether. Thus the public, the composer's critics, and the composer himself were willing to create out of *Les Indes galantes* an incomplete and deformed body, and in each case this transformation occurred in response to notions of genre: the public denied *Les Indes* was an opéra-ballet by influencing the physical state of the score, critics denied generic attributes so that the opera could be regarded instead as a sonata, and Rameau seized this opportunity to argue for a polyglot print meeting multiple generic interests.

To an unusual degree, critical language observed a reflexive, metonymic link between composer and work: the work stood in for the composer; the composer stood in for the work. In the implied equation, however, the advantage lies not with the composer, as some biographers of Rameau have believed, but with the work. Rameau's works dominated critical discourse. When they stood in for Rameau, as in the case of the print of *Les Indes,* this allowed critics to place certain words in the composer's mouth. The composer had willfully mutilated opera. When Rameau stood in for the work, it led to the same outcome. The composer was insensitive to opera's standards, proprieties, etiquette, and ultimately to its audience. Rameau himself did little to clarify this situation. He neither confided nor explained. If we want to understand him, we must interrogate his monsters.

I hope that by now my rationale for placing this print among Rameau's tragedies will have become evident. We evaluate many musical sources according to whether they provide authentic texts, setting for ourselves the task of following them back to an ideal source, the abstract musical work. The *Les Indes* print forces us to reconsider this process. By teasing out, in the most material way imaginable, the critical themes that would hound Rameau throughout his career, the print reminds us that even the most authentic documents inevitably bear traces of cultural beliefs, social rituals, and public scrutiny that interfere with our attempts to locate the idealized, abstract work. In this particular instance, these traces create both strong and weak representations of Rameau's opera, simultaneously providing us with a rich historical commentary on it while actively obscuring the original musical text.

If we admit that ideal musical texts are unavailable, the possibility remains that through the act of seeking them we can still arrive at a better understanding of how historical audiences listened to the works. What we learn from this print, then, is that Rameau's audiences did not receive operas passively, even those conceived as entertainment. Opera in this setting was more than a catalyst for escapism, abstract contemplation, sensual delight, or emotional uplift (though it invited—and continues to invite—these responses); like the best Enlightenment experiments, it provoked dissection, rumination, discussion, and argument. Writers as relatively far apart in time as Jean-Laurent Le Cerf de la Viéville and Gabriel Bonnot de Mably chided audience members who failed to give opera the attention it deserved, creating in their treatises didactic authority figures who instructed audience members on critical probity. Those controversies that excite the most interest among historians today—such as the *querelle des Lullistes et Ramistes* or the *querelle des bouffons*—are the most extreme cases of a critical impulse that was in continuous operation at least until the French Revolution. We might say that society expected operas to be consumed actively and to be thoroughly ingested into the cultural milieu. I should prefer instead to think of operas as being *read,* and in choosing this expression I again mean something more than a passive act. As the *Les Indes* print demonstrates, the public actively interpreted its operas. In this sense, composers, critics, journalists, politicians, parodists, and audience members from the parterre through the upper tiers of the Palais royal "read" operas. Through the act of perceiving them in performance and print, they produced meanings for them, built up repertories of meanings, and treated these presumed meanings as commensurate with the musical texts. As numerous accounts from the period indicate, an opera without a public quickly ceased to exist, passing (along with its composer) into obscurity.

The abstract musical work, then, was available no more to historical audiences than it is to modern ones. In following the issues that cut and scored away *Les Indes galantes* beyond recognition, we find that for Rameau's operas there was no single mode of hearing: the public had little concern for establishing the content of his musical texts or, what amounts to the same thing, for understanding his intentions. The opera was instead an event at which could be carried on the cultural work of arguing what an opera was, what a genre could be, and how an ambitious artist might fit into society. In the remainder of this chapter, I wish to chart the "monstrosity" of *Les Indes* not as an aspect or even as a failure of the composer's musical style but rather as a function of the competing representations of the work: the necessary by-product of confrontation between a public accustomed to determining the value of operas and a composer who desired explicitly to locate this value in music of the opera.

Genre, the bridge between the composer's intentions and an audience's judgment, is the crucial first step. Modern attempts to understand opéra-ballet as a genre, and as a general category made up of related subgenres, have focused on the taxonomy of stylistic attributes and generic characteristics in the manner criticized by Kallberg. James Anthony, for example, working with a model first provided by Paul-Marie Masson in 1928, lists these traits: "Most 18th-century definitions emphasized two structural features of the opera-ballet: (1) each act or *entrée* (the terms 'acte' and 'entrée' were used interchangeably when referring to the opera-ballet) has its own independent action; and (2) each act includes at least one *divertissement* of songs and dances. Therefore, the roots of the genre may be traced to both the opera and the 17th-century *ballet à entrées* in which each act developed its own intrigue."[42] This definition works well if one desires an encompassing view of the repertory or a summary outlook that reduces a substantial slice of history to sweeping conformity. By isolating generic features in this way, Anthony easily traces the genre's origins to a single cause, the *ballet à entrées*. He also shears away, however, *cultural* elements that Kallberg might have emphasized as constituting generic practice, among them the substantial financial requirements and increased emphasis on entertaining music and dance that made producing lyric tragedy a burden in the final years of the seventeenth century. As current issues, these events would have been far more significant to audience members attempting to understand a new genre than resemblances to the now-forgotten *ballet à entrées*, a genre that had died out in the 1670s. We could list a range of other general issues sheared away with Anthony's model, which does not explain conditions for the admissibility of new genres, for example, that would haunt attempts at creating French comic opera during the eighteenth century. Similarly, it fails to broach the evolving relationship between opéra-ballet and *tragédie en musique*, in which opéra-ballet quickly became the more popular genre—in terms of premieres and numbers of performances—than tragedy, which ideologically remained more respectable.[43] Further, Anthony's definition does not help us understand why or how genre was a significant critical tool in this context. It does not help us track how expectations differed for tragedy and opéra-ballet, affecting such concerns as appropriateness, acceptable levels of novelty, and even possibilities for enjoyment. Finally, in the case of the *Les Indes* print, the definition fails to tell any meaningful story at all. It provides no clues about what was wrong with this particular opéra-ballet, and it does not explain the relevance of the public's attacking recitatives when other musical passages elicited stronger documented responses (as, for example, in Cahusac's observation that early audiences could not sing "Brillant Soleil").

What Anthony's definition does succeed in capturing is something peculiar to seventeenth- and eighteenth-century France: the rigidity with which genre was wielded as a critical tool, drawing a sharp distinction between what opéra-ballet was and was not. We might, echoing Freud, imagine this distinction as *topographical,* that is, as describing genre by mapping out its terrain.[44] In accordance with this view, audience members located those features that best characterized this operatic landscape, and when they recognized familiar landmarks—a single action per entrée, prominence of divertissements—they took pleasure in knowing they were on familiar ground. Seen in this light, Anthony's definition offers a glimpse of "l'effet Boileau" in action. Abbreviated, cut, and shuffled, the print of *Les Indes galantes* becomes a metaphorical substitution for the actual ballet, capturing something of what audience members experienced at performances: the terrain of this opéra-ballet was unfamiliar. Nevertheless, such insights as afforded by Anthony's definition are coincidental. They have less to do with the rigor of either his methodology or his definition than with the parallel intentions of modern historians and historical audiences: musicologists wish to exclude works that are not opéra-ballets in order to understand the category *opéra-ballet* better, whereas eighteenth-century audiences wished to exclude unworthy works to achieve generic purity. Both goals are chimerical, ignoring the constant historical shifting that occurred in the horizon of the opéra-ballet (and which led from Campra's relatively straightforward *L'Europe galante* to more ambiguous, but equally important, subgenres like the ballet-héroïque). Generic assumptions had and have more play to them than a collection of stylistic attributes is able to demonstrate.

Following Kallberg and echoing Freud, we might more accurately conceptualize the generic attributes of opéra-ballet as *economic*: as an exchange in items and features of value. This view need not supplant topographical models of genre, and, given the vigorous allegiance to notions of genre that prevailed in eighteenth-century France, it indeed should not. Rather, the economic view offers an alternative vantage point to sift through familiar evidence in new ways. It allows us, first of all, to comprehend a more complex, less uniform set of values and a shifting scenario in which different audience members valued different genres and generic traits. Some, like Desfontaines's correspondent, dogmatically preferred the Lullian tragedy, while others, like Desfontaines himself, preferred newer forms of entertainment. Even those who agreed on the overall worth of a given work did not necessarily agree on what made it good or bad. Second, the economic model of the opéra-ballet helps us understand how values were placed on particular features within opera. Poetry had its place in opera, instrumental music had another, and dance, still another. Indeed, we may go further. Different kinds of poetry, instrumental music, and dance evinced different values, and one understood the overall worth of an opéra-ballet according to the merits one attributed to these contributions. What was scabrous noise to Desfontaines's correspondent was the music of Corelli and Vivaldi for Desfontaines. This leads to a third sense in which viewing the opéra-ballet economically is worthwhile: the way materials such as poetry, music, and dance circulated between opéra-ballet and tragedy. In general, the tragedy used a certain kind of poetry to tell a certain kind of story, while the opéra-ballet featured dance and instrumental music, or what Anthony refers to in his definition as divertissement. Yet in the most general stylistic terms, both genres, tragedy and opéra-ballet, possessed divertissements. It was not simply the presence of certain kinds of poetry, music, or dance that caused a work to represent genre successfully but also the balance between them and the manner in which audiences perceived them. By considering the economic viewpoint, we can better track the multiple characterizations of the printed score of *Les Indes galantes*: an opera containing poor recitative, an opera containing unperformable music, a sonata, a monstrosity, four concerts, a compilation of pieces for performance, a collection of keyboard suites. The generic markers used to arrive at these characterizations did not carry absolute, but functional, values that served to keep the operatic house in order. They were capable of permutation and constrained only by what composers were willing to attempt and what audiences were willing to accept.

Central to questions of genre in eighteenth-century opera was the relation between recitative and divertissement, which we might think of as a continuum with dramatic action at one end and instrumental music at the other. We see this historic economy replicated in the tensions that permeated discourse on opera, between old and new music, texted and untexted music, serious and frivolous music, well-formed works and monstrosities, as well as between tragédies en musique and opéra-ballets. These were the terms in which critics evaluated *Les Indes galantes,* and throughout the eighteenth century we find the opéra-ballet weighed according to this scale. Already in 1719 Nicolas Boindin had noted that "dance is . . . the soul of a ballet, and the less charged [the opéra-ballet] is with words [i.e., plot or recitative], the more there is of an appearance that it will succeed."[45] Similarly, those chroniclers of theater, the brothers François and Claude Parfaict, complained of the opéra-ballet *Le Triomphe de l'harmonie* that "[t]hough one would agree that the poem is well-written, some [dramatic] interest would have been desirable. It is not easy, even for those authors most experienced with this theater, to put more into an opéra-ballet. This type of piece . . . seems made for the mind rather than the heart and is, moreover, two-thirds dance."[46] With both works, the writers evaluated the genre not according to whether there was one story and one divertissement per entrée, but according to the balance between dramatic action and divertissement, assuming the latter to be the feature more important to the genre. Relatively conservative commentators, however, they also expressed a belief that opéra-ballet in general would benefit from greater emphasis on words. Saint-Mard was even more blunt about this: "Here is practically everything that constitutes a ballet: a little intrigue, a little recitative, some *ariettes,* lots of dance . . ."[47] For conservative operagoers the problem with the opéra-ballet, was that its plots were weak, but the popularity of the genre was not in question.

Such comments imply, moreover, that the opéra-ballet was an entertaining rather than edifying form of theater, and the distinction was important for participants in discussions of opera. According to the Parfaicts, for example, opéra-ballet appealed to the mind (*esprit*) rather than the heart. The distinction is a difficult one for modern readers to follow, since we tend to privilege the heart as the site of aesthetic reception, but it was borne out by Aristotelian conventions of the time. According to the conservative Rapin, seventeenth-century spoken tragedy affected the intellect most profoundly by first moving the heart, and this effect could only be accomplished in serious genres:

> The tragedy only becomes pleasurable to the spectator because he himself becomes sensitive to everything presented to him, because he enters into the different sentiments of the actors, because he is interested in their adventures, because he fears, hopes, grieves, and rejoices with them. The theater is cold and listless as soon as it ceases to produce these movements in the soul of those who attend it. But of all passions, fear and pity make the greatest impression on the heart of man, because of his natural disposition for frightening and moving himself: Aristotle chose them from among the others, the better to touch the intellect by these tender sentiments, caused when the heart allows itself to be penetrated.[48]

By this reasoning, what the Parfaicts seem to be saying is that one judged opéra-ballet intellectually, according to such broad generic characteristics as its divertissements. One might judge whether the music and dance pleased or whether they were performed well, but without having serious plots opéra-ballet inspired only a detached pleasure, devoid of the emotions that stirred an audience's hearts. By criticizing the genre's most prominent topographical feature—dance—critics forced it into a less stable, economic relationship of generic features, where one could consider the possibility of making the text more important and the divertissement less important. To this kind of commentator, the rejection of recitative in *Les Indes* implied that the work was nothing but divertissement, and when Rameau allowed the print to slide in the direction of lesser genres—from ballet to concert to detached pieces to *pièces de clavecin*—he too cast the work as simple entertainment. What is most peculiar, then, about the circumstances of the printed score of *Les Indes galantes*—what makes Rameau's response to removing recitative so odd—is that recitative should have been an issue at all. If conservative commentary is any indication, an audience member would not have had particularly high expectations for the recitative in *Les Indes*. That portion of the audience that included the Parfaicts might have wished that recitative scenes *in general* were more substantial in opéra-ballets, but there would have been no compelling *generic* reason to single out Rameau's creation for negative treatment because opéra-ballet was not about recitative. Indeed, the *Les Indes* print highlighted what had the greatest value in the underlying economy of opéra-ballet, preserving the divertissements that ostensibly formed the heart of the work.

We can begin to understand how Rameau inadvertently played into these competing tensions by returning to the second entrée, *Les Incas,* and, more particularly, to the great scene invoking the sun, which culminates in the chorus "Brillant Soleil." At first blush, this entrée would have much to commend it to critics like the Parfaict brothers; Voltaire, in fact, whose taste in opera was (as we will see) just as conservative as theirs, expressed admiration for it.[49] Cuthbert Girdlestone noted that *Les Incas* is "the only [entrée] with any dramatic interest and also the most spectacular." He was not alone in his judgment. Masson and Sylvie Bouissou have both drawn comparisons between the entrée's plot and characteristics of the tragédie en musique.[50] The observations of all three writers are well founded, for *Les Incas* is the only entrée in *Les Indes* to move beyond romantic dalliance, the standard subject of opéra-ballet, to the more serious issues of honor, loyalty, and commitment. We see this range in the opening scene, where the Spanish conqueror Carlos within a single statement challenges the patriotism, religious devotion, and sincerity of his lover, the Incan princess Phani-Palla:

CARLOS:
  Vous devez bannir de votre ame
  La criminelle erreur qui séduit les Incas;
    Vous l'avez promis à ma flamme:
  Pourquoi diférez-vous? Non, vous ne m'aimez-pas . . .

PHANI:
  Que vous pénétrez mal mon secret embarras!
  Quel injuste soupçon! . . . Quoi, sans inquiétude,
      Brise-t'on à la fois
    Les liens du sang & des loix?
  Excusez mon incertitude.

[CARLOS: You must banish from your soul the criminal error that seduces the Incas; you have promised (your soul) to my love. Why do you hesitate? No, you do not love me. . . . PHANI: How poorly you discern my difficult secret! What an unjust suspicion! . . . What? Without disquiet the bonds of blood and law are broken in a single blow? Pardon my uncertainty. (*RG*, 3:541).]

These conflicts would have been especially familiar to audiences of the time through a recent production of Voltaire's spoken tragedy *Alzire* (1733), which likewise dealt with the moral demands made on South American natives by imperial conquest.

After Phani's brief monologue—an apostrophe to Hymen—in scene two, the next scene brings the entrance of the priest Huascar. Almost immediately, in an aside that will become important, he confesses his love for Phani: "Tout ce que dit l'Amour est toujours pardonnable,/Et le ciel que je sers doit servir mon ardeur" (Everything love says is always pardonable, and the heaven that I serve must serve my desire). He then goes on to remind her of the duty she has as a princess:

> Obéissons sans balancer,
> Lorsque le ciel commande.
> Nous ne pouvons trop nous presser
> D'accorder ce qu'il nous demande;
> Y refléchir, c'est l'offenser.

[Let us obey without wavering when heaven commands. We cannot hurry too quickly to concede what it demands of us. To reflect on this is to offend (heaven). (*RG,* 3:542).]

These events lead to a prayer scene, yet another reminder of the tragédie en musique. As in many lyric tragedies from the time, including Michel Pignolet de Montéclair's *Jephté* (1732) and Rameau's own *Hippolyte et Aricie* (1733), the story halts so that a priest may call upon a god to intervene in human affairs. In *Les Incas,* this prayer scene is a full-scale *fête de soleil* in which Huascar, assisted by his countrymen, prays to the Sun, asking the deity in "Brillant Soleil" to avenge their servitude to European invaders:

> HUASCAR:
> Soleil, on a détruit tes superbes aziles,
> Il ne te reste plus de temple que nos coeurs:
> Daigne nous écouter dans ces déserts tranquilles,
> Le zéle est pour les Dieux le plus cher des honneurs.
>
> *Les* PALLAS ET LES INCAS *font leur adoration au Soleil.*
>
> HUASCAR:
> Brillant Soleil, jamais nos yeux dans ta carriere,
>   N'ont vû tomber de noirs frimats!
>   Et tu répans dans nos climats
>   Ta plus éclatante lumiere.
>
> CHOEUR:
> Brillant Soleil, *&c.*

[HUASCAR: Sun, your superb havens have been destroyed. A temple no longer remains to you except in our hearts. Deign to hear us in these tranquil deserts. Zeal is, for the gods, the most precious of honors. *The* PALLAS *and the* INCAS *make their devotion to the sun.* HUASCAR: Brillant Sun, never in your course have our eyes seen fall the black hoar-frost, and you shed in our climate the most magnificent light. CHORUS: Brilliant Sun, etc. (*RG,* 3:542).]

The presence of gods is in itself a sign of tragic plotting. Here, as in most tragedies, divine intervention arrives in the form of a divertissement, and here, too, it brings with it natural disaster, in this case a volcanic eruption. There is an unusual seriousness in this divertissement, providing not only the requisite entertaining music and visual spectacle one would expect but also the violent and painful resolution of the entrée's dramatic conflict.

The plot of the entrée, by employing features that marked tragedy as an ideologically significant genre, is more than a pretext for dance, and Masson and Bouissou correctly call attention to its resonances with the tragedy. It is little wonder then that Masson singles out the entrée for unrestrained praise. "In the act of the *Incas,*" he wrote, "the solemnity of the celebration of the sun, the violence of the passions, the redoubtable presence of the volcano, where the Indian Huascar, mad with rage, seeks and finds death confer on this part of the work a dramatic vigor, which Rameau rendered powerfully, making one dream of the strongest pages of his *tragédies lyriques.*"[51]

Yet, although this dramatic complexity may bring welcome relief to modern observers overwhelmed by eighteenth-century pleasantries, we must keep in mind that *Les Incas* was never singled out in its own time as exemplifying the serious dramatic action craved by conservative critics. Desfontaines's correspondent cast it aside along with the rest of *Les Indes galantes;* decades later another critic questioned the sophistication of its text (in an article for the *Mercure de France* suggestively entitled "Les paroles d'un Opéra sont-elles inutiles à la progression du Génie musical, & conséquemment indifférentes au succès du Musicien?" [The words of an opera, are they useless for the progress of musical genius and consequently irrelevant to the musician's success?]). This writer argued that revivals of *Les Indes* had failed precisely because its livret was so poor:

> *Zoroastre* no more concludes [the argument] against the necessity for good poems in tragedies than *Les Indes galantes* favors the musicians' indifference to words in opéra-ballets. Although [*Les Indes galantes*] was applauded at its original production, one knows how different its fortune was in revival. Observing . . . all works in this genre, one finds none where music constitutes the sole reason they sustained the trial of returning to the theater. Instead, numerous [other opéra-ballets] could be cited that, by favor of their poems, have obtained favor and obtain it still for their *slight* music, however pretended connoisseurs—who always affect out of vanity to devalue the national genre— qualify it.[52]

According to this argument, poetry rather than music affected the success of a revival, and by these standards *Les Indes* had failed miserably. To some extent, these judgments reflected the poor technical state of the poetry in *Les Indes*. Little more than a century later, Pierre Larousse's *Grand diction-naire universel du xixe siècle* would describe the librettist Louis Fuzelier as "better known for his fecundity than his talent," adding, "A *faiseur* in all senses of the word, he had pieces staged in most theaters."[53] (The word *faiseur*, which can mean either a "maker" or "hack," is in this instance an insult.) As we will see in chapter 4, critics held Rameau responsible throughout his career for the poor state of his livrets making the case that he did not care about words, chose inexperienced poets in order to receive a larger share of the box office, and bullied and prodded the poets to con-form to his musical designs instead of his conforming to theirs.

A more important argument for looking beyond the topographic aspects of poetic technique is the curious double bind created by the dramatic ac-tion of *Les Incas*, which undermines the very tragic values the entrée ap-pears to invoke. The opening scene encourages us to regard the dilemma of duty versus honor (belonging to Phani) in tragic terms, but in the third scene Huascar's passing remark—"Everything love says is always pardon-able, and the heaven that I serve must serve my desire"—emerges as the dilemma driving the story. Far from a passing hope that the desires of his deities parallel his own, Huascar confesses he is using his priestly office for personal gain, that is, to win the love of Phani. When, as the volcanic erup-tion begins, Carlos learns what has happened, even he is justifiably repulsed by Huascar's immoral behavior: "Ton crime ose paroître!" (Your crime dares show itself!) Realizing that the gods will not avenge his humiliation at the hands of the Spanish conqueror, Huascar, in a belated confession, calls on them to punish him instead:

> Abymes embrâsés, j'ai trahi les autels.
> > Exercez l'emploi du tonnerre;
> > Vengez les droits des immortels;
> > Déchirez le sein de la terre;
> > > Sous mes pas chancelans,
> > Renversez, dispersez ces arides montagnes;
> > Lancez vos feux dans ces tristes campagnes,
> > > Tombez sur moi, rochers brûlans.

[Burning abysses, I have betrayed the altars. Use thunderbolts; avenge the rights of immortals; rend the bosom of the earth. Beneath my tottering steps, overturn and scatter these arid montains; hurl your fires into this sad coun-tryside. Fall on me, burning rocks. (*RG*, 3:543–44).]

This time he gets his wish, and we are left to wonder at a setting in which the apparent values of the lyric tragedy in the end serve only to unite lovers at the expense of duty and honor. Phani's obligations to her homeland are irrelevant. (A year later, critics would belabor Rameau's character of Castor for desiring his murdered brother's fiancée: far from thinking of filial duty, he relents only when she demands that he enter the underworld and take his brother's place.) If *Les Incas* approaches tragedy, it does so only in order to overturn tragic values. If Fuzelier added elements of tragedy, possibly in the hopes of placating conservative critics, these turn out to be an economical grafting of disparate generic features, a chimerical combination that fails to result in a rational whole.

Rameau's musical response will not surprise analysts familiar with his work, but it is a curious one in light of the tensions we have been tracing. We see the response at the beginning of the *fête de soleil*, in Huascar's air, or short monologue, "Soleil, on a détruit tes superbes aziles." A brief statement in ternary form, this air consists of his initial prayer cited above: "Sun, your superb havens have been destroyed. . . ." It is both an admission of failure to stop the invaders and a plea for help in repelling them. Rameau captures something of this mood in the second phrase of the instrumental prelude, shown in example 1.1a.[54] Following a half cadence in A minor, this passage features a dominant prolongation, moving from a second inversion A-minor harmony in m. 4 to a strong dominant in m. 6, ultimately cadencing on the tonic in m. 7. Especially noteworthy is the descending chromatic progression in m. 5, framed by the root-position submediant and first-inversion tonic harmonies and outlining passing diminished triads. In his treatise *Observations sur notre instinct pour la musique* (1754), Rameau would consider the associations that accompany such chromatic descents, noting that "the *flat* [and here, because it descends, the D-sharp is technically speaking an E-flat] is cited as the sign of indolence, weakness, etc."[55] The descending chromatic line in example 1.1a is an apt characterization of this moment in the story: the position of the singer is one of subjugation to an invading force. At the same time, the musical gesture is also an intimate one, capturing something of Huascar's jealousy evident in the scenes immediately preceding.

Compare this with the corresponding passage at the conclusion of the A section, shown in example 1.1b. The phrase is foreshortened to end in three measures instead of four, a more lyrical balancing of the three-measure opening phrase, and as a result the harmonic progression of the prolongational m. 12 is compressed so that it reaches the dominant on its fourth beat. The root-position submediant of the prelude remains; Rameau has removed the diminished triad from the third beat and emphasized the passing tonic harmony by moving to it through a dominant harmony, which lends it a second-inversion feel. This places the diminished harmony on the second beat in an entirely new light: now a half-diminished seventh, its bass line resolves upward to the root-position dominant. Just as the descending chromatic line had dramatic implications, so too does the promi-

Example 1.1a. "Soleil, on a détruit tes superbes aziles," *Les Indes galantes,* entrée
2, scene 5, mm. 1–7

Example 1.1b. "Soleil, on a détruits tes superbes aziles," *Les Indes galantes,* entrée
2, scene 5, mm. 8–13

nent ascent have them. In *Observations* Rameau wrote, "The *sharp* or *natural* is the sign of strength, of joy,"[56] and Huascar's text at this point is telling: "Your temple no longer remains, except in our hearts." The chromatic reversal falls precisely on the word *temple*. We hear spiritual devotion in this moment: the Incas may indeed experience dejection, because the temples of the sun have been destroyed (descending chromatic resolution), but hope remains as long as those temples continue to exist in their hearts (ascending chromatic resolution). Further, the ascending diminished harmony may be intended ironically, since we know that Huascar's desires have overruled his devotion. Musically and semiotically, the passage in example 1.1b is sophisticated, forcing us to hear beyond the half-diminished seventh harmony as a coloristic detail and drawing our attention back to its initial statement in m. 5. It asks us at some level to listen recursively— to remember the original voicings of the progression and to infer dramatic conclusions from the difference between the two statements.[57] As though to drive the point home, the mode shifts from A minor to A major in the following movements, "Brillant Soleil" and the "Air des Incas pour la dévotion du soleil," suggesting the brighter possibilities of continued devotion and providing opportunities to repeat the ascending chromatic progression in E-major passages.

What interests me here is not simply the pairing of musical gesture with poetic image, which I take to be commonplace in French opera at this time, but rather Rameau's commitment to superseding this kind of elementary musical function and transgressing, in so doing, his audience's assumptions about the relationship between music and drama. To appreciate music's role in the *fête du soleil*, one must first accept the possibility that music is more than a divertissement or entertainment. One must accept it as a signifying system that participates directly in the drama. In an obituary for his teacher, Rameau's pupil Michel-Paul-Guy de Chabanon singled out the *fête du soleil* for this very reason, rejecting the traditional hermeneutic strategy of the pairing of musical gestures with poetic images:

> When the priests bow down with adoration before the sun, the melody and harmony unfold with a majestic gravity; when they bless this star which purifies their regions and pours out the most agreeable emanations, their songs paint rapture and give birth to it. The cry "Brillant Soleil" seizes and transports us when it is taken up again and repeated in turn by the different parts of the choir, while the other parts continue with the subject with the words "jamais nos yeux, dans ta carrière," etc. These are strokes of *art* and *workmanship* which produce their own effects. Yet how many untrained musicians there are who seek to find a relationship in this chorus between the diatonic descent of this melody and the *chute des frimats* ["fall of winter," from the poetic text]. In the present composition this is only an accidental circumstance,

and one which, as painting, is pointless or even contradictory. The musician must not paint winter when the sun is praised for dispersing it; and if there is anything to paint in this case, it is serenity rather than winter. Moreover, a descending diatonic series of notes no more paints the fall of winter than the fall of anything else. But a noble and simple melody, without difficulty traversing modulations dependent upon the key, like so many branches shooting out from the same trunk, opening up around it and crowning it—this is what speaks to the senses and the soul in the chorus "Brillant Soleil," and this above all is what must be felt. If one of these analogies called *peintures* must be found in it, the following will suffice: this chorus inspires a feeling of exaltation, a kind of ecstasy which accords with those who worship the sun. The music needed to paint nothing more.[58]

Drama, not word-painting, is of primary importance here. As we will see in chapters 2 and 3, when we analyze the assumptions underlying this kind of description in more detail, Chabanon could arrive at this conclusion only by treating music in a manner foreign to contemporary thought, that is, as a complete means of expression independent of poetry but equal to it in weight.

By finding in passages such as the *fête du soleil* grounds for a complex musical hermeneutics, Rameau participated directly in current debates on music's importance for opera, the role of divertissement in story-telling, and the significance of opéra-ballet as genre, but ultimately *Les Indes galantes* failed to make its case. If we take at face value the popular assumption that music and dramatic action were separate entities—opéra-ballet emphasizing the former, tragedy the latter—then music's presence *as* dramatic information assumes the economic view of genre that contemporary criticism hinted at. But it assumes it in a manner that would not have been recognizable to critics. The composer did not choose the obvious course: he did not simplify his music, keeping the focus on poetry. Instead, he composed music characteristic of neither tragedy nor ballet, allowing it to do the signifying work of poetry. Music breaks the seal separating divertissement from drama, and this rupture surely encouraged such responses as that of Desfontaines's correspondent. To accept a work like *Les Indes galantes,* one first had to accept music's ability to convey meaning, conferring upon it a radical new status among the sister arts. This concession would eventually become easier to make. Writing in 1756, in the wake of the *querelle des bouffons,* the abbé Marc-Antoine Laugier argued for just this expanded role of music:

Opera is not a monster, although people of bad humor submit that the assembly of so many parts is capable of forming only a monstrous whole. This sentiment can exist only for want of envisaging this spectacle from the point of view where all people ought dispassionately to regard it. It would be a monster, in effect, if all the parts composing it were to cede reciprocally its right to preeminence in order for each in particular to shine, without noticeable regard for the principal object that unites them. But if to the contrary music is envisaged as the art constituting the essence of this spectacle, and the other arts employed as subordinate to it—being only the means with which one makes it shine in all its parts—then the monstrous character of this spectacle will disappear, and one will see only a whole formed by parts that will converge in the perfection of a single, unique object.[59]

His terms are now quite familiar, but this attitude then was still some distance in the future, and it is questionable whether it ever reached widespread acceptance in the context of Rameau's operas. In 1735, at any rate, Rameau's music for *Les Indes* paralleled the odd conflation of generic values in Fuzelier's livret, creating not the desired, subtle shift in the horizon of opéra-ballet but a patchwork of unintelligible generic markers. The composer and the poet had participated in the economy of genres in a manner unrecognizable to their critics. Together they had created a monster.

Taken as a whole, the following chapters treat as themes the issues raised by the print of *Les Indes galantes*—the tensions between topographical and economic views of genre, the problems for the audience in hearing music *intrude* into the operatic experience, the composer's willingness to remake works ontologically in response to public criticism. These issues became features of his most important compositional activity, the production of tragedies. The most pressing consideration at this point is how these problems emerged within the context of Rameau's first opera, the tragédie en musique *Hippolyte et Aricie* (1733).

CHAPTER 2

Different Tragedies

THE PRINT OF *Les Indes galantes* illustrates in microcosm the role difference played, and continues to play, in discussions of Rameau's tragedies. By this I mean more than the disagreements that colored the reception of the tragedies. I refer rather to the larger distinctions arising from the drive or even need to constitute and reconstitute these works ontologically, the contradictions attending the desire of audience members and historians to establish once and for all what sort of objects the operas were musically, generically, socially, and culturally. Our modern understanding of them depends to some extent on determining a topographically stable tragédie en musique, originating in 1673 with Lully's *Cadmus et Hermoine* and ending either with Rameau's unstaged *Les Boréades* (1764) or perhaps with the decline in Lully revivals prior to the Revolution. According to this view, Rameau's first opera, the tragedy *Hippolyte et Aricie* (1733), was unusual, but still recognizable as the kind of lyric tragedy invented by Lully. We find support for this assertion in the very real desire among eighteenth-century commentators to treat French opera as artistically and ideologically stable, a fixed point in an evolving society. Nevertheless, the genre during this period was anything but stable. If some eighteenth-century writers treated it as a secure feature of French musical life, others viewed it economically, in the sense introduced in chapter 1, as being in flux during the years prior to the *Hippolyte* premiere. They viewed genre as a shifting medium in continuous decline in the early 1700s. In 1729, for example, the composer André-Cardinal Destouches reported in a letter to Prince Antoine of Monaco that the lyric tragedy was threatened by changing tastes, an increasing popularity of divertissements, and royal indifference:

> [A revival of Lully's] *Thesée* has been performed since 29 November. It is costumed and decorated magnificently. Nothing could be added to the beauty of execution, and I doubt that it was as perfect at any other time. Thevenard performs Egée to acclamation, though his voice is nearly worn out. Antier plays the role of Medée in the grand manner. Tribou and Pelissier, without having large voices, make the audience weep in the scenes of Eglé and Thesée. No one has as much talent as these two actors. Despite the unanimous praise the opera is given, [reception of] the performances [has] been extremely feeble for the past fifteen days. There is no longer any taste; the noble things no longer make an impression. Women, who are the compass for spectacles, give

no sign of sensibility to touching beauties. The charms of the music are lost;
only those of the dance are really known, and they are not sufficient to sustain us. *Alceste* succeeded modestly last winter and would have disappeared
without the help of a *pas de deux* that drew all Paris. The worst of the worst
is that there is no hope that taste will be renewed, unless the king takes an interest in the Opéra.[1]

Only twelve years later, in 1741, the Jesuit père Yves-Marie André would
view the decline of the tragedy in similar terms, lamenting that Lully's
tragedies grew stale and adding ominously that he would not mention "a
new musician who seems to divide all Paris."[2] Writers spoke of the Lullian
model with something more than concern; they looked on it nostalgically,
longing in vain for a return to its original, pristine state. Whatever was new
and different about Rameau's tragedies—and it is telling that André considered Rameau "new" eight years after the premiere of *Hippolyte*—it was
potent enough to disrupt both of these views, overturning a seemingly stable cultural achievement while at the same time revivifying a moribund pas-
time. Assessing Rameau's worth therefore entailed first agreeing upon
what kind of thing the tragédie en musique ought to be.

With *Hippolyte et Aricie,* contemporary audiences perceived opera to
have crossed a boundary and become something else. They avoided comparing Rameau to more recent innovators such as André Campra and
Destouches, with whom he had much in common, and instead looked back
to the source of French opera. Rameau, like Lully, had created something
different and new, but paradoxically, what he had invented was the tragédie
en musique. Perhaps no document captures this dislocation as well as the
review in the *Mercure de France* of the premiere of *Hippolyte et Aricie*. Like
most of the *Mercure* reviews, this one began by identifying poet and composer; establishing the degree of success the work had enjoyed, described
as "favorable"; and giving extensive excerpts from the livret. At its conclusion, however, the reviewer assessed the music, a rare if not unique commentary for a work by a new composer:

> The music of this opera has been found difficult to execute, but through the
> capacity of the symphonists and other musicians the difficulty has not hin-
> dered performance. . . .[T]he musician has forced the severest critics to agree
> that in his first lyrical work, he has offered a masculine and harmonious music
> of a new character. We would like to give an extract, as we have for the poem,
> and make [the reader] feel the wisdom of expression in the character airs, the
> tableaux; the happy and sustained intentions, as in the chorus and hunt scene
> of the fourth act, the *entrée* of cupids in the prologue, the thunder chorus and
> symphony, the parodied gavotte that Demoiselle Petitpas sings in the first act,
> the underworld in the second act, the terrifying appearance of the Fury with
> Thesée and the chorus, etc. In the third act, Thesée's monologue, his invo-

cation of Neptune, the shuddering of the waves. Phèdre's monologue in the
following act. That of Aricie in the fifth act, the *bergerie,* etc.[3]

The passage awkwardly pushes its way into the review, as though the writer
was unsure where to place it, but nevertheless felt compelled to describe
these musical events.

Three features of this passage illustrate the disruptive effect *Hippolyte* had
on operatic discourse. First, the novelty that this writer encountered sur-
passed his expectations. He had anticipated a lyric tragedy and found something else. Audiences had been familiar with what they regarded as Ital-
ianisms—plangent instrumental music, instrumentally conceived vocal
music, music that was difficult to perform—since the closing years of the
seventeenth century, yet what the reviewer heard in *Hippolyte,* which ostensibly exhibited those same qualities, was not merely different in degree
from older tragedies. It was altogether new. Without greeting *Hippolyte* as
warmly as the *Mercure* reviewer had, the Parfaict brothers later agreed that
the opera represented a new genre: "We arrive here at the first lyric work of
a musician who, despising or perhaps being unable to subject himself in
composing to the taste of those who preceded him, has wished to make us
see that profound science can, in this art, supply genius and natural talent,
even drawing some admirers and supporters. And following a new route,
which is peculiar to him, he undertakes to be for his [new] genre what Lully
had been in the [earlier] genre."[4] This entry then goes on to cite verbatim
the same passage from the *Mercure* review. A second striking feature of the
Mercure passage is that it provides a reasonably thorough inventory of *Hippolyte*'s principal musical events. In focusing on monologues, choruses, symphonies, dances, special effects, and tableaux, it embraces the set piece, divertissement, and musical entertainment at the expense of drama and
recitative, precisely the shift in values that had already concerned
Destouches in 1729. One might conclude from the review that Rameau's
recitative lacked substance or was perhaps even absent, for this catalogue
foreshadows the radical surgery that would be performed on *Les Indes
galantes* two years later, paring *Hippolyte* down to its most entertaining elements. Commentators could not fit dialogue and recitative into their experience of Rameau's operas. A third striking feature of the passage is the
reviewer's using a fragmented syntax to mirror this fragmentary content.
Critical response to *Hippolyte*'s music, as with *Les Indes,* ties the work to
metaphors of communication. Music's heavy intrusion into the opera and
into the review rendered the writer speechless. He wished to provide some
sense of the composer's musical expression—the most obvious means being
to provide an extract, common enough in the *Mercure*—but settled for an
incoherent inventory of it. Setting out to list his favorite moments, he began
by mentioning types of pieces (character airs, tableaux), and then shifted to

a miscellany, even a random account, of high points from each act. In a period when French writers willfully spliced grammatically complete sentences together with commas, semicolons, colons, and conjunctions, this passage instead dissolves into paratactic stuttering, a series of dependent clauses lacking subject or predicate, yet separated by periods. Language fails the reviewer in the face of this surprising musical presence, and in failing introduces more than a hint of the monstrous. Rameau's operas were threatening because of the way his music challenged the primacy of language.

Long after the novelty of *Hippolyte* had worn off, observers retained this sense of difference as a theme for narrating Rameau's career. Facts that we would consider fundamental to the reception of *Hippolyte et Aricie*—for example, whether the opera had been a success or failure—had long faded from public memory by Rameau's death in 1764. The notion that he had invented a new genre by musical means remained fresh, however, taking on a near-mythological status by the end of his life. In his obituary, the ever-diplomatic *Mercure* looked back at the premiere as a difficult but unqualified success:

> [The premiere of *Hippolyte et Aricie*] was the epochal event in the revolution that occurred in music and in its new progress in France. Monsieur Rameau ought to be and probably will be regarded as [its] author and principal cause. The sector of the public that judges and makes decisions only by impression was at first astonished by a music much more charged and fertile in images than they had been accustomed to hearing at the theater. This new genre was nevertheless relished, and they ended up applauding it. The avid desire for novelty, the real merit of the work, and even the contrariety of opinions: everything converged in the success of this first production by a great musician.[5]

If the *Mercure* writer remembered the premiere much as the reviewer had originally reported it, Rameau described it to his pupil Michel-Paul-Guy de Chabanon in rather different terms. In his eulogy for his teacher, Chabanon recounted, "The judgment of the multitude to which M. Rameau found himself subjected furiously rejected that to which he dared make it listen," and further, "The opera *Hippolyte* was decried; its performances were abandoned and deserted." However, Chabanon conceded that the work finally met with deserved success, describing its historical importance in some of the same terms as the *Mercure* had: "reform," "progress," "new," and "revolution." He even characterized the composer's eventual perseverance and success, another theme familiar from eighteenth-century accounts of Rameau's career, in terms of communication: "Our senses opened to the accents of genius, and our hearts appreciated the expression in them and felt their warmth."[6] What the *Mercure* had initially been unable to enunciate was now a primary feature of the story; Rameau and his music had found their way into operatic discourse.

The differences created by the premiere of *Hippolyte et Aricie* can be situated within an ongoing public debate over music's role in opera. By forcing its way into the public's conscious perceptions of the work, the music had upset a delicate balance in which it had formerly been counterpoised with words and drama. It posed the risk of incoherence. This created a double bind for audience members. On the one hand, the association of music with entertainment made it difficult for them to take Rameau and his tragedies seriously; on the other, the intrusive nature of his compositions produced an exciting and, for some, dramatic critical situation. Music could no longer be ignored. Rameau's music de-formed opera, rendering it simultaneously unfamiliar and familiar and locating it both within and outside of Lullian tradition.

As a result, Rameau and his works emerged as something more than composer and compositions. They became easily manipulated symbols for values and concerns defining opera, and they came at times to be used contrary to the composer's evident intentions. One well-documented example occurs in Rameau's collaboration with Voltaire on the unperformed tragedy *Samson,* begun shortly after the premiere of *Hippolyte.* Voltaire regarded Rameau less as a collaborator than as the embodiment of a particular set of musical values he could exploit for his own ideological ends. He needed Rameau, but only on terms that the composer would have found incompatible with his own views of music. At the same time that Rameau's tragedies were becoming symbols of the increasing importance of music over and against text, the composer himself was, in his theoretical writings, elaborating a system of values more consistent with the conservative tragic tradition. His audiences scarcely guessed that he was engaged in a sophisticated musical semiotics, the effects of which would influence the course of his career.

As Destouches's letter of 1729 has demonstrated, the surprise and discomfiture experienced by Rameau's earliest audiences was not restricted solely to his music; rather, they reflected the experiences individuals throughout the French-speaking world felt as their means for discussing music underwent a profound epistemological shift. At the beginning of the eighteenth century, representatives of French culture still treated music as a secondary art, incapable of the insights afforded by painting and spoken theater, and this attitude was to persist in some quarters through most of the century. At the same time, however, the public could no longer ignore the emerging popularity of a variety of musical styles, genres, and repertories. Music was entering into social life to an unprecedented degree, but the conceptual language for framing it had not kept pace. We have already observed this same tension at work in even the simplest statements about Rameau and *Hippolyte et Aricie,* but to appreciate fully the difficulties the composer faced, we must go further. We must gain some sense of the genuine difficulty this culture had in valuing music, beginning by looking at how similar problems emerged in early treatises on beauty and in some later commentaries on opera reform.

During the early eighteenth century, authors in the new field of aesthetics regularly incorporated music into their treatises, but doing so created problems not unlike those Rameau would later unleash with *Hippolyte*. One simply did not write about music without some sort of justification. Le Cerf de la Viéville's famous *Comparaison de la musique italienne et de la musique françoise* (1704–6), for example, had originated as a polemical defense of French values in response to the criticisms of François Raguenet's *Paralèle des italiens et des françois, en ce qui regarde la musique et les opéra* (1702). In the *avertissement* of Jean-Pierre de Crousaz's *Traité du beau* (1715), the author alerted readers to the imbalance that had occurred in his treatise from his decision to include music, and he apologized for it: "[This] work has grown in the writing through the application [I] believed ought to be made of the general idea [of beauty] to different kinds of *beauty* that appeared to merit the most attention. In order to draw from their true principles the reasons one finds beauty in music, a long digression on physics was necessary. This is what rendered the last chapter much longer than the others. If the principles posed there are true and the principles drawn from them clarify the subject, the chapter will not displease [readers]."[7] This is no exaggeration. The first ten chapters, bearing titles such as "Caractéres réels & naturels du beau" (Real and Natural Characters of Beauty), "De la beauté des sciences" (Concerning the Beauty of the Sciences), and "De la beauté de la vertu" (Concerning the Beauty of Virtue), take up 171 pages, while the final chapter, devoted solely to music, contains 131 pages, nearly doubling the treatise's length. In order to arrive at his rather simple points—that, like most arts, music appealed both to the senses and the intellect and that it exhibited unity in diversity—Crousaz felt the need first to range across such topics as why noises are easier to hear at night, how a whistling sound is produced by blowing on a key, the hexachord system, and other matters equally out of character with the rest of his treatise. This thoroughness related to the novelty of his proposition. It was not enough for him to assert that music was comparable to poetry, painting, science, or virtue in its beauty; he had to prove this rationally, a difficult task when music's qualities were so ephemeral:

> There are few subjects on which men are more divided than on that of music. If there are some that it enchants, there are also those who cannot stand it; it calms anxiety in some, while causing it in others; one sees some in whom it creates liveliness, and others whom it renders somber and pensive. Among

those who love it, what diversity of taste is not encountered? People want vaudevilles and airs for dancing, but perceive only noise in overtures, cha- connes, and other airs with this degree of vigor. Nations themselves divide on the preference that ought to be given to different species of music. If our prin- ciples allow us to discover reality in the midst of so much diversity—which, it seems, holds to such whimsy—this will be a new proof of their accuracy.[8]

Music, for Crousaz, was the extreme case, its features so diverse and re- sponses to it so contradictory that it defied reason.[9] Yet as Rameau was re- alizing at about the same time, this very unruliness held out the ultimate prize for would-be thinkers: the individual who could make music conform to rational principles could truly call himself a successful philosopher.

Wherever we look in the literature of this period, music does not coex- ist easily with its surroundings: it disrupts, spills over, and forces its way in. As in Crousaz's treatise, it expands to fill whatever space authors leave for it. Other writers may not have regarded whistling keys as germane to un- derstanding it, but they responded with similarly outsized digressions to the challenges of making music's value apprehensible to readers. The abbé Dubos devoted the entire final tome of his enormous, three-volume edi- tion of *Réflexions critiques sur la poësie et sur la peinture* (1733) to tracing the history of music's importance. The task took him into related areas such as declamation, dance, and theatrical gesture, and it led him from an- tiquity to the glorious days when Lully's tragédies en musique reigned supreme.[10] And even endeavors like these could not deplete their subject. Rameau went on to write forty-one articles and treatises on music without ever successfully exhausting the topic.

Whereas a twentieth-century observer has little trouble identifying music as the necessary detail without which opera lapses into spoken play, French critics struggled with the fact that operas were sung throughout. Charles de Saint-Denis, Seigneur de Saint-Évremond, one of opera's most famous opponents, found the notion of singing a drama from beginning to end abhorrent. It violated the principle of verisimilitude by requiring the com- poser to set both noble and trivial passages to music with equal care. In his popular and much-cited discourse *Sur les opéras* (1684), Saint-Évremond imagined with dismay an opera in which masters called on servants, friends confided in friends, and heroes killed foes, all while singing. Likewise, the omnipresence of song prevented the audience from concentrating on the story: "The intellect, being incapable of conceiving a hero who sings, seizes instead on the one who made the song, and that Lully is a hundred more times likely to be thought of than Thesée or Cadmus would be denied only at the Palais royal."[11] The effect of music on poetry was thus debilitating; language lost its ability to convey meaning when composers added music to it. The problem was sufficiently obvious to gain the attention of opera's proponents as well. Le Cerf de la Viéville, an early and ardent supporter, felt it necessary to have a character in his *Comparaison* address Saint-Évremond's criticism directly. The resulting refutation by analogy with the fable is more noteworthy for its passion than its logic:

> "Ah, M. le Comte," interrupted the Chevalier, "let us therefore show up your Saint-Évremond. In fact, it is not at all natural, if you wish, that what is put in song be sung. I admit that this is not plausible in itself, but it becomes plausible and natural through practice. The musician ought to suppose that it is [plausible and natural] and act accordingly, just as a poet treats subjects from fable as though they were historically plausible. It is well known that all these facts from the fables of antiquity are false, but they have established themselves, they are passed off as true in poetry, and an author who takes a subject for his tragedy from a fable is no less obliged to maintain exactly customs, characters, and proprieties than if he had taken it from the most authentic history. This is how the musician ought to go about it. It is permitted him—he is ordered—to believe that there is nothing except the natural and nothing that ought not be naturally expressed in what he sets to music. It is even necessary that he force himself to express most naturally the least natural things, to give them a form of plausibility by the naiveté of his song and to make spectators as delicate as M. de Saint-Évremond forget, if it is possible, that it strains nature and plausibility to sing these sorts of things."[12]

Saint-Évremond would not have been impressed. Clearly, the sticking point was the idea that singing an entire drama was unrealistic or unnatural, a palpable flaw that could not be overcome with mere enthusiasm. However popular the music had become in opera, it had to be accounted for and articulated in language to assure its commensurate cultural significance. Until these ideas could be expressed in an agreeable manner, opera itself would not take hold. For this reason Rameau's earliest theoretical arguments did not simply seek to elaborate a system for understanding music, but also went to great lengths to make the case that this system occurred in nature. The basis in nature allowed him to talk about those aspects of music that most interested him—how and why music worked—without having to justify his topic. If music was natural, then it was subject to rational inquiry. Rameau's detractors, nevertheless, though perfectly willing to concede that the composer had discovered a system for explaining music, remained unconvinced that anything so complicated could ever be more than sophistry.

Later enthusiasts would reclaim opera not by embracing the differences that music introduced into it but by proposing a new, poetry-based definition of opera with space opened up for music. This new rationale involved realigning the boundaries separating lyric tragedy from spoken tragedy, so that the former could no longer be conceived as a case of adding music to the latter. (It had, of course, never been anything of the sort. This was an argument that had suited its detractors.) What distinguished lyric from spoken tragedy was that it told a different kind of story. Opera had never really dealt with conflicts between duty, honor, and love in the same way as spoken tragedy had; rather, as conservative commentators like Nicolas Boileau, Jacques-Bénigne Bossuet, and Saint-Évremond complained, the livrets of Philippe Quinault allowed gods, strange creatures, and improbable events to mingle freely in a context where love, or at least dalliance, reigned supreme. The solution, then, was to tamper with the economy of genre and make opera's unusual features into generic ideals.

Two treatises from 1741 participate in this trend, Gabriel Bonnot de Mably's *Lettres a madame la marquise de P. . . .sur l'opera* and Toussaint Rémond de Saint-Mard's *Reflexions sur l'opera*. They are important because the authors shared relatively conservative views of opera. The authors treated Quinault's livrets as ideal French poetry, argued that opera resembled Greek tragedy by using music and dance, felt that the recent emphasis on music (beginning with Lully) had left opera in need of reform, and believed that lyric tragedy was a profoundly satisfying theatrical event. Yet they were also willing to sacrifice the highly respected critical positions of Boileau, Bossuet, and Saint-Évremond. Plausibility or *vraisemblance* was, for Saint-Mard, no longer an issue: "As soon as a god, a magician, or a fairy arrives, our heads are turned with special effects; we dispense with this plausibility so dear to us . . ."[13] Mably, meanwhile, suggested that audience members used the supernatural beings to justify music's presence: "These chimerical beings, of whom the spectator has no precise idea, all allow the musician the liberty of giving them a more musical language. It is rather natural to attribute to them more impetuous sentiments, and the poet himself is not obliged to compel his heroes to the essential proprieties when only a few men are introduced. [Lully's characters] Atys and Roland push their furor to an excess that would have been ridiculous in another theater, and one is not shocked that Renaud is intoxicated by Armide's charms and forgets his duty."[14] While claiming to respect the authority of Jean Racine and Boileau, Mably asserted that judging opera by the standards of spoken tragedy was like criticizing an eclogue for not being an ode. He affirmed that the poetic text was the most important feature of opera, but argued that this poetry should be judged by standards different from spoken tragedy: "Opera is a dramatic poem set to music, and for it to be good it suffices that it present an interesting action."[15]

Writers of a slightly later generation formalized Mably's and Saint-Mard's distinction. In *Les Beaux arts reduits a un même principe* (1747), for example, Charles Batteux juxtaposed the tragédie en musique with the two forms of serious poetry recognized in Aristotle's *Poetics,* epic and tragic: "Just as there are in the epic two sorts of greatness, the marvelous and the heroic, there can also be two species of tragedy, one heroic—simply called the tragedy—the other marvelous—called lyric spectacle or tragedy. The marvelous is excluded from the first kind, because there men act as men; whereas in the second, gods act as gods, with all the trappings of supernatural power. [In the latter case,] whatever was not marvelous would cease in some manner to be plausible."[16] Batteux reasoned that gods were exceptional beings and that music provided a means of conveying the difference between their conduct and that of mere mortals.[17] In *La Danse ancienne et moderne* (1754), Rameau's collaborator Louis de Cahusac argued that the tragédie en musique told a different kind of tragic story by virtue of its spectacular elements: "Gods—the first heroes, of whom the fable gives us such poetic and elevated ideas—Olympus, the underworld, the empire of the seas, miraculous metamorphoses, love, vengeance, hate, all the passions personified, the elements in motion, all of nature henceforth furnished the genius of the poet and musician with a thousand varied tableaus and the inexhaustible material for the most brilliant spectacles."[18] Cahusac makes his case for dance as a dramatic force in opera by taking for granted the spectacular topics found in livrets. Opera had not changed; it had simply found a suitable linguistic anchor.

Some scholars have characterized Saint-Mard and Mably as opponents of Rameau, participants in the *querelle des Lullistes et Ramistes,* but this ignores the significance that understanding music had for operagoers.[19] Saint-Mard and Mably did not engage in the kind of personal attacks common in the late 1730s; indeed, they did not mention Rameau by name, and what references they made to his style of composition were tangential to the larger task of prescribing what opera should be. They wanted to invent a form of opera that differed not only from Rameau's but from Lully's as well. In this respect, their position was similar to that of earlier commentators, like Destouches, who worried about intrusive music before hearing a note of *Hippolyte et Aricie*. Music was poetry's supplement. It was indispensable to the formulation of opera per se, but it was nevertheless something added onto an already complete poetic whole. Its position in the ontology of opera was illogical. The chimerical beings with which Mably justified operatic singing might just as easily have described the new genre he envisioned, a concoction of idealized and practical assumptions that testified openly to music's irrational presence.

For the reasons I have just outlined, Voltaire was no great fan of lyric tragedy when he attended the premiere of *Hippolyte et Aricie* in 1733. Only three years earlier, in the preface to the 1730 edition of his spoken tragedy *Oedipe* (1719), he had commented on the irrelevance of the Aristotelian unities to opera and criticized the features that later came to justify opera:

> Opera is a spectacle as bizarre as it is magnificent, where the eyes and ears are
> more satisfied than the intellect, where slavery to the music renders necessary

the most ridiculous faults, where it is necessary to sing ariettes during the destruction of a city and to dance around a tomb, where one sees the palaces of Pluto and the Sun: gods, demons, magicians, prestige, monsters, palaces formed and destroyed in the wink of an eye. These extravagances are tolerated, even loved, because [at the opera] one is in the country of fairies, and provided that there is a spectacle, some beautiful dances, some beautiful music, some interesting scenes, one is content. It would be as ridiculous to demand in [Lully's] *Alceste* unity of action, place, and time as to introduce dances and demons into [Corneille's spoken tragedies] *Cinna* and *Rodogune*.[20]

Voltaire's position was more conservative even than that of Mably and Saint-Mard. That gods, mythical creatures, and the ever-present monsters did not seem out of place merely signaled opera's banality; calling it entertainment for the senses ("eyes and ears") was tantamount to comparing it with furniture, food, or perfume, thereby effectively denying it the status of art. It comes as no surprise, then, that *Hippolyte et Aricie,* which contained most of the features disparaged in the *Oedipe* preface, was not well liked by the Voltaire circle. Madame du Châtelet confessed doubts in a letter to Jacques-François-Paul Aldonce de Sade: "You will surely have heard about Rameau and the different opinions that divide the public regarding his music. Some find it divine, above Lully, while others find it laborious, uniform and not at all agreeable. I am, I confess, one of the latter. I love [Destouches's] *Issé* a hundred times better than what is currently played."[21] Voltaire himself had written to Pierre-Robert Le Cornier de Cideville in just these terms after his first encounter with Rameau's tragic style: "Yesterday I attended the premiere of the opera *Hippolyte et Aricie.* The words are by the abbé Pellegrin and worthy of the abbé Pellegrin. The music is by someone named Rameau, a man who has the misfortune of knowing more about music than Lully. He is a musical pedant, exact and boring."[22]

However Voltaire felt about Rameau, something about *Hippolyte* and its reception caused him to reevaluate his attitude toward the tragédie en musique. Within the month, his friend Jean-Baptiste-Nicolas Formont was writing to Cideville, not without smirking, that "[o]ur friend [Voltaire] is writing a new opera entitled *Samson* for Rameau, for whom he has debased himself after having been so disgusted," and a month after that Voltaire wrote Cideville, "Did you know that during my illness I wrote the opera *Samson* for Rameau?"[23] Within six weeks of hearing *Hippolyte,* Voltaire was inspired to complete a new tragic livret, and sorting out the reasons for this abrupt change provides us with a vantage point for observing Rameau's own theories about poetry and music.

Disgust followed by self-abasement hardly sounds like a vote of confidence, yet we must recall that Voltaire's views on spoken tragedy and theater in general were more conservative even than Boileau's. With the premiere of his first tragedy, *Oedipe,* in 1719, Voltaire had established his reputation as a serious theatrical poet, his beliefs formed by the writings of René Rapin, François de la Mothe Fénelon, and André Dacier. Rapin, in his *Reflexions sur la poetique de ce temps* (1675), had demanded that tragedies serve a didactic function, as prescribed in Aristotle's *Poetics.* He regarded tragedy as "a public lesson more instructive than philosophy, because it educates the intellect through the senses and sets the passions right by means of the passions themselves, calming the trouble they excite in the heart through their emotion. Aristotle, who recognized two important faults to be corrected in man, pride and unkindness, found the remedy for them in tragedy, which renders man modest by showing him the humiliation of great people, rendering him sensitive and compassionate by making him see on stage the strange accidents of life and the unforeseen disgrace to which the most important people are subject."[24] Even admired playwrights like Pierre Corneille and Racine failed to live up to these standards. For Rapin, contemporary French tragedy was little more than an embarassment: "The modern tragedy works on other principles. Perhaps the genius of our nation could not easily sustain an action on stage by the movement of terror and pity alone. [Terror and pity] are machines, which move as necessary only by great sentiments and expressions, of which we are not nearly so capable as the Greeks. Perhaps our nation, which is naturally *galant,* has been obliged by the necessity of its character to create a new system of tragedy, in order to adapt itself to its humor."[25]

French love of gallantry debased the tragedy by introducing love as a recurring theme. "Nothing," Rapin writes, "appears to me to be of as little sense as amusing oneself in dallying with frivolous tendernesses when one can [instead] be admirable by [using] all the marvels of great sentiment and spectacle."[26] Rapin was not alone in his views. Fénelon, in his *Lettre à l'Académie* of 1713, suggested to the Académie française that France would be better off without the tragedies of Corneille and Racine, his words foreshadowing Voltaire's commentary on the tragédie en musique two decades later:

> As for the tragedy, I ought to begin by declaring that I do not desire these spectacles, where corrupted passions are represented only to be ignited, to be perfected. We have seen that Plato and the wise legislators of paganism sent fables and musical instruments, which could weaken a nation with their delights, far from their well-policed republic. What then ought to be the severity of Christian nations against these contagious spectacles? Far from wishing that these spectacles be perfected, I feel a true joy in knowing that ours are imperfect in their genre. Our poets have rendered them as languid, insipid,

and cloying as novels. One speaks in them only of the ardors, chains, torments [of love]. One wishes to die there, carrying on so. A very imperfect person is deemed a sun, or at least a sunrise. His eyes are two stars. All the terms are excessive, and nothing shows true passion. So much the better: the feebleness of the poison diminishes the evil. But it seems to me that one could give tragedies a marvelous force by following the very philosophical ideas of antiquity, without mixing in this inconstant and fickle love that causes so much havoc.[27]

Voltaire's choice of subject for his first tragedy, *Oedipe,* reflected Rapin's and Fénelon's belief that it was the ideal tragic story.[28] His "Lettres sur l'Oedipe," published at the end of the 1719 edition of Voltaire's play, showed the influence of Dacier at every turn, the younger writer alternately citing, praising, and arguing with the older critic's translation of and commentary on Sophocles's play.[29]

From these writers Voltaire developed a belief in tragedy's didactic potential, which he thought was marred by the popularity of romantic themes. In this way, *Oedipe* signaled the beginning of Voltaire's long and problematic relationship with the Comédie française. The actors felt that his earliest versions of the play had not contained sufficient romantic interest to ensure success, and they made the young poet rewrite it. It was an insult he never forgot: "When in 1718 it was a question of performing the only [version of] *Oedipe* that remained in the theater, the actors demanded some scenes where love was not forgotten . . . it was necessary to give in because these actors demanded it; it was necessary to subject oneself to the most contemptible abuse."[30] Encouraged by his stay in London (1726–28), where tragic theater was infused with didactic elements borrowed from Rapin, Dacier, and epic poetry, Voltaire hardened his position on theatrical love into one of seeming intransigence.[31] In his *Discours sur la tragédie,* published in 1730 with his tragedy *Brutus,* Voltaire argued that romantic dalliance was not sufficient; for love to be present in tragedy, it had to be "a truly tragic passion, regarded as a weakness and opposed with remorse. It was necessary that love lead to misfortunes or crimes to show that it is dangerous or that virtue triumph over it to show that it is not invincible. Without this, it is no more than an eclogue or comedy."[32]

He returned often to these themes. He concluded the *Dissertation sur la tragédie ancienne et moderne,* which accompanied the 1752 print of his *Sémiramis,* with a statement comparable to the arguments Rapin had made seventy-seven years earlier: "True tragedy is the school of virtue, and the only difference between purified theater and books on morality is that, in the tragedy, instruction is located completely in action. This is the nature of its interest, and it shows itself elevated by the charms of an art that was invented in the past to educate the earth and bless heaven, and which for this reason was called the language of the gods."[33] In Voltaire, then, we find the obverse of the relationship between spoken and lyric tragedy espoused by Boileau and Saint-Évremond. Whereas the earlier commentators had complained that opera was not sufficiently lofty to warrant the name *tragedy*, Voltaire now argued instead that even the typical spoken tragedy was not worthy of the title, and its failure lay precisely in that trait it shared with the lyric tragedy. His attitude toward tragedies like *Hippolyte et Aricie* was thus an extension of his interest in creating more serious forms of theater. Music aside, the preposterous stories, bizarre characters, and frivolous eroticism of the tragédie en musique were sufficient to assure Voltaire's disdain, and the musical torrent unleashed by *Hippolyte et Aricie* did little to mollify his opinion.

Nevertheless, at the time of the *Hippolyte* premiere Voltaire found himself in an especially vulnerable position with regard to these issues. Smarting from the failure of earlier tragedies like *Mariamne* (1723) and recent ones like *Ériphyle* (1732), he had made a major concession in *Zaire* (1732), allowing love a place in the tragedy. In a letter to Formont dated 29 May 1732, he announced, "I believed that the best means of forgetting the tragedy *Ériphyle* was to make another one. Everyone reproaches me for not putting love in my pieces. They will have it this time, I swear to you, and not just gallantry. I wish there was nothing so Turkish, so Christian, so amorous, so tender, so furious as what I versify at present to please them."[34] The juxtaposition of *Zaire* with the disastrous *Ériphyle* and criticism directed at his previous tragedies had indicated that the playwright was principally interested in theatrical success. Even so, *Zaire* was hardly a frivolous work: the slave Zaire must choose between her Christian faith and love for her master, and, though loyal to her master, she is murdered in his Othello-like fit of jealousy. As though to confirm Voltaire's worst fears, *Zaire* became his most popular tragedy.

During this period Voltaire cast an envious eye toward opera. Writing to Cideville in 1732, he gives the impression of despising opera as much as ever, but also complains that the extent of *Zaire*'s success at court did not satisfy him: "*Zaire* was played here again. Everyone was polite, and it was rather well received from what I'm told. It is not the same with Biblis and his brother Caunus [characters from Lacoste's opera *Biblis*], but one attends [it] even though it is said to be bad. The opera is a public rendezvous, where people gather on certain days without knowing why. It is a house where everyone goes, even if one speaks ill of the master and it is boring. To the contrary some effort is required to draw everyone to the Comédie, and I see nearly always that the greatest success of a good tragedy does not approach that of a mediocre opera."[35] If the offenses of operatic poetry were egregious, its popularity could not be ignored, and so Voltaire joined a long line of poets who disparaged opera publicly while experimenting privately with writing livrets. Boileau and Saint-Évremond had each done so, and in the summer of 1733, only months prior to the premiere of *Hippolyte,* Voltaire announced in a letter to Nicolas-Claude Thieriot that he too was writing an opera, the "tragédie pour être en musique" *Tanis et Zélide.*[36]

Hippolyte et Aricie could not have appeared at a better time. Voltaire saw in Rameau's new lyric tragedy the opportunity to make a statement about tragedy in general, and so he devoted himself to *Samson.* In the letter by Formont previously cited, Voltaire's friend reported to Cideville that "Rameau's opera has won a great deal of favor, and since what pleases in his opera is [duos,] trios, choruses, character airs, etc., [Voltaire] will put into his opera only a very little recitative and will attempt to leave to the musician occasions for exercising his sort of talent."[37] And in several letters from this time Voltaire himself reported much the same plan,[38] guided not by any particular insight into Rameau's music but by the assumption that music now could be more rigorously separated from poetry than ever before. Even after working with the composer for two years, he could not muster much enthusiasm for opera. He regarded music primarily as an instrument for drawing in audiences with the promise of entertainment: "Here is all the interest that I know in an opera. A beautiful, well-varied spectacle; some brilliant divertissements, lots of airs, little recitative, short acts—this is what pleases me." He remained convinced that music could not take part fully in an operatic narrative: "A piece can only be truly touching at the Comédie-française. *Phaëton,* Lully's most beautiful opera, is the least interesting."[39] For Voltaire, reforming opera meant reforming its stories. Love could be present. Indeed, in the preface to the *Samson* written for the 1752 edition of his works, he pointed out that "[t]he names of Venus and Adonis find in this tragedy a more natural place than would at first be believed: it is, in effect, on their terrain that the action occurs."[40] Nevertheless, *Samson* presented yet another opportunity to flirt with the possibility of turning love into a truly tragic emotion.

Volupté's opening speech in *Samson*'s allegorical prologue gives vent to Voltaire's ambivalence toward love as a tragic emotion and toward opera in general:

> Sur les bords fortunés embellis par la Seine
>> Je règne dès longtemps.
> Je préside aux concerts charmants
>> Que donne Melpomène.
> Amours, Plaisirs, Jeux séducteurs,
> Que le loisir fit naître au sein de la mollesse,
>> Répandez vos douces erreurs;
>>> Versez dans tous les coeurs
>>> Votre charmante ivresse;
>> Régnez, répandez mes faveurs.

[I have long reigned over the fortunate shores embellished by the Seine. I preside over the charming concerts that Melpomene gives. Cupids, pleasures, seductive games that leisure makes born in the breast of indolence, scatter your sweet errors; pour into every heart your sweet drunkenness; reign, dispense my favors. (*OCV,* 3:7).]

That voluptuousness ruled Paris in its leisure (*mollesse,* which carries connotations of weakness and flabbiness) could scarcely be construed as a compliment. In the prologue, Volupté's celebrants are momentarily taken aback by the appearance of that "severe nymph" Virtue, but Virtue assures them that she needs Volupté's assistance to tell Samson's sad story, because "Sans toi, l'on ne m'écoute pas" (Without you I am not heard). Virtue thus gives voice to Voltaire's position. The same interests that had motivated him to write *Zaïre* also drew him into the *Samson* project, and, as in the play, his purpose was to show that love could motivate tragedy without being frivolous. The prologue concludes with a lament by the followers of Virtue: "Chantons, célébrons, en ce jour,/Les dangers cruels de l'amour" (On this day let us sing, let us celebrate the cruel dangers of love [*OCV,* 3:9]). As in the prologue, so too throughout the opera: the sensual pleasures of the musical supplement drew the audience's enthusiasm but remained at best a vehicle for the poet's ideas.

Saint-Mard and Mably, Rameau and Voltaire—however much writers, critics, and composers desired a stable tragédie en musique, they found themselves instead trading in an unstable economy of poetry and music, drama and divertissement. Within this economy, Rameau's principal asset remained supplemental; it was extra, external to lyric tragedy, and therefore of questionable, or even dubious value to the public. Earlier composers, notably Campra and Destouches, had likewise invested in music's presence, yet done so without upsetting genre the way Rameau did by asserting purely musical value.

Hippolyte et Aricie offers the kind of operatic experience Michel Poizat and Carolyn Abbate have recently written about, in which music's nonreferential voice resists the easy conclusions of description and analysis.[41] One can argue with some conviction that at the moments of greatest dramatic impact (as when the *Trio des parques* tells Thesée that he will find hell on earth) poetry and drama become secondary to overwhelming musical utterance—the famous enharmonic plunge that musicians at the Opéra could not or would not perform. Music disrupts, spills over, forces its way in: this is what the *Mercure de France* reviewer conveyed when he had allowed musical events to intrude into his article without concern for syntax or logic. It is what Voltaire imagined when he wrote a livret in which action and divertissement were more widely separated than ever before. Yet when we speak of Rameau's operas in these terms, we are speaking less of particular dramatic, formal, or stylistic traces composed into the music than of ideological ones residing in the audience. Rameau's own notion of music's place in the operatic economy was not so neatly compartmentalized. Time and again he argued not simply that music had value but that it possessed significance independent of (but no less communicative than) language, and in making this argument he inverted common assumptions about his opera. As we will see, the weakest link in this exchange may have been not between work and audience, but between composer and public.

In 1765, the year following Rameau's death, the *Mercure de France* published an early letter from the composer to the famed poet Antoine Houdar de La Motte. Originally written in 1727, Rameau's letter appears to signal the end of a correspondence in which the composer sought to have La Motte write a livret for him. Rameau attempts to allay the poet's qualms about working with a well-known music theorist:

> One who speaks of a learned musician ordinarily means a man from whom none of the different combinations of notes escapes; but [this musician] is at the same time believed to be so absorbed in these combinations that he sacrifices everything: good sense, sentiment, intellect, and reason. Now, that is only a textbook musician, of the school where notes matter and nothing else, so that one is correct in preferring a musician inspired less by science than taste. Meanwhile, the latter, whose taste is formed only by the range of his senses, can at the most excel only in certain genres . . . relative to his temperament. Is he naturally tender? He expresses tenderness well. Is his character lively, playful, droll, etc.? Then his music responds accordingly. But if he departs from the moods most natural to him, you no longer recognize him. Elsewhere, as he draws on all his imagination through his affinity with [these] expressions, without the aid of art, he wears himself out. In his first inspiration, he was completely brilliant, but this inspiration consumes itself in proportion as he wishes to rekindle it, and one finds no more to his work than repetitions and platitudes. It would therefore be desirable to find for the theater a musician who studied nature before painting it, who, by his science, knew how to choose colors and nuances that his intellect and taste have made him feel agree with the necessary expressions.[42]

It would have been desirable, in other words, to find a musician like Rameau. The subtext is sufficiently clear to imagine the remarks leading to the composer's response: as a forty-four-year-old keyboardist he was rather old to begin a career at the Opéra, and as a theorist known for complicated arguments he was unlikely to write the simple, ingratiating accompaniments that La Motte required. Rameau's rejoinder, characteristically, was not to argue that he could in fact write such accompaniments, but to explain that La Motte did not understand composition. The ideal composer possessed both learning and taste. His task was neither to write notes nor to express sentiments; it was rather to compose music that *agreed* with the poetry. The composer must possess both a thorough knowledge of musical effects and the good sense to know how to use them appropriately. La Motte was apparently not impressed by this argument, for no collaboration ensued, but Rameau's argument, written about the same time as his treatise *Nouveau système de musique theorique* (1726), already shows a highly wrought notion of how music interacts with texts. In order for music to agree with poetry it must exist as more than an extraneous detail.

If the public could conceive of Rameau only as a learned compiler of notes, his theoretical writings painted a picture of someone who thought constantly about the links between music and text. He had broached this subject as early as the *Traité de l'harmonie* (1722), in which he addressed concerns like proper scansion—especially at cadences—and declamation. Even greater was his concern for mapping musical syntax onto poetic syntax: "Whenever possible, we must avoid using a final cadence on the last syllables of lines which do not conclude the meaning of the sentence." This matching of poetic and musical syntax, he observed, was especially important in recitative.[43] In the *Nouveau système* he developed this comparison more fully, creating from the analogy between poetic and musical syntax a theoretical principle that encompassed, but was by no means limited to, harmonic progressions: "Just as a discourse is ordinarily composed of several phrases, so too a piece of music is ordinarily composed of several *modulations,* which can be regarded as so many *phrases harmoniques.*"[44] In Rameau's lexicon, the word *modulation* incorporates multiple connotations, placing as much emphasis on the word *phrases* as the word *harmoniques.*[45] We may imagine modulation at its most general as addressing the flow or phrasing of the music as regulated by its poetry. In his very next sentence, Rameau moved beyond simile to state explicitly that in setting texts composers should reflect the phrases of the poetry within musical phrases, and he mentioned Lully's famous monologue from *Armide,* "Enfin il est en ma puissance," as a worthy example of this technique.[46] The chapter dealt extensively with tonal relationships between phrases and the ways in which cadences could be used to tie together and articulate these phrases. Rameau stated, "If these phrases [of poetry] are connected to each other, [then] one attempts to give them suitable harmonic progressions," and "There is also a choice to be made among *cadences,* conforming to the sense of the words."[47] The *Nouveau système* continued to value the grammatical or, better still, syntagmatic analogy between music and text.[48] What we now regard as the more intimate and profound compositional activity in setting text, what falls under the general heading of *expression,* is implied but secondary to the unfolding succession of poetic verses and musical phrases.

Rameau seems prepared to rectify this apparent imbalance between musical syntax and musical expression in the subsequent chapter of the *Nouveau systême,* entitled "The force of expression depends a great deal more on harmonic progressions than on simple melody." The title threatens to reroute us through that most favored of Rameau debates, the preeminence of harmony over melody, although it also demonstrates the composer's perception of the expressive element in texted music. In this chapter, Rameau adopts a more prescriptive and value-oriented tone than was typical for him: he criticizes all composers, including himself, for falling back on tried-and-true harmonic progressions, in the manner of the tasteful composer he described to La Motte, instead of exploring the full range of expressive possibilities offered by music. Yet, avoiding the underlying issues of musical expression, he confesses that if this range of possibilities is not in fact endless, it is nevertheless well beyond his own theoretical means: "If it is not absolutely impossible to determine the melodies, and consequently the *harmonic progressions,* that best agree with the most marked expressions [of discourse, then] it is, in other respects, an enterprise that demands more than the lifetime of a single individual."[49] He attempts to give some indication of the magnitude of the problem by presenting a table of sixty different ways in which the melodic interval g–c^1 might be effectively harmonized, the point being that such versatility gives the composer plenty of room to find just the right expressive nuance.[50] At the same time, Rameau takes care not to prescribe what those nuances are. Expressive text setting, according to this line of reasoning, is a matter of thoroughly understanding harmonic progressions and being willing to experiment, always with the poetic text in mind. Musical learning and taste go hand in hand.

Expression per se, then, is a particular aspect of the general notion of *modulation* described earlier, a singular musical gesture. It is still linked compositionally to musical syntax; indeed, more than merely linked, it is a constituent of this syntax, as revealed in Rameau's preceding chapter. Yet there is also a difference between the two chapters: whereas Rameau's material on *modulation* emphasizes its fundamental, practical importance for the composer, his discussion of expressive text setting emphasizes the more personal, even speculative, element in composition, bordering on what we might refer to as personal musical style.

We may surmise that the two chapters from the *Nouveau systême* tell us little about Rameau the composer. Their pedagogical tone, their emphasis on such topics as phrase length and cadences, and their exhortations to understand musical expression by studying harmonic progressions convey practical advice found in numerous contemporary music treatises. The point, as Rameau's eighteenth-century readers would have keenly felt, is that this advice is allied with a grounding of all musical gesture in nature, as part of a system of musical phenomena that is informed, controlled, and explainable. This places music on the same footing with poetry and theater, whose audiences might assume to find their sources in the simple and forth-right representation of natural phenomena. It requires placing music within the epistemology that informed, controlled, and explained all serious art.

Yet this also created problems for the composer-theorist. As we have seen, many readers in Rameau's time considered music quite different from other arts by virtue of its seeming irrationality, and Rameau appeared to be conceding some irrational features. Like Crousaz, he acknowledged music's polysemous elements—its ability to deliver countless, nuanced harmonizations that could radically change the meaning of even a simple perfect fourth—and he begged out of the claim to know and understand all its possible ramifications.

If music is irrational, then how could one hope to argue that its meanings are simple and forthright? Rameau would have us believe that, far from being irrational, music operates by virtue of its contiguity with poetry (through what Catherine Kintzler has described as its *parallelism* with verse).[51] Just as a syntactic unit within a sentence makes sense only in relation to what precedes and follows it, so too the expressive musical gesture must be conceived in conjunction with the unscrolling of its poetry in performance. This is not to deny the impact of the simple, denotative musical gestures that feature in so much of Rameau's music. The unusual melodic interval or dissonant harmony that directs our attention to a particular word or gesture has a rich and undeniable place in Rameau's operas and in those of his contemporaries and predecessors. But what he tells us again and again is that such gestures alone do not make a musical setting expressive. A narrowly denotative gesture cannot truly represent the emotional situation of a scene, but rather it calls attention only to the individual words and phrases. With a more explicitly connotative approach, Rameau hopes to capture the substance of the dramatic scene in the process of its unfolding.[52]

To appreciate what Rameau intended by this approach requires probing the curious semiotic paradigm that he elaborated over the course of his career, both theoretically and musically. It maintained the well-established value of poetic text in the tragédie en musique, but did so in an artificial manner, by maintaining an overtly musical value, one that was at odds with contemporary aesthetics. To many audience members and critics in Rameau's day, music was to be a transparent addition to poetry. Any expressive or descriptive musical addition beyond the simplest of gestures threatened to overturn meaning by rendering the poetry opaque. Rameau argued that by virtue of the analogy between poetic and musical phrasing, the musical setting of any given poetic text ran parallel to the poetry, commented on that poetry, but was ultimately exterior to it because it also maintained a self-sufficient musical grammar in its *modulation*.

The best model I have found for describing this paradigm for producing meaning is Roland Barthes's distinction between those visual references based on an *anchoring* process and those based on a *relaying* process. Anchoring, the simpler form of signifying reference, may be thought of as a form of labeling: a word or short phrase anchors the meaning of a corresponding visual image or gesture by fixing or labeling it. This occurs, for example, with the captioning of a picture. Next to a painting on a museum wall we are likely to find a small card answering such fundamental questions as who made this? what is it called? whom does it belong to? and what media does it employ? In the same way, we have tended to view Rameau's expressive musical gestures in a one-to-one referential system that labels isolated fragments of poetry. For example, in French opera of this time, the word *chaine* is often labeled musically with a melisma, the word *larmes* with dissonant harmony. Music, in these examples, may be said to fix or label the text, presumably assuring us of its sincerity in utterance. Relaying, on the other hand, involves two continuing, independent systems of signification that contribute mutually to a larger narrative act. Barthes cites as example film, in which closely connected spoken and visual narratives each contribute to the story through chains of signification, coextensive with but independent of each other.[53] This relaying seems closer to what Rameau had in mind. Semiotically, the word *chaine* might just as convincingly label the melisma as vice versa, the word *larmes* the dissonant harmony; the instability created in the space between the parallel sequences of discharging signifiers—as meaning moves back and forth between poetry and music—keeps our attention locked not on one to the exclusion of the other but rather on the details of the story being told. Rameau described something like this situation in attempting to privilege harmony vis-à-vis melody: "Harmony is sounded here before melody, which is the product of [harmony], in order that it inspires in the singer the sentiment with which he ought to be affected *independently of the words,* a sentiment that will strike all unbiased [listeners] who willingly entrust themselves to *the pure effects of nature*" (emphasis added).[54]

The opening to act one of *Hippolyte,* Aricie's monologue "Temple sacré, séjour tranquille," provides an example of the refractory ways we might hear and analyze music operating in this relaying kind of relationship with poetry. The composer's setting creates an ambiguous alternative to the livret, offering neither the full presence of its meaning—which Rameau agreed was impossible—nor the relative absence of meaning presumed by operagoers. Instead, modulation functions parallel to poetry. "Temple sacré" hints at significations relevant to the story through the kind of relay described by Barthes; much like Rameau's original audiences, however, we cannot be certain of the meanings we glimpse. For the analyst who desires a single, concrete interpretation of a musical passage, there is little of note to be found in this monologue, but Rameau's theories create what

Lawrence Kramer has called a "hermeneutic window," an invitation to speculate about potential meanings.[55] As the composer explains in the *Nouveau systême,* music is rife with meanings, whether or not they can be specified, because meaning itself results from music's regular ordering in nature. To dismiss the puzzling features of "Temple sacré" is to ignore the rich semiotic traces invoked by the name Rameau on the title page.

Example 2.1 presents the first sixteen measures of the vocal part to "Temple sacré."[56] What we make of this passage depends greatly on whether we look first at its melody, which bears the text, or at its *phrases harmoniques,* which would have drawn Rameau's interest. The melodic line presents two periods in D major (mm. 21–28 and 29–36), in which Aricie outlines the conflict between religious devotion and romantic attraction that will occupy the first act.

> Temple sacré, Séjour tranquille,
> Où Diane aujourd'hui doit recevoir mes voeux,
> A mon coeur agité, daigne servir d'azile
> Contre un amour trop malheureux.

[Sacred temple, tranquil sojourn where Diane today will receive my vows, deign to serve as refuge for my agitated heart against a love too unfortunate. (*H livret 1733,* 1).]

We hear, first of all, similarities between the periods: the opening rhythmic figures, a half-note followed by two eighth-notes and leading to a dotted half-note (mm. 21–22 and 29–30); the rising fourth from a to d[1] near the beginning of each (mm. 21–22 and 30–31); and the descending-third figures at the medial cadences (mm. 24 and 32), which draw attention to the rhymes *tranquille* and *azile.* These impressions are initially maintained as we look to the harmonic underpinnings of the two periods, because each opens with a descending tetrachord from d to A (mm. 21–23 and 29–32). Looking more closely, we must question what we hear, however, for the *modulations* are actually quite different in each case. In the first tetrachord, the basse continue descends in three measures, using its c# in m. 21 to support a passing dominant harmony and leading to the subdominant on the second beat of m. 22; this subdominant, sustained into m. 23, leads to a perfect-authentic medial cadence in D major in m. 24. In the second period the pitch content remains the same, but the descending tetrachord is redistributed metrically to create four equally strong downbeats. It modulates, in the modern sense, descending to a medial cadence in A major. Rameau emphasizes these differences through an elaborate reorchestration of the material in the second period: the basse continue drops out, the descending tetrachord moves into the second violins, and an upper-register flute accompaniment lavishly ornaments the whole. Rameau directs the listener's attention to the second period, and in this way musical details that sound simple and pleasant enough in performance intrude into our perception of the passage. Seemingly parallel musical gestures are overdetermined through a surplus of musical detail, and the farther we proceed into the second phrase, the more obviously different the two periods become. We thus encounter one of the central problems for modern critics who are studying Rameau's work: how contemporaries could hear unassuming passages as difficult or complex. Whether we admire this subtle pairing of the two periods or remain unimpressed, we discover something like the gratuitous play of musical gesture that both attracted and repelled Rameau's audiences. As the composer Campra put it in a widely circulated remark, there was enough music in *Hippolyte et Aricie* for ten operas.

But there is another way of hearing this material. In listening to the second period, if we recall the first one—if we engage in the complex, recursive listening I described with respect to "Soleil, on a détruit tes superbes aziles"—we find meaning in the differences we encounter. The beginning of the second period marks an important change in Aricie's text. The hyperbaton at the beginning of the third verse—"For my agitated heart, deign to serve as refuge," rather than the more direct "Deign to serve as refuge for my agitated heart"—draws attention away from Aricie's impending ordination as priestess and toward her actual state of mind. She is less concerned with the sacred temple or tranquil refuge than with her anxieties. In this context, the recursive hearing encouraged by the two musical periods—the first looking forward to the second, the second looking back to the first—allows us to hear the second descending tetrachord as a lament topos. The indirectly stated material of the first period allows Aricie's sadness to emerge gradually in the music, just as it does in the text. Rameau encouraged just this sort of recursive hearing when he discussed *modulation* in the *Nouveau système*, asserting that music resembled language because the two shared such referential properties:

> Let us suppose that one is setting words to music. It is therefore necessary to consider the connection that the phrases of the discourse have between them that express these words and to make the connection of the *modulations* conform to them as much as possible.
>
> If one wishes a phrase to have a great deal of connection with the one that precedes or succeeds it, then these two phrases must be given the most closely related *modulations*. For the same reason, if these phrases have little connection between them, one attempts to give them [more distantly] corresponding *modulations*.[57]

In just this way, Rameau links the two opening phrases of "Temple sacré" with similar modulations but then subverts these links in order to show that the two couplets are not as closely linked as they appear. He counts on the ability of musical signifiers to refer not only to events but also to other musical signifiers as well.[58]

Example 2.1. "Temple sacré, séjour tranquille," *Hippolyte et Aricie* (1733), act 1, scene 1, mm. 21–36

Example 2.1, *continued*

Contre   un A - mour   trop   mal - heu - reux.

The intention I ascribe to Rameau appears reasonable if we compare the linking to a similar passage in Lully's *Atys*, act one, scene four. As James Anthony has observed, Lully uses a descending tetrachord in Sangaride's "Atys est trop heureux" to denote lament,[59] its presence emphasizing the ironic cast of her speech:

> Atys est trop heureux!
> Souverain de son coeur, maître de tous ses voeux,
> Sans crainte, sans melancolie,
> Il joüit en repos des beaux jours de sa vie;
> Atys ne connoît point les tourments amoureux,
> Atys est trop heureux!

[Atys is too happy! Sovereign of his heart, master of all his desires, without fear, without melancholy he enjoys the beautiful days of his life in repose. Atys does not know amorous torments: Atys is too happy! (*RG*, 1:110).]

Though ostensibly speaking of joyful matters (that is, Atys's well-being), Sangaride is sad in fact that he does not suffer "amorous torments" as she does; her lamenting ground bass, therefore, undercuts her text's most obvious meaning. Rameau must have admired how this music provides information only indirectly available in the poetry. Nevertheless, this scene alone would not support his setting of "Temple sacré." Where he placed the burden of Aricie's meaning on a single descending tetrachord, Sangaride is steadily accompanied by them; when she ceases to speak, the tetrachords cease as well, and when she begins again, they do also, so that perceiving her underlying emotional state becomes unavoidable. More interesting than this act of simple denotation are the connotations of the single descending tetrachord when it reappears in a following scene, during Atys's entrance (shown in example 2.2).[60] Having just learned of Sangaride's pain, we are reminded

Example 2.2. Lully, *Atys,* act 1, scene 5, m. 5 through scene 6, m. 6

through the music that she feels it each time she sees him.[61] Here, as in the example from *Hippolyte,* the listener is expected on some level to hear a musical detail recursively, to recall earlier music and use it in a present interpretation.

What we take away from "Temple sacré, séjour tranquille" is the rift that existed between the composer and his critics. Rameau wagered on his theoretical position, presenting a text setting that radically compressed the musical effect and believing that the musical topos would have its desired effect whether or not the listener consciously noticed it. He assumed, as he put it in his letter to La Motte, that a composer could "disguise art with art itself,"[62] using musical taste to disguise the effects of musical learning. But the wording of this phrase (*cacher l'art par l'art même* [p. 39]) points to a glaring inconsistency in his beliefs, for eighteenth-century French thought in general opposed art to nature. If the learned and tasteful composer drew too heavily on artifice to create music, then nature itself was surely lost and no amount of theorizing would restore it. Even such reasonably knowledgeable collaborators as Voltaire heard in Rameau's music the intrusion of musical effect, "art itself." An asymmetry important for understanding Rameau thus emerges in his relationship with the public. He did not simply believe something contrary to public opinion but something inconceivable within that context. He believed himself part of the Lullian tradition because he used music to support what that tradition valued most. But the public deemed music could never be more than an ornament, a pleasant addition secondary to drama in importance. To draw attention to music's presence was to reconfigure the tragic genre in terms of entertainment, and this was more than a nominal distinction. To maintain the position that music revealed poetic meaning, and Rameau had already invested a great deal in this position by the time of the premiere of *Hippolyte et Aricie,* could lead only to crisis, and we find the evidence of this crisis as we sift through the revivals of his three middle tragedies, *Castor et Pollux, Dardanus,* and *Zoroastre.* As we might expect, the crisis was at least in part one of communication.

CHAPTER 3

Rameau's Twins

HAVING ESTABLISHED a new compositional voice by emphasizing music's presence, Rameau could easily have continued composing scenes in the vein of "Temple sacré, séjour tranquille." To be sure, *Hippolyte* had met with controversy. Musicians refused to perform portions of it, and, as we will see, they forced poet and composer to alter other scenes during the earliest stages of the production. Yet, in spite of this, Rameau's status as a composer was now sufficiently strong to provide opportunities for pursuing music's newfound role. The Académie royale de musique, plagued as always by financial difficulties, could scarcely ignore the attention he had generated with his first opera: at a time when successful new tragedies were rare, the promise of a continuous flow of controversial works was far better than having no new works at all. When, in late 1739, Rameau's new tragedy *Dardanus* ceased to be profitable, the directors of the Opéra caused a stir by replacing it not with the anticipated Lully revival, but with another work by Rameau, the opéra-ballet *Les Fêtes d'Hébé*. Some members of the public feared—not for the last time—that this new composer was in fact taking over.[1] Further, we cannot overlook that a substantial portion of the audience found *Hippolyte* genuinely enjoyable and, unlike Voltaire, believed this was reason enough to attend performances. Ramistes may not have been as outspoken as their Lulliste counterparts, but the Lulliste screeds suggest that Rameau's fans were not declining in number. As though to prove this point, rewards followed on the heels of *Hippolyte*. Rameau found protection in the household of the wealthy tax-farmer, Alexandre-Jean-Joseph Le Riche de La Pouplinière.[2] As the object of Voltaire's newly discovered interest in opera, the composer no longer had to struggle to impress the likes of Antoine Houdar de La Motte and Simon-Joseph Pellegrin. And throughout all of this, Rameau's reputation as a theorist continued to grow with the publication of his articles in the *Journal de Trévoux* and *Le Pour et contre* and of his *Génération harmonique* (1737). Whatever doubts existed about his music, Rameau's place in Parisian musical life was secure in the years following his first tragedy.

Still, despite these successes, it would have been difficult for him to remain unaware of the divisions his music was causing among audiences. Lingering questions about whether theorists could be good composers, incidents such as the printing of *Les Indes* without recitatives, and frequent appearances of new epigrams lambasting Rameau and his works were reminders that his theory and practice had failed to mesh with public imagination. The resulting gap between the composer and his audience intensified in the 1730s, reaching its zenith with a brief pamphlet war on the occasion of *Hippolyte*'s revival in 1742, nine years after its premiere.[3] For all his success, Rameau may well have wondered at the price of attitudes, opinions, styles, and theories that did not produce their intended effects even among his supporters, and there is evidence that he took steps to address these issues. Indeed, I will argue that finding a means of bridging the gap between theory, practice, and critical response came to consume his principal efforts as a composer, tying up much of his creative energy during the 1740s and 1750s. Entering into the experimental spirit he had encouraged in the *Nouveau système* (1726), Rameau chose to explore the text-music relationships that informed pieces like "Temple sacré," searching for a plan that would please audiences while conforming to his own theoretical tenets.

Confronted with the failure of some of his most cherished ideas, Rameau did not so much refine as redefine his compositional procedures, the criteria for good text setting changing in the course of his career. He responded to criticism of—or deafness toward—his conception of music's role with extensive revisions of his older works. While it was not uncommon at this time to revise operas, Rameau seems to have been especially fascinated with the creative opportunities these revivals offered for new versions. Given the chance, or else grasping at it when it availed itself, he made over entire operas, perhaps with the hope of "getting them right." He did more than add new ariettes, dances, or other divertissement material, as often happened with Lully revivals from the same period.[4] He focused as much or more of his attention on the most dramatic portions of the work: its monologues, recitatives, airs, and scenes. As with the *Les Indes* print, in which the suppression of narrative material had caused the work itself to spiral out of control and into a series of generic anomalies, the revisions made it difficult in the end to determine what sort of social function the print, and hence the work itself, was to have. With the lyric tragedies, Rameau's propensity for transformation led to versions that shared the same title, and at least some superficial resemblances, yet ultimately twisted the composer's theoretical and practical ideas into new and striking shapes. The volatile ontology of opera, so important to Rameau and his audience, also came to look remarkably unstable within the limits of the composer's own *oeuvres*. Even now, to speak of works like *Hippolyte, Castor et Pollux, Dardanus,* or *Zoroastre* is to blur and confuse them, for each exists in two or three versions from the composer's lifetime. It is to speak ambiguously of doubles and twins. It is to speak of works possessing recognizable, yet also fundamentally altered features. By reevaluating the parallelism between music and poetry, by focusing on the parts of the opera to which narrative was most important, Rameau came to reimagine or "re-image" his older works in radically new ways.

To trace this process of doubling I will pursue a different methodology: whereas to this point I have allowed the publicly espoused attitudes of Rameau and his critics to situate his works culturally, I now reverse this process and look at how private compositional decisions responded to public criticism. Here and in the next chapter I will speculate on why Rameau and his poets engaged in these revisions and what they hoped to gain from them. As years of sketch studies have demonstrated, it is next to impossible to divine why a composer would choose one version of a musical passage over another, but by now it should also be evident that the circumstances involving Rameau are somewhat different. In the case of a Beethoven sketch, we have the final version of the work for comparison. In the case of Rameau, we have something more. We have an extraordinarily detailed selection of writings by critics and composers that deal with rigorously stated values, the values I have outlined up to this point. We have a sense of what the public liked and disliked and, more importantly, of how it responded to a form of opera that was difficult to comprehend. Moreover, we have some notion of what the composer valued and how that fit into his theoretical position. A gap may have existed between critics and composer, but it is a gap we can measure with some surety because, unlike a Beethoven sketch, the values brought into play by a Rameau opera have been articulated fairly well.

For the present, I wish to pursue the issue of text setting as we find it in recitative scenes and in pieces like "Temple sacré"; in chapter 4 I will return to the larger issue, first outlined in chapter 1, of the shifting balance between poetry and music, between drama and divertissement. Both chapters will focus on the central tragedies in Rameau's career, *Castor, Dardanus,* and *Zoroastre*. With regard to text setting, the issues are how this practice changed in the course of his career and how these changes functioned within the various operatic ideologies we have been tracing. We will find that the first versions of Rameau's tragédies show a concern for the kinds of semiotic practices broached in the *Nouveau système* and practiced in such pieces as "Soleil, on a détruit tes superbes aziles" and "Temple sacré." In subsequent versions of these tragedies, however, these same practices were in various ways attenuated. Even as, in the early 1750s, Rameau was mounting his most impassioned theoretical arguments for a semiotics of text setting, he seems already to have experienced some doubts about its practical effectiveness. Thus it is that we find chimerical figures not only among the doubles that attach to a title like *Castor et Pollux* or *Dardanus,* but also in the composer who went about redefining himself with the same zeal he devoted to his compositions.

A key text for understanding Rameau's positioning of himself and his tragedies is his second commentary on Lully's "Enfin il est en ma puissance" (from Lully's *Armide,* act two, scene five), which appears in his treatise *Observations sur notre instinct pour la musique* (1754). It is an unwieldy discussion. Long and extravagantly detailed, it betrays the awkwardness of describing music measure by measure. Moreover, it uses a singular method. In the *Nouveau systême* Rameau had argued that musical details affected meaning, extrapolating outward from his theories and offering sixty harmonizations of a single ascending fourth. In the *Observations* he reverses this process, moving inward by providing a detailed exegesis of a substantial passage of music. No trill, no cadence, no change of key lacks significance in this discussion. The apparent reason for this sudden reversal in method is that the *Observations* text comes as a response to Jean-Jacques Rousseau's *Lettre sur la musique françoise* (1753).[5] As we will see, the importance of Rameau's commentary on "Enfin" lies not only with its application of the composer's theories but also with the circumstances under which it was written and, ultimately, the timing of its appearance.

I refer to Rameau's presentation of "Enfin" as a discussion or commentary in an effort to resist its resemblance to modern theoretical practice.[6] The temptation is great: here at last in the history of music theory is an event that looks much like what we do when we analyze music, especially opera.[7] Yet Rameau was uncomfortable, as we have seen, committing to definitive statements about musical representation: he may have pointed eagerly to certain harmonies and progressions—as he did, for example, with the chromaticism in "Tristes apprêts," from *Castor et Pollux*—but he usually avoided comprehensive analyses of the kind we practice today. In the *Nouveau systême,* he had halted before coming to such an explanation, pleading (in terms that Jean-Pierre Crousaz would have appreciated) that music's potential meanings were too diverse to be inscribed irrefutably on the printed page. In that text he had offered instead a transcription of "Enfin" with an additional staff indicating its fundamental bass (*NS,* 41, 79–90; *CTW,* 2:51, 89–100). As Alan Keiler has observed, this strategy afforded Rameau a relatively safe means of presenting material by allowing him to comment on music through musical notation.[8] Rameau could give readers the impression that he was revealing natural truths rather than presenting his own views. He had not explained Lully's music; rather, Lully's music had explained itself. The circumstances were different twenty-eight years later, after Rousseau had undertaken a detailed commentary on "Enfin" in his *Lettre.*

Rousseau made it clear that in commenting on "Enfin" he was attacking not only the French operatic tradition in general but also Rameau's praise for Lully's monologue in the *Nouveau systême:* "I remark first that M. Rameau rightly cited ["Enfin"] as an example of an exact and well-linked *modulation,* but this eulogy, applied to the piece in question, truly becomes satire. Were [the musical passage by] Rameau himself, he would merit similar praise, for can one think of a more poorly conceived [setting] than this scholastic regularity in a scene where outburst, tenderness, and the contrast of opposed passions place the actress and the audience in the most lively agitation?"[9] What Rousseau disliked about "Enfin" was the avoidance of overt musical expression, in the highly emotive sense that twentieth-century readers would understand by this phrase. Far from revealing the dramatic content of Quinault's poetic text, Lully's unobtrusive musical setting seemed to exist for its own sake as a distracting musical artifact: "Armide, furious, comes to stab her enemy. In his presence, she hesitates, she allows herself to be moved, the knife falls from her hands; she forgets her designs for revenge, but does not for a single instant forget her *modulation.* The silences, the interruptions, the intellectual transitions that the poet offered the musician have not been seized upon a single time by the latter."[10] Neither harmony, tonality, melody, ornamentation, nor declamation, according to Rousseau, come to Armide's rescue, and he thus could portray her as concerned more with her music than with her situation.

An interesting trajectory has emerged from the various commentaries on "Enfin." In the *Nouveau système* Rameau's goal had been to explain his theories. He had offered up "Enfin" to show how Lully had followed the rules of music as they occurred in nature. Rousseau then returned Rameau's theories to him in inverted form, disrupting the very foundations of the composer's argument. Rousseau's goal was nothing less than to demonstrate the poverty of expression in all French opera. He contended that the expressive means of French opera had failed in one of the most admired passages in the history of the tragédie en musique, and they should be replaced with stylistic attributes and aesthetic values more consistent with those of Italian opera. The philosophe pursued Lully's lack of sensitivity for twelve full pages, dwelling particularly on the composer's treatment of tonality. The gist of his argument was that Lully had composed music hopelessly anchored in E minor throughout. By conflating Rameau's theoretical position with Lully's music, Rousseau attributed to the tragic tradition the very qualities associated with Rameau's music: attention to musical detail made at the expense of textual clarity. By admiring Lully's setting, he argued, Rameau had accomplished something that would have been difficult for his contemporaries to imagine. He had made himself into an advocate for bland music. The composer's position in the *Observations* was thus one of answering criticism, a position formulated not of his own volition but rather of necessity.

Rameau found himself in the enviable position of defending his theories and traditional French opera in the same breath, producing a declaration that is more old-fashioned polemic than modern analysis. He used the opportunity to align himself further with the very tradition that treated him as an outsider, and this position gives his remarks a passion and a practicality that reflect his own complicated status within and outside traditional French culture. To appreciate fully Rameau's remarks, then, we must keep in mind their function as a reply to a reply, an answer to Rousseau's indirect attack on the *Nouveau système*. Rousseau had constructed his critique of "Enfin" as a verse-by-verse reading of the first fifteen lines of poetry, skipping at the end to a verse from later in the scene. In response, Rameau addressed Rousseau's commentary with couplets rather than single verses, consistent with the sensitivity he had displayed in the *Nouveau système* for links between poetic syntax and musical *modulation*. Rousseau had forced him to center his argument on complete syntactical units and to integrate it with *modulation* to an unprecedented degree.

Example 3.1 reproduces the first example from the *Observations* of Rameau's extended discussion of "Enfin." It consists of the first two verses of Quinault's text:

> Enfin il est en ma puissance,
> Ce fatal ennemi, ce superbe vainqueur.

[Finally, he is in my power, this fatal enemy, this proud victor.][11]

Rousseau criticized two aspects of Lully's setting of the first verse: first, the trill, which he regarded as a needless ornament, along with its closely related *repos absolu* (both on "puiss*an*ce"), and second, the lack of musical connection between the first and second verses. He had less to say about the second verse, observing only that he could pardon Lully for having moved to another key in this passage if the composer had done so more often when necessary (*LSL*, 81–82; *QDB*, 1:753–54). Rameau countered Rousseau's first point by both agreeing and disagreeing with his terminology. First, Rameau stressed the importance of the word *trille*, agreeing with Rousseau that it, and not *cadence*, was the appropriate expression in this instance. This allowed him to separate the notion of trill, *qua* trill, from its routine deployment at cadences in French music, a practice that caused the ornament itself to be referred to in common parlance as a *cadence*.[12] Lully had used this particular trill, Rameau argued, for expressive rather than cadential ends. He wrote that it is "justly similar to [those trills] of trumpets in victory songs" and therefore expresses Armide's sense of triumph at having her enemy within her grasp. As for the closely related problem of Rousseau's *repos absolu*, Rameau argued on the basis of the expressive trill that "there is not a ghost of one" in the passage, and this by Rousseau's own principles. Rameau cited specific pages and lines from Rousseau's articles in the *Encyclopédie*, showing that there Rousseau had treated the concept of *repos* as virtually synonymous with *cadence*.[13] He was thus able to accuse Rousseau of succumbing to the same conflation of ornamental and cadential functions that Rousseau had condemned in his *Encyclopédie* article on *cadence*: on seeing the trill at the end of the first verse, Rousseau had erroneously leapt to the conclusion that it signaled a cadence dividing the two verses.

Example 3.1. Lully, "Enfin il est en ma puissance" (as cited in *Observations,* p. 70), mm. 1–4

Les notes de Basse, que ne sont point de Lulli, ne changent rien au fond.

Having proved that Rousseau conflated two unrelated musical gestures, Rameau could then argue that the first verse was musically connected to the second. Looking at the first two full measures of example 3.1, we see that the first verse is set in the voice part as an arpeggiation of an E-minor harmony, supported throughout by the fundamental pitch E in the bass, with no cadential motion whatsoever; neither harmony nor key begins to change until well into the second verse, on the downbeat of m. 3 ("enne*mi*"). Further, the brief pause of two eighth-rests between the two verses, which, it might be argued, drives a wedge between them, in fact serves the practical function of separating the sibilant syllable "ce" that concludes the first verse from the one initiating the second. Rameau was thus able to maintain that continuity between the two verses was strong, just as Rousseau (and, in the *Nouveau système,* Rameau) had argued it ought to be (*OSN,* 72–73; *CTW,* 3:302–3).

This linking of the verses in turn lends significance to Lully's passing from the key of E minor to G major during the second verse. The major mode is virile and vigorous, according to Rameau, whereas the minor is soft and weak because it is derived from the major mode.[14] The shift from minor to major in the course of these two closely connected verses therefore opens up possibilities for a more subtle interpretation: "To avoid all repose from the beginning to the end of the second verse—in order to make perceptible the sense [of the verses] (since the same tonic continues up to the hemistich of the second [verse])—this is already a great deal, but to employ first the minor mode, for its softness as opposed to the vigor of the [second,] major [mode], adds there a new goad and increases [it . . .] in the moment that this major [mode] terminates in absolute repose on the words, 'ce superbe vainqueur'—this is the grand stroke of a master."[15] For Rameau the tonal gesture was suggestive. He concluded from it that Armide's "proud victor," rather than her "fatal enemy," bore the brunt of her spite: Renaud had wounded her more by conquering her heart—while remaining oblivious to her beauty—than he had by conquering her soldiers in battle (*OSN*, 72–76; *CTW*, 3:304).

Rameau's interpretation of Lully's tonal and modal nuances may or may not have been what the older composer had in mind when he composed this music, but it is consistent with the highly personal, speculative approach to musical expression developed in the *Nouveau système*. He interpreted the passage according to how he himself would have composed meaning into it, grounding his interpretation in a system where musical syntax parallels poetic syntax. Musical meaning was made possible for Rameau by employing the notion of *modulation* in the full range of its meaning, from the particular idea of harmonic progression to the more abstract idea of flow or phrasing.

All the more reason, then, for us to follow the gesture begun in the first couplet of "Enfin" through to its completion. Example 3.2 contains the second segment of Rameau's commentary, the next two verses of the monologue (*OSN*, 78; *CTW*, 3:305):

> Le charme du sommeil le livre à ma vengeance.
>
> Je vais percer son invincible coeur.

[The enchantment of sleep delivers him to my vengeance. I am going to pierce his invincible heart.]

Rousseau's criticism of this passage dwelt first on what he considered to be Lully's inappropriate setting of the first verse. Specifically, he denounced the composer for sacrificing emotional content in order to paint the word "sommeil" musically through a chromatic bass line, and he pointedly remarked that Renaud was not the only sleeping figure involved in the scene: "The words *charme* and *sommeil* were an inevitable trap for the musician; he forgot Armide's *furor* in order to take a little nap here, awakening himself only on the word *percer*."[16] For the second verse, Rousseau returned to a familiar theme, criticizing the cadence in the final measure of example

3.2 and its accompanying trill on the brief syllable, "invin*ci*ble" because they fail to describe Armide's "impetuous agitation."

In response Rameau first accused Rousseau of cutting the poetry into units too small to make syntactic sense. To focus on the hemistich "le charme du sommeil" was to miss the manner in which the music carried the phrase through to its true point of completion, "le livre à ma vengeance." Far from being asleep at the reins, Lully began this phrase within the key of the subdominant (A minor), moving from its dominant in the first complete measure of example 3.2 to its tonic on the downbeat of the second ("som*meil*"), and then he "enjambed" this arrival, pushing past the A-minor prolongation to a cadence on B major ("ven*gean*ce"). Rameau's use of *enjambment* in this context is telling, for it provides further illustration of his belief that the properties of language were analogous to those of a musical setting, especially in leading the composer to reflect the syntactical phrasing of the poetry within the musical phrasing. A form of musical enjambment here mirrored the poetic. As for the anticlimactic, descending vocal line on the crucial words "le livre à ma vengeance," this too indicated Lully's forethought, for it made the sudden ascent in the next verse, "Je vais percer son invincible coeur," all the more exciting (*OSN*, 78–79; *CTW*, 3:305–6). More important, the end of the first verse at "le livre à ma vengeance" and on B major should have had a significant effect on listeners. According to Rameau, this B major, the dominant of the scene's initial E-minor tonal area, "makes [the listener] desire a new repose on the tonic, which ought to follow it," the anticipated return to E minor, and in doing so, it reveals to the listener that Armide has something left to say.[17] The composer went to considerable lengths to direct the listener's attention to the next verse, "Je vais percer son invincible coeur," which in fact closes with a return to E minor coinciding with the completion of the four opening verses. Rameau seems to have cared little about Rousseau's quibble regarding the trill in "invin*ci*ble," but he did take pains to note that Lully departed from standard French declamation at this point. From a purely dramatic point of view, he observed, the voice should have descended on the word "son." Instead, Lully conceded to purely musical demands, ascending through the syllables "invin-" in order to descend to the important cadential trill on "-*ci*ble" (*OSN*, 82–84; *CTW*, 3:307–8).

More than a difference of opinion separates the two writers: they project music's significatory potential onto the monologue in radically different ways. For Rousseau, this relatively simple music does no more than anchor the poetry. It fragments the text into a series of isolated gestures that border on nonsense. A trill routinely marks a cadence, while a chromatic bass line labels the word *sommeil* at the expense of Armide's intemperate state. For Rameau, however, the situation is far more complicated. He ekes from these brief eight measures a case for viewing music and poetry coex-

Example 3.2. Lully, "Enfin il est en ma puissance" (as cited in *Observations,* p. 78), mm. 3–8

tensively. In this short span, triumph, anguish, and anticipation succeed each other at a rapid pace, their presence established neither by music nor poetry alone but by the significatory relay between the two. Although the passage brims with the very qualities that Rousseau sought, the philosophe had failed to perceive them because he had not noticed the larger, underlying musical and poetic shapes. From something as unremarkable as the progression from subdominant to dominant to tonic, Rameau establishes the basis for a recursive view of the scene's unfolding: he asserts that the listener must refer back to the earlier tonic even as he is thinking back to earlier emotional nuances. The arrival on B major at "vengeance" would mean little without the verses in E minor that preceded it.

What is remarkable about Rameau's commentary is that it goes beyond analysis or polemic to provide a theoretical dimension that can only be described as exegetical or hermeneutic. Indeed, since Rameau's analytical language and theoretical principles differ markedly from our own, this exegetical dimension is what leads us to see parallels with modern endeavors and to draw meaning from purely musical gestures, using them as a basis for interpreting drama. It makes Rameau's commentary on "Enfin" self-revelatory in a way that theoretical passages from the *Traité de l'harmonie* and the *Nouveau système* were not, even though they dealt with the same issues. At the heart of Rameau's analysis lies an attitude toward musical phrasing, *modulation,* that goes well beyond such matters as whether perfect authentic cadences lined up with grammatical periods or dissonant harmonies lined up with dissonant emotions. The composer's task required careful scrutiny of the poetic and dramatic contents of the livret. This in turn leads him to decide when to press forward and when to pause, when to change color and when to maintain one, when to increase musical tension through harmonic and tonal prolongations and when to release that tension through a return to the tonic. In creating a musical setting the composer takes an active role in shaping the dramatic scene, sculpting the time in which it transpires while leaving space for the actor to further interpret the text through declamation and gesture.

In his 1930 study, *L'Opéra de Rameau,* Paul-Marie Masson broached a view of the composer's musical constructions that emphasized the forward-flowing, kinetic elements of Rameau's scenes. Substantial conceptual differences from the case I have presented here are also evident in Masson's views, perhaps best illustrated by the analytical passage from Rameau that he chose to cite. Masson avoided the long, complex discourse of the *Observations* and instead selected a much briefer set of remarks on "Enfin" from the *Code de musique pratique* (1760). In that passage, Rameau reviewed the portion of "Enfin" represented in examples 3.1 and 3.2 solely in harmonic or tonal terms:

> The monologue begins in E minor and passes to its relative major, a third away on G, in order to give more force to the epithets with which Armide characterizes her hero. Thereafter, in order to make felt her reflection on the accident which has placed him in her possession ("Le charme du sommeil le livre à ma vengeance"), immediately comes a G-sharp, which justly [leads to] the key a fourth away from the principal key [of E minor], that is to say, A minor. Then, delivering herself to her transport, she states "Je vais percer son invincible coeur" in this principal key [of E minor]. One feels all of the effects of this beautiful *modulation* without knowing the cause, without ever being occupied by it: how felicitous![18]

Citing this passage from a chapter entitled "On Expression" as a basis, Masson suggested quite rightly that the composer used harmony and tonality to shape scenes. Though he was able to offer some short examples of how Rameau put this into practice, Masson despaired of giving this subject the attention it deserved, owing to the degree of detailed commentary and quantity of musical examples such study would entail.[19] What is not made clear by using this isolated passage as a theoretical basis for interpreting music is the degree to which such decisions about harmony and tonality continued, for Rameau, to be informed by poetic (and, hence, through the concept of *modulation,* musical) syntax. Masson, in his brief excursus on how Rameau shaped scenes interpretively, appears to have examined only the chapter in the *Code* on expression and, perhaps, the chapters on continuo realization. Thus he could view text setting narrowly, as a matter of harmonic and tonal plotting. Moreover, this understanding of *expression,* as it was treated in the *Code,* would have led Masson to understand Rameau's definition of *modulation* (offered at the beginning of chapter 10 on *modulation*) only in its narrow harmonic or tonal sense: "One calls *modulation* the art of conducting [*de conduire*] song and its harmony both in a single key and from one key to another."[20] To define *modulation* in this manner, however, is to miss the importance of *conduire.* The chapter preceding this quote reflects on the problem of establishing continuity in music and is filled with words like *enchainement* and *conduire*; at its conclusion, Rameau offers to solve the problem by turning to *modulation* ("Passons à la Modulation"). The full title of chapter 10 is "On modulation *in general*" (emphasis added). The chapters immediately following then take up more specific aspects of this encompassing topic *modulation,* as is evident from their titles: chapter 11, "On the connection of keys, their interweaving, the length of their phrases consequently to their connections, the moment of their beginning, and [their] fundamental progress"; chapter 12, "Notes on ornament or taste, in which modulation is still treated"; chapter 13, "On composition in several parts"; and, finally, chapter 14, "On expression."[21] To end the general subject of *modulation* with the specific issue of expression is telling. Rameau grounds expression as the most particular case within the general subject of *modulation,* while broader matters of musical process, flow, and phrasing continue to be addressed. The logical progression of thought matches that of the *Nouveau systême.*

Although one must be wary of drawing facile comparisons between Rameau's theoretical writings and his musical practice, it is not difficult to find passages from his tragedies, even works written two decades earlier, that reflect this parallel between *modulation* and the syntagmatic underpinnings of dramatic poetry: the tragedies of the 1730s were rife not only with the kind of musical representation noted in "Temple sacré," but also with the elaborate harmonic and tonal play the composer advocated in 1754. The opening to act four, scene three, of the 1737 version of *Castor et Pollux* is such an example. In this scene the immortal Pollux enters the underworld to take the place of his mortal twin, Castor, so that Castor may return to his beloved Télaïre. It is a long and involved scene in which several key events must occur: the brothers reunite, Pollux announces that Castor will return at his expense, Pollux gives a synopsis of what has happened to Télaïre since Castor's death, Pollux confesses his own love for Télaïre, and the brothers agree on a course of action.

In the early measures of the scene (see example 3.3), during the long passage in which the brothers discover each other, Rameau puts into practice his theoretical notion of *modulation* as a harmonic and tonal parallel to poetic and dramatic syntax.[22] Just prior to the point where the example begins, Pollux has delivered his entrance speech reassuring the spirits of the underworld that he means them no harm. It concludes with a strong perfect authentic cadence in B minor. The music that follows, as the brothers recognize each other, refers obliquely to this B-minor cadence. Castor speaks first:

> Mais qui s'offre à mes yeux!
> Est-ce luy que je vois! ô Castor! ô mon Frere!

[But who offers himself to my eyes? Is it him I see? O Castor, my brother! (*C livret 1737*, 29).]

Rameau characterizes Pollux's increasing joy with a chromatic line in the basse continue rising from D# to F#, the final harmony a half cadence in the previously established key of B minor. Castor, however, quite rightly doubts his eyes and his ears—"Qu'entends-je! ô mon frere est-ce vous?" (What do I hear? Oh my brother is it you?)—and disrupts Pollux's B minor, pulling the music instead to an authentic cadence in E minor (mm. 19–20). A wave of tonal instability ensues as Pollux responds,

> J'ay donc flêchi du Sort la cruauté sévere.
> O moments de tendresse!

[I have moved destiny from (its) severe cruelty. Oh moments of tenderness! (*C livret 1737*, 29).]

His music moves through weak cadences in A major (m. 22) and D major (m. 23), gradually drawing his bewildered brother back toward B minor. They sing the next verse together—"O moments le plus doux!" (Oh sweetest moments! [*C livret 1737*, 29])—ending with a half cadence on F-sharp (m. 25). Even at this point, however, Castor still cannot believe what is happening. He asks again, "Oh my brother is it you?" first leading away from B minor with a deceptive resolution of the F-sharp dominant (m. 26) and then resolving once again in the key of E minor (m. 27).

Rameau conflates the harmonic and tonal goals of this passage with the poetic grammar and dramatic situation of Pierre-Joseph Bernard's livret. The half cadences on F-sharp punctuate the questions posed by Pollux while also acknowledging his agency in the scene and in the plot of the opera. The B-minor tonic returns only when he pushes aside his joy at seeing his brother in order to explain his presence in the underworld: "C'est peu de te rendre la vie,/Le sort t'éleve au rang des Dieux" (It is a small thing to give you life. Destiny elevates you to the rank of gods [*C livret 1737*, 30]). The tonal arrival at this point has been overdetermined, as though to ensure its audibility as an event. The music reaches a cadence in F-sharp at "vie" (m. 33). The verse revealing Pollux's sacrifice is then delivered; in B minor throughout, it is the most stable phrase tonally since

Example 3.3. *Castor et Pollux* (1737), act 4, scene 3, mm. 15–35

Example 3.3, *continued*

the beginning of the scene (mm. 34–35). Whatever Lully's intentions may have been in "Enfin"—and as we have seen, he gave considerable thought to text setting—Rameau's setting of this reunion gives full expression to his own theoretical beliefs.

In scenes like this one we begin to understand the attitude of Rameau's pupil Chabanon toward musical expression, as cited in chapter 1. Chabanon, it will be remembered, had nothing but contempt for those who saw word painting in "Brillant Soleil," linking the diatonic descent in the melody with the "chute des frimats" of the poetic text. What impressed him about the chorus was the way the music "paint[ed] rapture and gave birth to it," inscribing the overarching emotional content of the scene and, in so doing, rendering it real. Such musical acts could succeed only if one conceived music in terms contrary to those of Saint-Évremond. Music did not have to erase meaning from poetry; it could just as easily support, highlight, and even redirect it. If we were to end our discussion here, however, in the fullness of music's semiotic presence, we would miss an important aspect of Rameau's development. The composer may have argued theoretically for this kind of text setting, and he may have practiced and taught it to his pupils. When it came time to revive his tragedies, nevertheless, his thoughts turned to the criticisms the earlier versions had received. He then endeavored not to adjust, polish, or recreate the original works, but to substitute for them duplicates that harbored rather different notions of music's capabilities.

To return to the point made at the beginning of the chapter, one must wonder whether the mere existence of his highly nuanced settings would have satisfied Rameau. Certainly, Voltaire remained oblivious to them, and Antoine-Gautier de Montdorge, Rameau's poet for the opéra-ballet *Les Fêtes d'Hébé* (1739), looked on the composer's interest in musically plausible scenes as little more than interference. In his *Réflexions d'un peintre sur l'opéra* (1743), Montdorge cited a letter written by Rameau during one of their collaborations not as an example of the composer's concern for drama but as an illustration of hubris:

> First, the declaration of love that you have given me for the third scene of the second act does not work. Everyone finds it pretty. . . . Everyone admires it. It is necessary to render justice on this count. But a declaration ought always end with a sustained cadence, and there is no means with your syllable; it is necessary for me to have one that finesses, for example, like *prendre*. I would easily be able to place my cadence above that. In the name of God, some felicitous syllables and I respond to all.
>
> I am counseled to end the third act with a quartet. I need some words, but all that is necessary are some verses linked to one another so I can make my four parts "fugue" [*fuguer*].[23]

It is difficult to know whether this text is authentic, but it does suggest a strong familiarity with the demands composers placed on poets. The call for verses and syllables resembles the requests for material that Mozart sent to Varesco or Verdi to Piave. To the eighteenth-century French reader inclined to view poetry and music as opposing terms, however, the letter was symptomatic of Rameau's lack of concern for poetry: a composer requesting syllables to better suit the music or, worse, verses for a new musical number could not truly respect poetry. Both Montdorge and Voltaire viewed themselves in the long run as having abandoned poetic ideals for musical ends. Even the composer's most ardent supporters, the Ramistes, could not be counted on to perceive his musical nuances. Baron Friedrich von Grimm implied that Rameau's partisans defended the composer in terms he would not have appreciated: "Rameau has been reproached for not understanding recitative. It appears to me even that some of his friends, daring at first to justify him on this account, have preferred to advance [the argument] that anyone can compose recitative, in order to sustain his good will. Nevertheless, it is well established that nothing is so difficult for most people as composing recitative."[24] The nuances of Rameau's text setting were not directly perceptible, and audiences gave no evidence of responding to them intuitively, despite his arguments to the contrary.

It is difficult then not to imagine a crisis emerging from this gap between Rameau's theories and their practical application, between what he believed should occur when audiences listened to his music and what actually did occur. This crisis manifested itself in revised versions of scenes (such as the reunion of Castor and Pollux) for the 1754 production. Even as Bernard was abbreviating the scene's poetry, Rameau was stripping it of its most striking musical effects. By the time they were finished, the initial, highly emotional encounter between the two brothers was missing altogether, and without this semiotic grounding, there was nothing for the remaining music to refer to. It did little more than support the poetry, offering a simplified presentation of the text without attempting to interpret it further. In such instances, what had changed was not Rameau's musical style, but the way in which he used music as a signifying system. Whatever he may have argued in the *Observations,* he had stripped the music he was staging in 1754 of some of its strongest parallels to the poetry and drama. Without this semiotic foundation Rameau's musical accompaniments threatened to devolve into the kind of simplistic labeling of words with musical effects that he had long considered a secondary and relatively unimportant aspect of musical setting.

We find evidence already in the multiple versions of *Hippolyte et Aricie* of Rameau's reappraisal of musical signification. This opera set the tone for Rameau criticism, and, as we have seen, it was not without its difficulties. The composer revised *Hippolyte* during its original production and then again for its 1742 revival; indeed, the revisions were so extensive that we cannot always date them accurately. Among the earliest, however, were those included in an appendix to the 1733 engraved score, which he had introduced to mollify the performers.[25] It is quite possible that some of those substitutions predate the work's premiere, so that the composer may have begun reinterpreting the work musically even before its first public performance.

In his earliest layer of substitution, the composer's inclination was already toward greater accessibility. We see this, for example, in Phèdre's monologue "Espoir, unique bien d'une fatale flamme," which replaced the opening monologue in act three, "Cruelle mère des amours." The original monologue brings to mind the role made famous in Racine's spoken tragedy *Phèdre,* a tale of guilt and remorse consistent with Phèdre's incestuous desire for her stepson Hippolyte:

> Cruelle Mere des Amours,
> Ta vangeance a perdu ma trop coupable Race;
>   N'en suspendras-tu point le cours?
> Ah! du moins, à tes yeux, que Phedre trouve grace.
>   Je ne te reproche, plus rien,
> Si tu rends à mes voeux Hippolyte sensible;
> Mes feux me font horreur; mais mon crime est le tien;
>   Tu dois cesser d'être inflexible.
> Cruelle Mere des Amours, &c.

[Cruel mother of the Loves, your vengeance has lost my too-guilty race. Why do you not suspend your course? At least in your eyes, Phèdre finds grace. I (will) no longer reproach you for anything if you make Hippolyte sensitive to my desires. My passion horrifies me, but my crime is yours. You should cease being inflexible. Cruel mother of the Loves, etc. (*H livret 1733,* 25).]

Brimming with irony and self-contempt, these verses depict a tragic love similar to the one Voltaire advocated in his *Discours sur la tragédie,* "a truly tragic passion, regarded as a weakness and opposed with remorse." Rameau's setting took this emotional climate as a point of departure and seized as its focal point Phèdre's confession, "Mes feux me font horreur; mais mon crime est le tien;/Tu dois cesser d'être inflexible." The composer sets the passage with a striking chromatic accompaniment. Echoing a passing chromatic inflection from the monologue's prelude, the music plunges a full chromatic octave in the the the basse continue, moving from A to A^1, and Rameau supports this outburst with a sudden reentry of the orchestral accompaniment. To echo Chabanon's views, this musical setting paints Phèdre's emotional state and in painting it intensifies a dramatic reality. Nevertheless, as Voltaire had learned by this time, tragic emotions did not play in the theater as successfully as romantic dalliances, and what was true of the spoken tragedy was even truer of its lyric counterpart. Though "Cruelle mère" was listed in the 1733 and 1742 livrets and in the 1742 print, it may never have been performed publicly. Its replacement, "Espoir, unique bien d'une fatale flamme," was not only shorter but also decidedly less tragic. The new verses stressed romance at the expense of drama:

> Espoir, unique bien d'une fatale flâme,
> Pour la premiere fois viens règner dans mon âme.
>> Je sentirai mieux que jamais
>> Quel est le prix du diadême,
> S'il attache sur moi les yeux de ce que j'aime;
>> Doux espoir tu me le promets;
>> Unique bien d'une fatale flâme.

[Hope, sole benefit of a fatal passion, reign for the first time in my heart. I will feel more than ever the cost of the crown if it draws to me the eyes of the one I love. Sweet hope, you promise him to me; sole benefit of a fatal passion. (*H score 1733*, appendix).]

Pellegrin replaced the incestuous mother's remorse with hope, of all things, and Rameau's clever setting disappeared along with the tragic emotion. "Espoir, unique bien d'une fatale flamme" was shorter and simpler, and it contained no disturbing harmonic progressions. The neophyte composer, like the experienced poets around him, had given in to criticism.[26]

The 1742 *Hippolyte* gives further evidence of the contradictions that had come to inhabit the work. Both monologues written for act three, scene one, were replaced by a long, highly modulatory *ritournelle* that recovered some of the original mood of "Cruelle mère."[27] At the climax the furious bassoon obbligato, which had dominated the movement, leads the instruments sequentially from D minor through A minor, G major, and F major to a climactic E-diminished triad before closing back in D minor. The following short recitative for Phèdre undercuts some of this effect, however, by continuing to dwell on her romantic hopes:

> Mes destins sont changez, Arcas m'a fait entendre
> Que sur les sombres bords le Roy vient de descendre.
>> Je suis maitresse de mon sort;
> A l'ingrat Hippolite offrons le Diademe,
> Il và se rendre icy; Mais Si le rang Suprême
> Ne peut rien sur son coeur, Je n'attens que la mort.

[My fates are transformed. Arcas informs me that the king has just descended to the sombre shores. I am mistress of my destiny. To the ungrateful Hippolyte let us offer the diadem, he will come here; if supreme rank does nothing for his heart, I await only death.][28]

Having already presented his dramatic commentary in the instrumental introduction, the composer set the recitative in an uncomplicated manner; he included only a brief chromatic rise in the basse continue from F# to

A, at Phèdre's words "Si le rang Suprême ne peut rien sur son coeur," which would have been simpler to compose and less dissonant than his earlier, more extended descending chromatic progression. Rameau had reinvested his hopes for dramatic representation in the instrumental music this time, where bold statements were more acceptable.

Other scenes in the 1742 *Hippolyte* reflect Rameau's contradictory goals of creating dramatic accompaniments while writing accessible music. Of the two versions of act one, scene two, where Hippolyte and Aricie confess their mutual love, the 1742 version is musically the richer. In 1733 Rameau had developed this expository scene as a relatively straightforward recitative scene culminating in a duo; in the later version, he added two airs for Aricie and, in one of them, even lavish orchestral accompaniment.[29] Moreover, he added a semiotically more effective modulation to the later version. Example 3.4a presents one of the more harmonically complex passages from the earlier version.[30] We see a brief, ascending chromatic progression as Hippolyte begs Aricie not to resist his love. When she registers surprise, he responds with astonishment, "Je pourrois vous haïr! quelle injustice extrême?" (I could hate you? What extreme injustice! [*H*

Example 3.4a. *Hippolyte et Aricie* (1733), act 1, scene 2, mm. 45–51

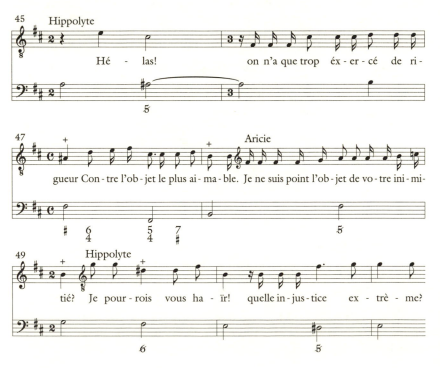

Example 3.4b. *Hippolyte et Aricie* (1742), act 1, scene 2, mm. 10–14

livret 1733, 4]). At this point the accompaniment makes an unexceptional change of key from B minor to E minor. As we see in example 3.4b, the later version offers a simpler text for this passage but suffuses the whole with chromaticism. The change is from an uncomplicated harmonic anchor on the word "Hélas" to a characterization of the two verses as a whole, the rising progressions complementing the couple's realization that they are in love. Aricie first hints at it, and Hippolyte, seeming to have heard the clue in her accompaniment, responds vigorously.

In this passage Rameau supported the notion that musical content could parallel poetic content, but later, in act four, scene two of the 1742 version, he moved in the opposite direction.[31] As we see in example 3.5a, in the 1733 version when Hippolyte confesses Phèdre's monstrous crime, he does so to an impressive burst of descending chromaticism that Aricie then picks up on in her reply: there can be no doubt she understands what he cannot state openly.[32] This passage would have been difficult to perform, requiring the actor playing Hippolyte to sing a c# against a C-natural in the basse continue (at "porter *les* yeux"). The 1742 version of the same passage, as we see in example 3.5b, did not lack expressive techniques, but it avoided the harmonic references of the earlier version. The initial tritone in the basse continue signals Hippolyte's mood, while the rising chromaticism at "Le respect me force à me taire" marks his mention of Phèdre's actions, which he cannot state aloud. But the effect of the simpler progression and easier vocal part is to recant the elaborate modulation (in its historic sense) of the earlier version. Aricie's answer, not included in example 3.5b, remains essentially unchanged, and without the earlier chro-

Example 3.5a. *Hippolyte et Aricie* (1733), act 4, scene 2, mm. 29–37

Example 3.5b. *Hippolyte et Aricie* (1742), act 4, scene 2, mm. 15–20

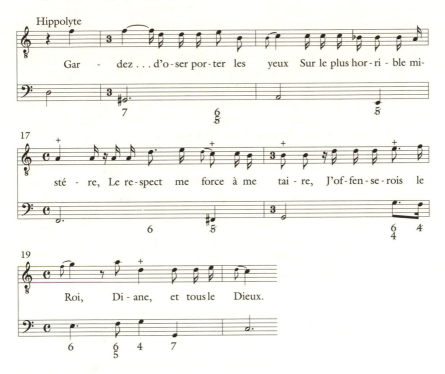

matic descent as a reference, it too becomes a passing gesture, labeling the expressive words without explicating them. To the extent that Rameau requires recursive listening from his 1742 audience, the attention he requires is closer to the elementary gestures of "Enfin" than to his own more complicated experiments. The later version replaces the task of matching the modulation to poetic and dramatic discourse with the simpler one of enhancing isolated words and expressions.

As examples 3.4 and 3.5 indicate, I am not arguing that expressive music or complex harmonization disappears from Rameau's tragedies in the 1740s. The tradition of using harmony to anchor key words within a scene was far too well established to fade altogether. Rather, what I find intriguing is that in the next wave of revivals the composer chose to transform the semiotic function of such progressions. It matters little in this context whether he did so to address problems of length or performability, because he could have accomplished either of those tasks without altering his basic belief in the discursive parallels between modulation and poetry. What we find in the versions of *Dardanus* in 1744 and *Castor et Pollux* in 1754 is the decline of the *relay* text, that is, the complex, recursive gestures that had previously linked poetry and music. Rameau's audiences evidently were not making the necessary connections between the poetic and musical signifying systems, and so he frequently returned to an old-fashioned form of signification in which isolated musical gestures denoted and anchored isolated words and dramatic gestures. Thereby erasing his earlier efforts, he felt it necessary to move closer, ironically, to the musical processes Rousseau had criticized him for in the *Lettre*.

We first see this new circumspection in the 1744 revival of *Dardanus*, where an overall simplification of musical material seems to be in force. For example, in both versions of Iphise's monologue "Cesse cruel Amour, de regner sur mon ame" from act one, scene one, she sings about being in love with a mortal enemy. Her words thus capture some of the same conflict between duty and love that we encountered in "Temple sacré, séjour tranquille." Rather than pining over her love life, she expresses a deep sense of guilt:

> Cesse, cruel Amour, de regner sur mon ame;
> Ou choisis d'autres traits pour te rendre vainqueur.
> Où m'entraîne une aveugle ardeur?
> Un ennemi fatal est l'objet de ma flâme;
> Dardanus a soumis mon coeur.

[Cease, cruel Love, to reign in my soul or choose other ways to render yourself (its) conqueror. Where does this blind ardor carry me? A deadly enemy is the object of my desire; Dardanus has conquered my heart. (*D livret 1739,* 1).]

Because these verses remained the same in the second version, the reasons for rewriting the monologue could not have included a change in emotion, as they had in the case of "Cruelle mère des amours." As example 3.6 (a and b) illustrates, in fact, the 1744 version does not include many musical alterations of the 1739 material.[33] The monologue remains in the key of G minor, and its melody remains close to the original in form and contour. Indeed, its middle section, not shown in the example, has the same vocal part and accompaniment as before.

The principal difference is that the 1744 version of the monologue is shorter and relies on a simpler form of phrasing. The 1739 version, shown in example 3.6a, is a lavish setting, as befits the first scene of an opera. Its accompaniment is rich in expressive dissonances, and its orchestration sets the flute timbre prominently against the violins in mm. 23–24. The music rises from an opening tonic phrase, appropriately in minor mode (mm. 20–23), through expressive changes of key in the following two phrases. The first of these is a standard move to the major mediant, B-flat major (m. 27), the shift in mode perhaps supporting the word *vainqueur*. The second modulation ends in C minor (m. 31), the subdominant of the opening G minor, a noteworthy shift in that, according to Rameau's hermeneutics, it could suggest weakness or hesitation. The return to the G-minor tonic in m. 34, though expected, has the effect of compounding the minor mode of m. 31 and of returning the music to the piece's opening sentiments. The whole is a musically rich depiction of Iphise's guilt over loving an enemy, a theme that will acquire particular importance in subsequent acts, and the contrasting settings of the recurring text give the passage a quality of rumination, as though she were examining her conflicting feelings from different angles. In the 1744 version, shown in example 3.6b, most of the dissonances disappear along with the lush orchestration, the flutes now doubling the violins throughout. The composer offers a reading of the poetic and musical material that we might describe as an antecedent-consequent period, a phrase structure that had become increasingly popular in *pièces de clavecin* during the 1730s. Taken together, the simpler texture, balanced phrases, unadorned melody, and more memorable melodic shape rely on principles having less to do with drama than with instrumental music.

The same principle of simplification is apparent in "Troubles cruels, soupçons injurieux," from the prologue of *Dardanus,* which raises once more the question of how tragic a tragédie en musique should be. The poetry of this prologue embodies the operatic values Voltaire and his predecessors had found detestable, and it delivers them with none of the irony of the *Samson* prologue. In *Dardanus* the court of Amour, with Vénus and Les Plaisirs in attendance, is thrown into disarray by the arrival of La Jalousie and her followers. Amour banishes these monsters, but shortly thereafter a lethargy falls on his company. Only Vénus finds the strength to fight it off. She calls on Jalousie and her troupe to return and prevent love from languishing; they succeed only too well, and in the end she must restrain them:

> Troubles cruels, Soupçons injurieux,
> Vous, que l'orgueil nourrit, que le caprice guide,
> Qui rendez & l'Amant & l'Amour odieux,
> Devenez une ardeur délicate & timide,
> Dont le respect épure, et modére les feux:
> Inspirez par l'Amour, guidez par sa lumiére,
> N'entrez dans les coeurs amoureux,
> Que pour y réveiller l'empressement de plaire.

[Cruel troubles, injurious suspicions, you whom pride nourishes and caprice guides, who render lover and love loathsome, become a delicate and timid ardor whose passions respect refines and moderates: inspired by Amour, guided by her light, enter into amorous hearts only to reveal there the eagerness of pleasure (*D livret 1739,* viii).]

Vénus's speech is the turning point in the prologue, and mortals then join with Amour's court to celebrate Vénus's victory over Jalousie. The spectacle following is to be their entertainment.

Example 3.6a. "Cesse cruel Amour, de regner sur mon ame," *Dardanus* (1739), act 1, scene 1, mm. 20–35

Example 3.6a, *continued*

ner   sur   mon   a - me,   Ou choi - sis   d'au - tres

traits   pour te   ren - dre vain - queur.

Example 3.6b. "Cesse cruel Amour, de regner sur mon ame," *Dardanus* (1744), act 1, scene 1, mm. 17–24

In keeping with this speech's pivotal role in the prologue, Rameau's 1739 setting turns it into a highly dramatic moment, elevating greatly the otherwise insubstantial proceedings. Its opening measures are shown in example 3.7a.[34] With its parataxis, declamatory style, and descending leaps, the vocal part in these first measures may have reminded audiences of a famous lament heard two years earlier, Télaïre's "Tristes apprêts, pâles flambeaux" from *Castor et Pollux* (1737). Vénus's speech, however, differs in scope from the earlier piece. It is set not as an elaborately accompanied monologue but as a recitative with violin accompaniment, its modulation pursuing a rather different sentiment. We hear this texturally in the complex opening gesture, with its imitative relationship between violins and voice; we notice it again melodically in the diminished fourths of the opening interval (mm. 2, 4); and we observe it harmonically as well, in the use of the resulting C-sharp

Example 3.7a. "Troubles cruels, soupçons injurieux," *Dardanus* (1739), prologue, scene 1, mm. 1–13

Example 3.7b. "Troubles cruels, soupçons injurieux," *Dardanus* (1744), prologue, scene 1, mm. 1–16

Example 3.7b, *continued*

nez une Ar - deur dé - li - cate et ti - mi - de.

as the root of fully diminished seventh chords. The dramatic issue here is not
mourning but strife. The opening dissonances initiate a chain of complementary dissonances spreading over the next three verses. In m. 8 the vocal
line once again provides the altered pitch, on the weak syllable "capri*ce*,"
stressing perhaps the lax sensibilities of Jalousie's cohorts. (Recall here
Voltaire's ironic celebration of *volupté* in the *Samson* prologue. Rameau's
setting in *Dardanus* subtly inverts the courtly inanities of its prologue.) The
dramatic mood continues with two more surprising dissonances in mm.
11–13 ("Deve*nez* une ardeur délicate *et ti*mide"). First, an abrupt shift from
C major to A major sets up a chromatic passage in the bass, which then culminates in the intrusion of a B half-diminished seventh harmony, also subtly outlined in the descent from f^1 to b in the vocal part. These dissonances
abruptly divert the music at the climactic moment from its D minor-F major
track onto the dominant of A minor, and the sudden move to the sharp side
is in keeping with Rameau's theories. In her poetry Vénus has moved from
a depiction of Jalousie's retinue to the demand that they "become a delicate
and timid ardor." Out of Jalousie's chaotic influence, Vénus orders nobler
and worthier sentiments, carrying the day through moral suasion.

By the 1744 revival, however, the composer appears once again to have
questioned the value of this kind of modulation. As example 3.7b indicates,
the second version of Vénus's speech is no longer a recitative but a *galant*
air accompanied by violins and flutes in thirds. The opening measures of
the vocal part resemble the outline of their 1739 counterpart, but the descending intervals have been changed to perfect fourths and stripped of
their imitative texture. Only the ornamental dissonances at "l'Amant et
l'Amour odieux" and the modulation to G minor at "Devenez une ardeur

délicate et ti*mide*" hint at musical dramatization. Stripped of a context in which musical strife parallels poetic strife, the change in key now sounds less like a command than an immersion in sensual pleasures. Rameau has chosen simply to paint the underlying mood of delicacy and timidity. Whereas his first version had characterized Vénus's stance as courageous, the new one anchors an easier and, for some at least, more troubling message of unbridled sensuality.

The 1754 revival of *Castor et Pollux* bore similar changes, and still another reunion between major characters, this one in the fifth-act scene in which Castor returns to his beloved Télaïre, allows us to trace Rameau's shifting attitudes. Given Télaïre's importance in both versions of the opera—as the impetus in 1737 for Pollux's decision to find his brother and as the Euridice-like signifier of broken betrothal in 1754—this scene had the potential for a *coup de théâtre*. Indeed, given that in the 1737 version Castor was murdered before the first act began, this reunion would have been keenly felt: it was the first time in the story that the lovers Castor and Télaïre had shared the stage.

As act five, scene two, of the 1737 *Castor et Pollux* opens, Télaïre does not yet know that Castor's return is temporary. Unable to allow Pollux to make such a great sacrifice, Castor wishes only to see Télaïre once more before returning to the underworld so that his brother may live. Télaïre reacts joyously at the sight of him, whereas the audience knows that his return is not permanent. The scene is thus rife with the expressive opportunities Rameau favored:

> TÉLAÏRE:
> Le Ciel est donc touché des plus tendres amours;
> Au jour que je quittois, votre voix me rappelle,
> Vous vivrez immortel, & vous vivrez fidele,
> Pour ne mourir jamais, & pour m'aimer toûjours.
>
> CASTOR:
> Hélas!
>
> TÉLAÏRE:
>   Mais, pourquoy ces allarmes?
> Vous m'aimez, je vous vois . . .
>
> CASTOR:
>   Télaïre, vivez.
>
> TÉLAÏRE:
> Qu'entends-je! quels discours!
>
> CASTOR:
>   Télaïre,

TÉLAIRE:
                              Achevez.
Helas! de si beaux jours sont-ils faits pour des larmes!

CASTOR:
A d'éternels adieux il faut nous préparer!

TÉLAIRE:
Que dites-vous, ô Ciel!

CASTOR:
                    Il faut nous séparer.
      Je retourne au rivages sombres.

[TÉLAIRE: Heaven is thus touched by the tenderest of loves. On the day I gave up, your voice called me back. You will live immortally, and you will live faithfully, never to die and to love me forever. CASTOR: Alas! TÉLAIRE: But why this alarm? You love me. I see you. CASTOR: Télaïre, live. TÉLAIRE: What do I hear? What are you saying? CASTOR: Télaïre, TÉLAIRE: Explain yourself. Alas, are such beautiful days made for tears? CASTOR: It is necessary to prepare ourselves for eternal goodbyes! TÉLAIRE: What are you saying? Oh, heaven! CASTOR: It is necessary for us to separate. I return to the somber shores (*C livret 1737*, 35–36).]

Drama aside, the poetry itself would have been inviting for a composer interested in text. Bernard set it so that Castor's interjection, "hélas," disrupts Télaïre's regular Alexandrine verses, resulting in a succession of heavily enjambed exclamations, half-stated explanations, and incomplete thoughts. One can easily imagine an equally disjunct musical setting.

Rameau's 1737 version of this passage is provided in example 3.8a.[35] Already, in the four-measure instrumental *prélude de basse,* he hints at a conflicting relationship between C minor and E-flat major that will come to dominate the scene. While the prelude is, to be sure, securely in C minor, tonicization is weak, especially for Rameau. The opening measure presents the tonic in first inversion, and the music does not arrive at a strong tonic harmony until the downbeat of m. 2. A compressed version of the same gesture occurs at the cadence in m. 4. The G-major dominant harmony on the final beat of m. 3 resolves not to root-position C, as Rameau espoused in his theoretical writings, but to another first-inversion tonic, which then resolves downward stepwise to its tonic note. In the *Traité de l'harmonie* (1722) Rameau referred to cadences that avoided conventional voice-leading through inversion as "imperfect" or even as "imitations of cadences," a means of varying the succession of ordinary perfect resolutions.[36]

Télaïre's opening verse (mm. 5–8) replicates the prelude's bass line in a higher register, but with important differences that further weaken the C-minor tonal center. The vocal part at first appears to arpeggiate a C-minor harmony, much as it did in the prelude; on closer inspection, however, the pitches e^{b1} and g prove to be dissonant suspensions figured as ninths, so that pitch classes important for perceiving the C-minor key now take on secondary, ornamental functions. The phrase nevertheless ends on a half cadence in C minor (m. 8), and we can reasonably anticipate that what follows will begin in that key. Instead, the next phrase foregrounds the latent tonal ambiguities of the *prélude de basse*. Rather than answering the half cadence with a continuation of C minor, the music of Télaïre's second verse veers suddenly into E-flat major (mm. 9–11). The resolution is especially noteworthy because it creates a chromatic descent between the two phrases, implied in the natural and flat signs in the figured bass at mm. 8–9, moving from B-natural to B-flat. There are conflicting musical messages here. On the one hand, as we have seen, the minor mode implies tenderness or weakness in Rameau's theories, as do descending chromatic lines; on the other hand, shifting to major mode implies strength or hope, which is well suited to Télaïre's words, "Au jour que je quittois, votre voix me rappelle." E-flat major is important to Télaïre. She has every reason to be hopeful, and she uses every musical device within her grasp to convey her joy. The accompaniment of her next phrase (mm. 12–14) edges painfully toward G major in mm. 11–13—at her unknowingly ironic words, "Vous vivrez immortel, et vous vivrez fidele"—but she pulls it back to E-flat major with a deceptive cadence.

Unfortunately Télaïre does not fully understand what is happening, and with Castor's interjection, her musical hopes unravel. His two-syllable "hélas" pushes the accompaniment abruptly to the sharp side and back to C, the tonal center of the prelude, now heard in major mode (m. 15). Rameau appears to be letting the conflicting tonal centers of C and E-flat represent two people who, however much they wish to be in agreement, are hopelessly at odds. E-flat major is Télaïre's key, associated with her hopes for life and love; C minor introduces the reality principle, inexorably pushing her toward the realization that Castor will not stay. We hear this in mm. 16–19. Over an E-flat-major harmony, Télaïre cries out, "Vous m'aimez, je vous vois," and Castor echoes her melodic line as he urges her to keep living (mm. 17–18). She senses what is about to happen—"Qu'entends-je! quels discours!"—and as Castor calls her name, the accompaniment sinks from E-flat major to C minor (mm. 18–19). To an E-flat major cadence (m. 21), Télaïre asks whether this happy moment is made for tears, and when Castor tells her to prepare for a final farewell, his accompaniment responds with a chromatic line rising to the dominant of C minor. Again she avoids moving it toward C minor at "Que dites-vous, ô Ciel!" (m. 24), but when Castor finally gets his point across, "Je retourne au rivages sombres," his music cadences instead in the pivotal key of G minor (m. 27).

Bernard's poetry remains largely the same in the 1754 version of this passage, now located in act five, scene one. The final two verses of Télaïre's four-verse opening speech have been telescoped to create eight-syllable and six-syllable verses, respectively, but the message remains the same:

> Vous vivrez, pour m'être fidele,
> Et vous vivrez toujours.

[You will live to be faithful to me, and you will live forever (*C livret 1754*, 43).]

Significantly, Bernard retained the future tense for Télaïre's unknowingly ironic words. The ensuing patchwork of interjections and enjambed verses, in response to Castor's "hélas," remains largely intact, though the contrast has lessened now that Télaïre's opening speech is no longer completely in Alexandrines. The single alteration is the dropping of another "hélas"—in the verse "De si beaux jours sont-ils faits pour des larmes?"—rendering it a ten-syllable line.

Such minor alterations in no way prepare us for Rameau's revisions. The 1737 music could have been adjusted to the 1754 libretto with little difficulty, and there was no obvious reason for him to compose new music; yet that is precisely what he did, writing music bearing little substantive resemblance to the earlier setting. Here as before, the outcome is the weakening of the long-range effects of modulation, creating a setting in which isolated words, phrases, and ideas take precedence over the scene's larger dramatic issues.

We hear these changes already in the prelude, which is no longer a four-measure outline of musical and dramatic mood but a full-scale, twenty-eight measure ritournelle scored for strings and double reeds, as befits the beginning of an act.[37] The ritournelle, in C minor throughout, is simpler than its predecessor; the earlier, carefully plotted conflicts between C minor and E-flat major are now conspicuous to us for their absence. The most notable resemblances to its earlier version are the choice of key and, perhaps, the recurring bass line, which may have derived from the basse continue of Télaïre's opening line (cf., example 3.8a, mm. 4–8).

As we see in example 3.8b, the differences become even more pronounced as the scene begins in earnest; the musical gestures that characterized the 1737 version have now been removed or neutralized. Télaïre's opening verse begins similarly, and the basse continue is much the same (mm. 29–32; cf., example 3.8a, mm. 5–8), though the initial dissonant ninth has been removed. The vocal part now places more emphasis on the leading tone, which strengthens its half cadence (m. 32). Major alterations, however, do not begin until the next phrase. The chromatic shift from G major to E-flat major between the two phrases has vanished, and in its ab-

Example 3.8a. *Castor et Pollux* (1737), act 5, scene 2, mm. 1–27

Example 3.8a, *continued*

Example 3.8b. *Castor et Pollux* (1754), act 5, scene 1, mm. 29–57

Example 3.8b, *continued*

sence, Télaïre's opening period becomes a pair of four-measure, antecedent-consequent phrases in C minor (mm. 29–36). As in the 1744 "Cesse cruel Amour, de regner sur mon ame," the composer has replaced expressive modulations with phraseology and progressions more characteristic of the newest instrumental music. It evokes a musical world of regularity and predictability, with little or no explicit link to the drama. We could argue that what happens musically at Castor's "hélas" is expressive, but if so, it is not expressive in the same way as the 1737 version. Castor's remark pulls the music from E-flat major into F minor (mm. 40–41), and Rameau then creates further tension with his second remark, "Télaïre vivez," by ratcheting the music up another whole step into G major (mm. 43–44). Without the complex tonal context of the earlier version, the effect is little more than a coloristic inflection of the passing words.

It is worth pausing here to consider the musical values at work in these revisions. Once again, what has changed is the relationship between signifying systems. Meaning no longer relays between poetry and music; rather, it is anchored to the poetry in one-to-one correspondences: agitated tonal progressions underscore agitated, emotional outbursts. In the process of revision, the recursive musical references of the earlier version have vanished, their syntagmatically ordered modulations giving way to the commonplace denotative gestures of the tragic tradition. No longer devoted to dramatic narrative, the music now paints individual words and verses. Having arrived in G major, the musical accompaniment becomes temporarily rooted there. As Télaïre comes to realization, Rameau introduces a five-measure dominant prolongation (mm. 46–50), distinctive for its diminished harmonies and chromatic descent in the basse continue, and then concludes with a strong melodic cadence in m. 51. When Castor's revelation follows in the key of E-flat major, the key no longer bears the optimistic significance it carried in the 1737 version because no context has been provided in which it could accrue such a connotation. It has not been defined over and against C minor, and so it simply acts as part of a larger tonal progression, inflecting the text without engaging it on an equal footing.

More was involved in the revision than a shift in compositional technique. To make the move from the 1737 version of *Castor* to the 1754 version, Rameau had to redefine music's referential properties in ways that had wide-ranging implications for his treatment of poetry. He now had to acknowledge, at least to himself, that music perhaps could not perform the tasks he had professed it could. As a result, he forced himself to think less about poetry and more about traditional musical processes; his new music no longer effected elaborate parallelisms between poetry and drama, but instead placed premiums on simple, straightforward elaborations of the text. While this was what audiences had expressed enthusiasm for all along, it was for Rameau a form of retreat, and in the context of his development as a composer it signaled that poetry had become in some sense less important. It no longer received the lavish attention he formerly gave it, raising important questions about music's theoretical significance for Rameau in the early 1750s. He could scarcely have been unaware that in presenting the 1754 *Castor* he was effacing over three decades' worth of theorizing about the relationship between poetry and music, and whatever illusions he had held about this practice would have been laid to rest while writing his rather optimistic commentary on "Enfin" for the *Observations*. Even as he was defending Lully's monologue on theoretical grounds, he was embracing in his own work some of the very practices that had earned Rousseau's contempt.

Thus the very gaps that emerge between theory and practice or between musical ideals and audience perception lend Rameau's career its characteristic shape. They provide his life with the texture of events actually lived and cover the operas themselves in a patina of glimpsed intentions, imperfectly grasped perhaps but nevertheless present. Throughout it all there were decisions that made sense—initiated out of the desire to please and win over the public—and decisions that did not—initiated out of the composer's desire to instruct or edify the public. As in any life, there were contradictions. We would be better off speaking not of the shape of Rameau's career, but of its shapes. Two different but equally informative chronologies will illustrate my meaning.

The first chronological shape we can give to Rameau's career tracks the composer's evolving attitudes toward musical signification. According to this perspective, during the earliest part of his career Rameau devoted his text-setting efforts to developing the sophisticated modulations we have observed in the earliest versions of *Hippolyte et Aricie* (1733) and in the first versions of *Castor et Pollux* (1737) and *Dardanus* (1739). This practice was in relatively close alignment with the theories espoused in his earliest theoretical writings, the *Traité de l'harmonie* (1722) and *Nouveau systême* (1726), and later in the *Observations* (1754). In the late 1730s and the 1740s, however, during the most intense years of the Lulliste-Ramiste debate, Rameau came in some manner to doubt the efficacy of these techniques. Revivals of *Dardanus* (1744) and *Castor et Pollux* (1754) withdrew the elaborate theoretical parallels between poetry and music and replaced them with simpler musical settings. (This process may also have included Rameau's incorporation of arrangements from his *Pièces de clavecin* [1724] into the operas *Les Fêtes d'Hébé* [1739] and *Dardanus* in an effort to create more accessible instrumental music.)[38] Rameau's principal concern in the 1740s was with making his operas easier to understand, and in this context, his opera *Zoroastre* emerges as an important work: we have yet to see whether its 1749 production and 1756 revival reflect the optimism of the 1730s or the ambivalence of the 1740s.

Yet one might argue that this chronology takes us too far from the music itself, offering us notions, narratives, and value systems in place of carefully reasoned music analysis. In our second chronology, we might attempt the more fundamental task of matching dates to actual compositions and watching for patterns to emerge. As we have observed, however, in Rameau's case this does not yield the kind of information we anticipate. Instead of allowing a manageable perspective to emerge from Rameau's tragedies, it produces yet another speculative narrative, this one consisting of uncanny doubles and duplicitous twins. By the 1733 premiere of *Hippolyte et Aricie,* Rameau had already learned harsh lessons about writing successful tragedies, and yet he chose not to follow the course they dictated in either *Castor et Pollux* (1737) or *Dardanus* (1739). Each time he composed a new tragedy, he initiated the process all over again by reintroducing in some form the innovations of the first *Hippolyte.* With each new tragedy he repeated this same trajectory, returning to his complex system of musical references in the first version only to abandon it in the second. His hesitation first becomes evident in the *Hippolyte* of 1742, where he removed some difficult passages but added still others; it emerges fully as a feature of the second versions of *Dardanus* (1744) and *Castor* (1754). Doubt had entered into Rameau's work, and he enacted it as part of his revisionary process. This chronology does not trace the stylistic or ontological transformations of the tragédie en musique but rather a series of reflexive gestures or compulsively repeated acts of erasure. It is an unruly chronology in which ideas, compositional gambits, arguments, and values seemingly subtend one another. It is a chronology not of events but of gaps between events. The two versions of *Zoroastre* from Rameau's lifetime raise still more questions. Had he finally learned his lesson? Did he repeat once again the proffering and withdrawal of musical favors that had characterized his earlier tragedies? And what of *Les Boréades,* the tragedy left unperformed at his death in 1764? It is the opera *without* a revision, the tragedy without a twin, and we will question its place in this series of operations more thoroughly in chapter 5.

Both of these chronologies influence how we view what happened to Rameau's works beginning in the early 1750s. With the first chronology, his evolving attitudes toward musical signification, the composer had to respond to earlier criticism by addressing the creative crises of the 1730s and 1740s. The desire for correspondence between his theoretical claims and musical practice led him to fill the void left by his earlier referential model, and he sought to do this by using music more traditionally to anchor larger dramatic events. With regard to the second chronology, the chronology of innovations proffered and withdrawn, Rameau appears, at least in the end, to have viewed his multiple versions as individual works, seizing upon the instability of the opera and using it to his advantage. The tragedies of the 1750s mark the end of one innovative approach to signification in music, but at the same time that he was stripping scenes of this paralleling function for some music, he was also trying out his new, tradition-based system of anchoring text to music in others. He sought to effect drama by musical means not by aligning musical modulation with poetic syntax but rather by allowing it to function simply as music, relying on the very faith in music per se that his audiences had been more than willing to acknowledge as part of his philosophy all along.

It is likely that emerging trends in the staging of tragédies en musique influenced both of these processes. By the 1740s, the very period in which

Rameau was replacing his older practice, the Opéra had long been engaged in the practical adaptation of Lully's operas in their revivals. Although this adaptation primarily entailed adding, shifting, and replacing the music of the divertissements, it also involved changes in the recitative scenes. Audiences had become less appreciative of narrative scenes in the course of the eighteenth century, whatever Lullistes believed to the contrary, and what was perceived as the enormous length of Lully's lyric tragedies had become a problem. (Le Cerf and the abbé Jean-Baptiste Dubos attributed this impatience to a gradual slowing in performance.)[39] As a result, recitative scenes were abbreviated. Lois Rosow has shown with respect to *Armide* that this practice often took the form of streamlining airs through the elimination of musical and textual repetitions.[40] For Rameau, the logical extension of this practice involved processes of abbreviation, but the composer saw the opportunity to increase dramatic effect by placing greater emphasis on styles of accompaniment and techniques of orchestration. Thus, while some passages in the 1754 *Castor* are most noteworthy for the way in which they abandon earlier techniques, others begin instead to build up the denotative anchors of Lully and his successors, using isolated musical gestures to highlight the poetry. The already loose distinctions between recitative, accompanied recitative, and air became even less precise as Rameau refocused his attention on passing musical effects—preludes, lyrical phrasing, orchestral accompaniment—not as complex signifiers in themselves but as markers for anchoring the listener's attention.[41] I will attempt here only to sketch these innovations as they pertain to the 1754 version of *Castor et Pollux* and 1756 version of *Zoroastre*, leaving to chapters 4 and 5 a more detailed consideration of how the composer's creative strategies changed in the 1750s.

In *Castor*, the strategies involved compressing some airs until they were no longer at all song-like. Compare, for example, the settings of the following maxim in the original and the revised versions of *Castor*: "La Vangeance flatte la gloire,/Mais ne console pas l'amour" (Vengeance flatters glory, but does not console love [*C livret 1737*, 2]). In 1737 this speech occurred in act one, scene two, as part of Télaïre's response when Phébé advises her to ease her sorrow through revenge. As we see in example 3.9a, Rameau set the words as the second part of an air and, by dwelling on them through textual and motivic repetitions, was able to make this brief statement last fully ten measures.[42] In 1754 these same words occurred in act two, scene five, under similar circumstances: Pollux has avenged Castor's death and expressed the hope that his victory will sweeten Télaïre's sorrow, and Télaïre once again uses the maxim to explain that revenge for her is meaningless. Here, as we see in example 3.9b, the same two verses barely filled a single measure. Though none of the traditional features suggestive of an air is present, the passage is still set off from its musical surroundings. Activity in the basse continue abruptly increases, as does the harmonic rhythm, causing the passage to differ from its surroundings. What changed in this situation were the assumptions the composer made about music's capacity for signification. Straightforward, formal structures went the way of the elaborate recursive gestures of the 1730s, marking a flight from text-oriented features to musical features treated *qua* music. To the extent that modulation affects our hearing of the 1754 passage, it does so not by asking us to draw inferences from subtle voice leadings, but rather by forcing us to notice how perfectly some audible features of the music highlight the text. Similarly, act one, scene five of the new version employs lyricism to mark Pollux's magnanimous decision that Castor and Télaïre's love should take precedence over his royal claims. "Que vos fronts soient couronnés" is devoid of musical and textual repetitions, relying instead on its basse continue and harmonic rhythm to capture the listener's attention. By virtue of brevity and intensity, such moments function as extensions of traditional expressive practices. They do not refer back to and contextualize earlier musical gestures; instead, they *anchor* phrases and verses, much as old-fashioned musical accompaniments had highlighted isolated words.

A logical extension of this practice was Rameau's greater willingness in 1754 to use the orchestra to accompany recitative in *Castor*. As in "La Vangeance flatte la gloire" and "Que vos fronts soient couronnés," he abjured the more obvious technique of allowing formal repetition to underscore important texts and instead relied on audible features of musical texture, in this case timbre, to capture the audience's attention. For example, in the newly composed confidante scene for act one, scene one, Phébé and Cléone confer in simple recitative up to the point when Phébé must narrate her relationship with Télaïre, a key plot element originating outside the frame of the opera:

> Filles du Dieu du Jour, par quels présens divers
> > Le Ciel marqua notre partage!
> Je reçûs le pouvoir d'évoquer les Enfers;
> Que Telaïre obtint un plus doux avantage!
> Elle commande au coeurs où mon art ne peut rien;
> > Un coup d'oeil lui rend tout possible,
> Je ne fais qu'étoner ce qu'elle rend sensible.
> > Que son pourvoir est audessus du mien!

[Daughters of the god of day, with what different gifts did heaven mark our individuality! I received the ability to call upon the underworld, while Télaïre obtained a sweeter advantage! She commands hearts, where my art can do nothing. A glance renders everything possible for her. I can only amaze those whom she renders sympathetic. How far above mine is her power! (*C livret 1754*, 8).]

The additional musical emphasis communicates a dramaturgical change from 1737 in the relationship between Phébé and Télaïre: they are now

Example 3.9a. *Castor et Pollux* (1737), act 1, scene 2, mm. 41–54

Example 3.9b. *Castor et Pollux* (1754), act 2, scene 5, mm. 1–10

sisters, adding weight to the jealousy evident in this passage. They also have been elevated to the rank of gods, diminishing the isolation of Pollux found in the earlier version of the opera. Similarly, the reunion between Castor and Pollux—act four, scene seven, in the 1754 version—contains two new accompanied recitatives at key moments in its conclusion, first as Castor agrees to Pollux's plan and then as Pollux calls on Mercure to take him to Télaïre.

In the revivals of the mid-1750s, Rameau's earlier experiments at simplifying text settings thus take on a new agenda, asserting a new relationship between words and music by offering direct, easily perceived relationships between the two: music labels text. This paring of musical effect to its barest essentials reaches its peak in the 1756 revival of *Zoroastre*. We see this, for example, in act one, scene three, when Amélite's companions seek to cheer the lovelorn princess. Her first air, "Les plaisirs et les jeux ne m'offrent plus de charmes," has been deleted, even though its text remains dramatically plausible and the material preceding it is unchanged. Meanwhile, eleven measures of textual repetitions were simply removed from her second air, "Reviens, c'est l'Amour qui t'appelle." Rameau added orchestral accompaniment to these short, lyrical passages with striking effect. In the evil Abramane's air "La Haine, qui sait agir," from act four, scene four, the orchestra accompanies the three-measure refrain:

> La haine, qui sait agir,
> Est toujours assez puissante.

[Hate, who knows to act, is always rather powerful (*Z livret 1756*, 57).]

But it drops out in the middle section:

> Les trésors de mon art à vos yeux vont s'ouvrir,
> Le danger s'affoiblit, quand le courage augmente.

[The treasures of my art unfold before your eyes. Danger is weakened as courage grows (*Z livret 1756*, 57).]

The relationship between text and music is the simplest imaginable: the accompaniment is at its peak when the evil wizard Abramane explains the power of hatred, and then diminishes as he explains how he will use hatred to diminish the power of his foes. A more intriguing example occurs in act three, scene eight.[43] After Zoroastre saves the dying Amélite, she awakens with a brief, unaccompanied air:

> Ah! c'est vous que l'amour offre encore à mes voeux!
> Je vous revois. . . . Je meurs contente.

[Ah, it is you that love yet offers to my prayers! I see you again. I die content (*Z livret 1756*, 51).]

When Zoroastre must then leave her, he does so with a fond farewell, "Tendre Amelite, cher amante,/Adieu" (Tender Amélite, dear loved one, goodbye [*Z livret 1756*, 52]), set to the kind of chromatically descending modulation Rameau had avoided in the 1740s. (It is the only such progression in this version of the opera.) As we see in example 3.10, what is equally noteworthy is the setting of the text to a brief accompaniment in the bassoons (also used in act two, scene three, when Zoroastre learns Amélite is in trouble).[44] On the one hand, the use of instrumentation to call attention to text resembles the kind of gesture one finds in "Temple sacré, séjour tranquille" and "Cruelle mère des amours," where Rameau had likewise used shifts in orchestration to underscore surprising modulations. On the other hand, it bears witness to the composer's mounting lack of confidence in modulation alone. Used in isolation, such progressions require added accompaniment. No longer does Rameau trust their effects to the instinctive responses of audience members. It is telling as well that the reference to an earlier passage is timbral rather than harmonic. *Zoroastre,* then, repeats the pattern of earlier revivals, but without the apparent ambivalence of those cases. Rameau had found a satisfactory means of reintroducing music into dramatic situations.

Example 3.10. *Zoroastre* (1756), act 3, scene 8, mm. 39–42

By this stage in Rameau's musical development, he was setting listeners a task substantially different from the one he had extended to them in the 1730s. Whereas before he had hoped to influence their experience through subtle, but presumably natural properties of music, he now expected, much like any other composer, that audiences would pay attention to the words. Rameau's thoughts on text setting during the mid-1750s ensured his success as an opera composer not by recreating poetic syntax in music, but simply by ornamenting poetry musically. The plasticity of his material came to hold as much or more value than any particular connotations it might stir up in performance. The implications are numerous for our reading of contemporary discussions of his career. Perhaps, like the modulations available for accompanying a single interval, they are too numerous to recount. We can, however, imagine some of the ramifications. Consider for example the following passage in the *Mercure* from Rameau's obituary: "[W]ith the exception of *Les Indes galantes, Les Fêtes d'Hébé,* and *Zoroastre,* all the works that our illustrious musician has placed in the theater never had in their novelty an abundance of spectators as sustained and continuous as in their subsequent reprises and above all the most recent."[45] When later writers looked back nostalgically on the wonders of Rameau's tragedies, which versions were they remembering? When they recalled the composer's achievements, which composer they did they recall? It is altogether possible that when they cited with approval Rameau's earliest tragedies, they were not thinking of those works at all but their twins, the changelings the composer had left in their place.[46]

CHAPTER 4

Rameau Mise-en-Scène

RAMEAU'S SHIFTING ATTITUDES toward text setting repeat the fundamental contradiction we have been tracing all along. On the one hand, if he truly believed he was composing tragédies en musique in the Lullian tradition—and at least on some level he wished to believe it—then he was presenting nothing particularly new in his tragedies: the surprising harmonizations and elaborate orchestrations, however mesmerizing their effect on audiences, were the logical extensions of musical techniques already familiar to operagoers. This belief in tradition complemented his belief that his theories were not newly invented but something in the natural universe that he had discovered, as the title *Observations sur notre instinct pour la musique* implied. Indeed an important pretext for his argument in the *Observations* had been to agree with Rousseau that Lully and Rameau were cut from the same cloth. They both worked within music's immutable, natural laws. On the other hand, by the late 1740s and early 1750s Rameau's mounting ambivalence toward his own text-setting practice underscored the fact that his compositions, like his theories, were creations he himself had built: they had less to do with nature or Lullian tradition than with the intellectual broodings of an individual.

Thomas Christensen recently traced the continual transformation of Rameau's theories and the way that, as he was exposed to new ideas and philosophies, he incorporated their perspectives into his writings—and what Christensen has found applies equally to Rameau's development as a composer.[1] Explaining over and over the simple harmonic underpinnings of "Enfin il est en ma puissance" must have made Rameau aware of how different his own approach was in pieces like "Troubles cruels, soupçons injurieux," and if juxtapositions with Lully did not bring this self-awareness, then surely the act of revision would have. It is difficult to avoid the conclusion that Rameau wanted to build a musical tragédie that would complement his theoretical edifice.

Rameau wanted to have it both ways. He wanted to be accepted into the Lullian fold, but he also wanted credit for the originality and cleverness of his theoretical and musical ideas. This ultimately led him to reinvent not only his works but also, in a paradoxical manner, himself. The earliest versions of his tragedies attempted to project a composer who took literary traditions seriously, whereas the later ones suggested a more approachable composer whose works were openly entertaining. In the process of changing himself, he had to give up some of his most prized text-setting techniques to win any attention at all. It should perhaps come as no surprise then that scholars and modern performers have evinced greater enthusiasm for the later versions of some of Rameau's tragedies. Masson expressed astonishment that a revival of *Dardanus* in 1907 had not used the 1744 version, and Sigiswald Kuijken chose for a complete recording of *Zoroastre* the later version of 1756, calling it "undoubtedly an improvement" over the 1749 version.[2] Similarly, scholars have lined up to express their preference for the later version of *Castor et Pollux*. Although he called the earlier *Castor* "the best French opera livret of the eighteenth century," Masson believed that Pierre-Joseph Bernard and Rameau in revising it had tightened its dramatic structure. Graham Sadler has commented that the 1754 opera is "dramatically more taut" than the original: "none of his other operas is so well constructed, nor so rich in emotional contrasts; in no other are music and drama so consistently well integrated." Cuthbert Girdlestone criticized the earlier livret because it did not conform to the strictures of genre, observing that it is "not strictly tragic, and [is] . . . more narrative than dramatic." He took it for granted that in the 1754 version Rameau and Bernard had sought to remedy these defects by adding to the action the surefire elements of "jealousy and bloodshed."[3] Thus, while seducing his audiences, Rameau has seduced us as well. Accustomed to Italian opera, we too prefer to get through the recitative expediently so that we can enjoy our favorite musical events. (The recurring image of "tautness" certainly encourages this view.) In doing so, however, we cancel out the more complicated and more interesting historical subject—the composer who wanted to preserve the lyric tragedy through musical means—and we praise instead the entertainer. We replicate the judgments of Rameau's original audiences.

Both aspects of Rameau's thought, his affinity for tradition and his drive for novelty, betray considerable ambition, and questions arise over what he thought his various innovations were about: new genres or old values, new social roles for composers or the established ones for musicians, new dramatic roles for music or the primacy of poetry. Rameau's answers were never very clear, and his inability to articulate definitive statements about what his work represented forced him to inscribe and reinscribe his tragedies within larger, more ambiguous issues. They attracted attention by blurring the distinctions between mutually exclusive categories: entertainment and edification, frivolity and ideological commitment. It is not enough to catalogue the curious duplicities of Rameau's text settings. We must return to the issues first raised with respect to *Les Indes galantes*: how text is set against music in Rameau's tragedies, how scenes of drama are set against those of divertissement, and how the tensions between poetry and music play themselves out in scenes and acts. These issues are of fundamental importance to understanding Rameau. They limn the regions of narrative, drama, diversion, and pleasure. At the same time, however, we must also turn away from a topography where generic features emerge with geological predictability, in favor of an economy in which those same features circulate, exchange, transpose, and supplant one another. We must discover what Rameau was about when he went about composing, and we must do so while keeping in mind his own subtle transformations of himself and the tragic genre.[4]

This is a speculative area, because as a musician Rameau's principal task was to compose music, not to arrange scenes or dispose the elements of a drama according to his whims. He was dependent to a large extent on what poets gave him to work with, and we could easily argue that he played little part in decisions involving "dramatic tautness" and "bloodshed." Yet as we have seen in the machinations surrounding *Les Indes galantes* and *Samson,* by virtue of the music he wrote, Rameau was dragged into these larger debates and even credited with single-handedly inventing a new genre. The composer was so closely identified with his operas that each was difficult to separate from the other, and, as the following story reported by Jean-Marie-Bernard Clément suggests, Rameau's contemporaries showed little inclination to distinguish between composer and work:

> A British lord—having presented himself at the fifth performance of *Zoroastre* to obtain a seat in the balconies, the loges, or the amphitheater—was told by everyone that all the seats had been taken. "Here is the strangest and most singular thing I have seen in my life," he said. "I do not enter a house in Paris without hearing there horrible ills spoken of this opera, and I have come four times in a row to see it without being able to find a seat. In the whole world only the French are capable of these contradictions."[5]

To understand such contradictions, one would first have had to understand the public's complicated relationship with Rameau. Audiences certainly were not flocking to the Opéra to read Louis de Cahusac's first attempt at a tragic livret; they went to hear what the composer had wrought with his fourth tragédie en musique and his first new one in a decade. Whatever it was, it was to be disliked as a matter of course. At such moments, Rameau was "staged"; he became part of the spectacle audiences anticipated.

In this chapter I consider how Rameau, in his capacities as composer and public figure, influenced the design of the lyric tragedy. As it happens, *Zoroastre* (1749) is the obvious place to begin this appraisal, given the noteworthy pairing in it of poet and composer. Cahusac has become a focal point of critical and historical commentaries in recent years because his theories of theatrical dance complemented aspects of Rameau's thought. Both men wanted to take features of the tragedy traditionally associated with entertainment or divertissement—music and dance—and treat them as serious dramatic elements; as a result, Cahusac's influence on the unusual design of *Zoroastre* was substantial. At the same time, however, many of the features that make the first version of the opera appear unique did not in fact originate either with Cahusac or *Zoroastre*. They had been taken up in one form or another by Rameau's various collaborators as ideally suited to his newly invented tragédie en musique, and we find aspects of them even in *Hippolyte et Arice* (1733). They were part of how one staged the work of a highly musical composer like Rameau. At the very least, the identification of composer with work and work with composer establishes important patterns in the way the public perceived Rameau's tragedies and the opportunities they provided for transforming or reforming the tragic genre. At the other extreme, this blurred identity of composer and work is a hint that Rameau himself was instrumental in designing the shape and content of his operas. It is possible that he set out to use his shockingly innovative music to reinstate markedly conservative values in the tragic genre and thus came to dominate the repertory in tangible but less than obvious ways.

Zoroastre was the culmination of a period of intense compositional activity. From 1744, the year of the *Dardanus* revival, through the premiere of *Zoroastre* in 1749, Rameau composed four opéra-ballets (*Les Fêtes de Polymnie* [1745], *Le Temple de la Gloire* [1745], *Les Fêtes de l'Hymen et de l'Amour* [1747], *Les Surprises de l'Amour* [1748]), two pastorales héroïques (*Zaïs* [1748], *Naïs* [1749]), two actes de ballet (*Les Fêtes de Ramire* [1745], *Pigmalion* [1748]), the comédie-ballet *La Princesse de Navarre* (1745), and the comédie lyrique *Platée* (1745). In this same period various works, old and new, were revived as well: *Le Temple de la Gloire* (1746), *Les Fêtes d'Hébé* (1747), *Les Fêtes de l'Hymen et de l'Amour* (1747), and *Platée* (1749). The composer gives every indication of having found a secure compositional strategy, but the precise nature of that strategy and its effects on his subsequent tragedies remains unclear.

Given this largesse, we should not be surprised that by the end of the 1740s observers feared Rameau's increasing influence over the world of opera. In January, 1749, amid increased worries that the Opéra was going bankrupt, René-Louis de Voyer de Paulmy, marquis d'Argenson, reported on Rameau's growing support at court: "The marquise de Pompadour, who supervises spectacles, has just judged that within two years we would have only Rameau at the Opéra, whatever displeasure the public shows for it. An opera on *Médée* was sent [into storage] already completely learned and rehearsed. Good-bye to good taste and to good French music!"[6] There must have been some truth to the rumor, for in the following July Charles Collé recounted a ruling against Rameau by the *secrétaire d'état de la maison du roi*, Marc-Pierre, comte d'Argenson (brother of the marquis), indicating just how closely the public identified Rameau with the success and failure of opera as an institution:

> It is claimed that Monsieur d'Argenson, who presently has the Opéra in his department, explained to the directors that he did not wish to give more than one opera by Rameau each year. Partisans for [Rameau's] music are furious at this order and proclaim that this minister wants the Opéra to fall—that this great genius [Rameau] alone sustains it—in order to take it over from the current directors and give it to [the composers François] Rebel, [François] Francoeur, and [the singer Pierre] Jélyotte, whom he protects. One adds that Rameau is stung to the quick, swears to work no longer, and that he has withdrawn a tragedy by Cahusac and him, which he had provided for this winter [presumably *Zoroastre,* which premiered that December].
>
> I believe all this is exaggerated, and Monsieur de Boizemont, who is always at Madame d'Argenson's house, told me that Monsieur d'Argenson in truth did not wish to have more than two operas by Rameau per year and that this was in order not to discourage other composers, but that [d'Argenson] thought it neither here nor there to bother the current directors by giving the Opéra to this triumvirat [of Rebel, Francoeur, and Jélyotte].[7]

Exaggeration or not, by the end of the year the comte d'Argenson had transferred financial responsibility for the ailing Opéra to the *prévôt des marchands,* Bernage. As for the fear that Rameau would dominate the repertory, it was probably well-founded: in March, 1751, Collé reported that Rameau had three tragedies, two opéra-ballets, and three single-act works ready for performance, if only Bernage would allow them.[8] Two months later, a desperate *prévôt des marchands* made an ill-fated visit to inquire whether the composer would provide the troubled institution with some new operas. Rameau offered him several in exchange for a pension of one thousand écus, which d'Argenson refused to grant.[9]

Rameau's social and professional status in the early 1750s was thus problematic. At the height of his compositional powers, and precisely because he was at the height of them, he entered into a particularly difficult relationship with the Opéra that appears to have influenced the remainder of his career.[10] His works continued to be performed, to be sure, but neither at their former rate nor at the rate he was actually producing them. Often the performances and revivals were scheduled for private performances at the court in Fontainebleau, rather than in Paris at the Académie royale de musique. Further, in addition to the tragedies *Linus* and *Les Boréades* at least three *actes de ballet* remained unperformed at his death: *Nélée et Myrthis, Zéphyre,* and *Io.* It seems likely from Rameau's remarks (as reported by Collé) that still other unperformed operas existed as well, which have never been discovered.

In this dispute over creativity, dominance, and suppression, genre was an important factor. Only one extant tragédie en musique, *Zoroastre,* dates from mid-century, leaving us with a catalogue of ten lighter works (fourteen, counting revivals) performed over the five-year period from 1745 to 1749. Rameau's compositional strategy had thus changed drastically from the preceding decade. Earlier in his career he had sought credibility by devoting his energies primarily to the tragédie en musique. He wrote three major tragedies in the 1730s, four including *Samson,* and only two opéra-ballets; the early 1740s saw the revival of two of the early tragedies and brief consideration of yet another tragedy project with Voltaire, *Pandore.*[11] Rameau's reward for five productions of tragedies (and two failed productions) in the period from 1733 to 1744 had been a steady stream of critical abuse; however, after turning to lighter genres in the late 1740s, he quickly came to enjoy the kind of attention he had always craved. *Zoroastre,* as a return to the lyric tragedy, thus marks a significant decision by the composer, a resolution encouraged perhaps by his growing popularity. The draw of the tragédie en musique was still strong. We cannot identify the three tragedies mentioned by Collé in 1751, but if Thomas Green's conjectural dating of Rameau's remaining tragedies holds up, and it seems likely to, then the composer's best-known later projects were composed soon after *Zoroastre*'s premiere. These included the missing tragedy *Linus,* the parts and score of which were lost, stolen, or perhaps discarded after a rehearsal in 1751 or 1752; the revised *Zoroastre* and *Castor et Pollux,* apparently completed around the same time; and *Les Boréades,* possibly begun as well during this same period.[12] (And this list does not take into account the abortive *Hippolyte et Aricie* scheduled for the 1751–52 season [see n. 4].)

The nexus of compositional events and activities revealed in the early 1750s—Rameau's mounting difficulties with the Opéra's administration, shifts in genre, and prodigious compositional output; the argument in the *Observations* for a link between Rameau and the Lullian tradition; and ongoing reevaluation of the relationship between text and music—may not be coincidental. It explains the grounds for the crisis we have seen developing in Rameau's career, leading to this point when exhaustive reconsideration of what constituted opera and the tragédie en musique had become inevitable for the composer.

Cahusac's influence throughout this period appears to have been great. Between 1744 and 1749, he had authored two of Rameau's opéra-ballets, *Les Fêtes de Polymnie* (1745) and *Les Fêtes de l'Hymen et de l'Amour* (1747), and the two pastorales héroïques, *Zaïs* (1748) and *Naïs* (1749), as well as *Zoroastre.* Furthermore, scholars have conjectured that he was the poet behind *Les Boréades,*[13] which as we have noted may date in its earliest conception from about 1751 or 1752. By the late 1740s and early 1750s Cahusac was known as one of the handful of poets, including Voltaire, with whom Rameau had worked repeatedly, and the public associated him with the composer's recent successes in light genres. Still, though success seemed attainable for Cahusac, the shift in Rameau's compositional activity that *Zoroastre* signaled and the resulting transition to writing poetry for tragédies en musique proved difficult. In July, 1749, several weeks before the premiere of *Zoroastre*, he wrote the *Mercure de France* to squelch the rumor that he had not authored Rameau's forthcoming tragedy: "Perhaps when the work becomes known, I will be quite happy that one wishes to credit it to another, but whatever the judgment of the public may be, the disgrace or honor ought to reflect on me alone, and I await my destiny with a constant desire to recognize my faults, to correct them, and to please."[14] Cahusac was right to be guarded in his comments, for reactions to his livret followed the long-established pattern of abuse directed at Rameau's poets. Clément, for example, recorded an epigram suggesting there was something almost grandiose in the failure of the *Zoroastre* livret:

Ombre de Pellegrin, sors du fond du Ténare,
Pauvre rimeur sifflé si long-tems & si haut;
L'Opéra t'a vengé, ta gloire se répare.
Le Poète Gascon, à qui l'on te compare,
Est au-dessous de toi, plus que toi de Quinault.

[Shade of Pellegrin, depart from the base of Taenarus, poor rhymer, whistled so long and so loudly. The Opéra has avenged you; your glory is restored. The Gascon poet, to whom you are compared, is as far beneath you as you were beneath Quinault.][15]

The comparison with Pellegrin was an apposite one. Though Pellegrin had been a well-established livret poet when he set about writing *Hippolyte et Aricie* for Rameau, the public still treated his works as a high-water mark for bad poetry. (Voltaire, it will be recalled, had written with typical irony that the livret for *Hippolyte* was "by the abbé Pellegrin and worthy of the abbé Pellegrin.")[16] The choice of Rameau's first collaborator for comparison with Cahusac was undoubtedly not coincidental. The epigram traces a steady decline in the tragédie en musique from Quinault, revered by eighteenth-century critics, to Pellegrin and on down to Cahusac, subtly linking the problems associated with the lyric tragedy to Rameau.

In the weeks prior to *Zoroastre*'s premiere, however, Cahusac had reason to believe that his forthcoming work would bring him honor rather than disgrace, for the aspirations of the livret were grand. He had selected a story that elaborated on sources from antiquity in the time-honored manner, and, in the preface to the 1749 livret, he assured readers of the scholarship that had gone into writing it: "In offering on the lyric scene so celebrated a personage, neither research nor care should be spared to assemble the principal traits that distinguish him in ancient history, and it is on this material that his character and the plan of this work have been traced." The story also allowed Cahusac to design a plot of magnificent proportions. He evoked a sense of profound conflict by stressing Zoroastre's role as the inventor of good magic as opposed to Abramane's, a worshiper of dark magic: "This [latter] personage and the contrast he furnishes are drawn from the sources of the subject itself. Zoroastre had combated and destroyed the idolatry then spreading through Persia, just as [it spread] through the rest of the world."[17] The story was meant to depict a cataclysmic battle between good and evil, the livret abounding with metaphors of light and dark, which he emphasized for the reader through italics and footnotes. In the final scenes of the story, Cahusac even split each page of the livret into parallel columns so that the relationship between the opposing speeches of Zoroastre and Abramane would be as clear as their actual positioning in performances—at each end of the stage.

As modern commentators (including Kintzler, Russo, and Sadler) have pointed out, the 1749 *Zoroastre* is noteworthy for the stark relief with which Cahusac presented his characters and incidents. Foregoing the traditional prologue, the opera begins *in media res*: act one opens onto destitution, the countryside of a ravaged Bactria, the waves of its river lashing at the banks. This beginning is reminiscent of both the prologue to the 1737 *Castor et Pollux,* in which loveless war threatens to destroy the world, and the first act, which starts with mourning for a principal character, Castor. The first scene of *Zoroastre* opens not with a leading female character singing a monologue or exchanging information with a confidante but rather with an exchange between the villain Abramane and his confidant Zopire. Abramane is crushing Bactria to force its people to choose as ruler his candidate, Érinice, over the presumed heir Amélite. Érinice enters. She wants revenge on Zoroastre, who does not return her love. The villains vanish at the approach of Amélite, whose friends introduce a divertissement to cheer the troubled princess. Érinice interrupts the celebration, and the act concludes with a chorus of evil spirits carrying away Amélite. The joyful second act is an extended divertissement of songs, choruses, and dances, in which the natives of idyllic Hindustan, Zoroastre's adopted home, welcome the sunrise. Here again celebration is interrupted as a flaming cloud descends and a voice from within it calls Zoroastre to glory:

> Zoroastre vole à la gloire:
> Triomphe, éclaire l'Univers.
> La *Lumiere* attend la victoire,
> Sur les *Ténebres* des Enfers.

[Zoroastre flies to glory: triumph, enlighten the universe. *Light* awaits victory over the *twilight* of the underworld (*Z livret 1749,* 33, emphasis in original).]

Zoroastre and the cloud depart for Bactria. There, in the third act, he finds the Bactrians living in the shadow of Érinice's palace. Much like Voltaire's Hebrews in act one, scene one, of *Samson* (or the Incas in the second entrée of *Les Indes galantes*) the Bactrians cry out to the gods to ease their torment. Zoroastre uses his good magic to bring light to them; then, suddenly possessed by a horrible vision, he rends open the walls of Érinice's palace, revealing Amélite in chains and Érinice poised above her with a knife. Amélite faces her assailant bravely, but Érinice flees. As Zoroastre releases Amélite from her chains, they acknowledge their love. Abramane appears and warns the Bactrians to fear him. To calm them, Zoroastre calls on spirits, the "elemental people" (*les peuples elementaires*), to introduce a divertissement. The fourth act counterbalances the second: whereas the second act was preoccupied with sunrise and the dawning of Zoroastre's powers, the fourth traces the fomenting of Abramane's dark schemes in his subterranean temple. Abramane reassures Érinice that hatred overwhelms love. He conjures up Vengeance, Haine, Desespoir, Jalousie, Colère, and two Furies, who present a divertissement. In the first scene of act five Amélite sings a monologue explaining how the "doux espoir" of Zoroastre's love sustains her; he enters, and they reaffirm their love. The Bactrians reenter and enjoin Amélite to assume her rightful throne. A noble ruler, she states that she is less touched by her birthright than by the tender sentiments of the Bactrians. Abramane arrives, and the positioning on stage then splits in two as previously mentioned, with Zoroastre and the Bactrians on one side, Abramane and his troops on the other, and Amélite caught in the middle. Zoroastre wins the battle, and a celebratory divertissement concludes the opera.

Cahusac's dramaturgy results in a notably different balance between music and drama, especially in the second and fourth acts. One could in fact view these two acts as devoted almost solely to divertissement. In act two, we encounter Zoroastre's retreat in Hindustan through a series of songs and choruses, the characters accumulating on stage in the manner of a Classical finale; entrées and dances emerge as a matter of course, depicting the routine happiness, love, and sun-worship that go on in a land unblemished by evil. Act four brings the contrast of darkness, treating us to a similar crescendo of activity as Abramane worships his evil spirits, confers with various characters who enter, calls upon priests and evil spirits, and then allows them to take over the stage with their demonic songs, dances, and choruses. The two acts do not develop the plot in any real sense. We do not need to know much about Hindustan or Abramane's evil kingdom in order to follow the story. Nevertheless, they are rich in a certain kind of dramatic information, revealing much about the eminence of the characters Zoroastre and Abramane. They are a clever attempt at establishing mood and at heightening the contrast between good and evil.

This unusual *combination* (as opposed to juxtaposition) of dramatic action and divertissement within single acts suits Rameau's musical style and turns out to have been a principal goal in Cahusac's theorization of dance. In articles for the *Encyclopédie* and in his treatise, *La Danse ancienne et moderne* (1754), Cahusac proposed moving away from the ornamental function of simple dance, which he compared to flower arranging, and toward his newly conceived *danse en action,* a theatrical event that would revolutionize lyric theater:

> Our tragedy and comedy have an extent and duration sustained by the charms of discourse, the finesse of the details, the variety of flashes of wit. The action is divided into acts; each act is divided into scenes; the scenes lead to situations; the situations in their turn provide the warmth, form the intrigue, lead to the end and prepare it.
>
> Such ought to be, but with even more precision, the tragedies and comedies in dance. I say with more precision, because the gesture is more precise than discourse. Several words are necessary to express a thought; a single movement can paint several thoughts and sometimes the most vigorous situation. It is therefore necessary that theatrical action always move with the greatest rapidity, that there be no useless entrée or figure. A good piece of theater in dance ought to be a compressed extract of an excellently written dramatic piece.[18]

Cahusac wanted dance to cross its traditional boundary and become part of the drama, thereby exceeding its usual role as a necessary but nonpoetic supplement. Like Rameau, he envisioned the semiotic potential of elements normally considered secondary to the literary discourse of French theater, and, like Rameau, he argued for the capacity of this semiotic system to transform familiar entertainment into something richer and more serious. His remarks in the article on dance for the *Encyclopédie* tie this process to the kind of natural, instinctive responses Rameau had discussed in the *Observations*:

> In its development, the song so natural to humankind inspired in others, who were struck by it, gestures related to the different sounds with which the song was composed. The body then acted, the arms opened or closed, the feet formed slow or rapid steps, facial expressions participated in these diverse movements, the whole body responded with positions, shakings, attitudes to the sounds by which the ear was affected: thus the song, which was the expression of a sentiment, made a second expression develop, which was among humankind what was called dance, and these were the two primitive principles.
>
> One sees by these few words that voice and gesture are not more natural to the human species than song and dance, and that both are, so to speak, the instruments of two arts to which they have given place.[19]

Dance answered text in the same way that music answered it in Rameau's theories. Much as the music in Rameau's earliest operas operated as a signifying system parallel to written text, so too dance created its own relay, a signifying system that operated in conjunction with the other two. Coordination of these systems was therefore of paramount importance. Cahusac wrote in *La Danse ancienne et moderne*: "If the general plan of the opera is well made, as are for example all those of Quinault, [then] each of the parts that compose it relate to the principal action. Consequently, in order for it to be well executed, it is necessary that each dance taken separately be connected [to the principal action] and thus make, in some manner or another, part of this action."[20] Like Rameau in the *Nouveau systême* and the *Observations*, Cahusac appropriated authoritative works from the seventeenth century to support his case. A distinguishing feature of the third volume of *La Danse ancienne et moderne*, where he presented his theories in greatest detail, is its parade of famous operatic episodes drawn from Quinault and Lully, passages which might have been and still could be enhanced by allowing dance some measure of narrative control. The second and fourth acts of the 1749 *Zoroastre* thus put Cahusac's beliefs into practice, creating passages of continuous divertissement while presenting information more or less relevant to the drama. Extravagantly produced, the 1749 *Zoroastre* was perhaps the last and greatest staged attempt at providing a forum for the contributions of music and dance to tragedy.

As a result of Cahusac's theories, French scholars in the past decade have come to accept the first version of *Zoroastre* as the defining point in Rameau's career, the time when he found himself in the company of a poet complementary to and worthy of his own elaborate musical conception. With Cahusac, Catherine Kintzler argues, the tragédie en musique gave in to its essential tendencies and became devoted entirely to divertissement. Grand, marvelous themes replaced dalliance. Concern with character development ceased, the dramatis personae becoming placeholders for the elemental forces that surrounded them, such as good and evil, and the tragédie en musique abandoned its crisis-oriented plots, derived from spoken theater, in favor of confrontations between those elemental forces. Cahusac had realized the latent possibilities of Rameau's new genre by simplifying narrative and giving primacy to the magnificence of the spectacle.[21]

If Kintzler is correct in her assessment, the story nevertheless does not end with Rameau enjoying his moment of glory (and the 1749 *Zoroastre* is by all means a remarkable collaboration), for there still is a revival to take into account. Like Rameau, in 1749 Cahusac had run a risk by conflating the traditionally separate roles of edification and pleasure, threatening once again a monstrous fragmentation of the familiar, the intelligible, and the predictable. His ideas encompassed an impossible figuring of genre, but as with Rameau this figuring involved pleasure, a problematic surplus capable both of appealing to and offending large sectors of the public.

In a pattern that is by now familiar, the most remarkable features of the 1749 version stand out in particular relief only once they have vanished in *Zoroastre*'s revision. In 1756 *Zoroastre* tells a completely different story, and it adopts different narrative strategies in order to tell it. Cahusac replaced the struggle between good and evil with an emotional framework of the traditional lyric tragedy and, in effect, neutralized the features that had formerly made the work so striking. In act one, scene two, of the 1749 version, for example, Abramane had been the coolly calculating villain:

> La raison plus que la colere
> Eteint les feux dont je brûlois;

[Reason more than anger appeases the fires with which I burned (*Z livret 1749*, 14).]

In the 1756 version of the same passage, he becomes the exact opposite, a figure ruled by the basest passions:

> De mon coeur, ma juste colere
> D'un ingrate efface les traits.

[My righteous anger at an ingrate effaces the features of my heart (*Z livret 1756*, 16).]

Anger here replaces reason. Similarly, the motivation for Érinice's character devolves from revenge to a hopelessly confused state motivated principally by her love for Zoroastre. As she is about to strike Amélite down in act two, scene five, the mere sight of Zoroastre causes the knife to fall from Érinice's hand:

> Elle vivra pour toi: tu ne vis que pour elle.
> A l'excès de ma rage, à ma douleur mortelle,
> Connois du moins, ingrat, l'excès de mon Amour.

[She will live for you: you see only her. In the excess of my rage, in my mortal sadness, at least know, ingrate, the excess of my love (*Z livret 1756*, 32).]

In act three, scene one, she confesses as much to Abramane, who doubts her resolve. She is quick to reassure him, but act five, scene one, finds her seeking instead to save Zoroastre: "Malheureuse! . . . est-ce à moi de trembler pour sa vie?" (Unfortunate one! am I to tremble for his life? [*Z livret 1756*, 65]). When he enters in scene two—"Il approche. . . . Enfin je respire" (He approaches. . . . Finally I breathe [*Z livret 1756*, 66])—

she begs him to hide his disgust for her and flee while he has still the chance:

> Tu vois le désespoir où mon ame se livre,
> Sois touché de mes pleurs, fui cet affreux séjour.
> Mes malheurs, tes mépris, ma mort qui va les suivre,
> Je te pardonne tout, ingrat, si tu veux vivre,
> Et c'est l'unique prix qu'exige mon amour.

[You see the despair to which my soul delivers itself. Be touched by my tears. Flee this frightful place. My misfortunes, your scorn, my death, which follows, I pardon everything, ingrate, if you wish to live, and that is the only price my heart exacts (*Z livret 1756*, 68).]

Just then she hears a brilliant symphony; realizing that the Bactrians have chosen Amélite as ruler, she returns to Abramane.

The final events of the opera are emblematic of the differences between the two versions. In 1749 the focal point of the fifth act is less the romantic reunion of Zoroastre and Amélite than Amélite's election in scene three as ruler of Bactria. Zoroastre's presence is secondary to Amélite's magnanimity toward her new subjects. The final battle erupts, and Zoroastre must prove once again that good triumphs over evil. To be sure, love is present in the final scenes of 1749, but much more space is given over to the joys of living under wise rule:

> Douce Paix, regnez dans le monde.
> Les Cieux triomphent des Enfers.
> Que nos chants de victoire éclatent dans les airs,
> Et que la terre nous réponde.

[Sweet peace, reign in the world. The heavens triumph over the underworld. How our victory songs sound in the air, and how the earth responds to us! (*Z livret 1749*, 72).]

In 1756, as we have noted, the selection of Amélite takes place offstage. The forces of evil kidnap her again. A battle ensues but it is quickly dispensed with: the earth opens up, swallowing Abramane and his evil forces. The remainder of the act is given over to Zoroastre and Amélite's love, which they express in words that had been uttered thousands of times in French opera:

> ZOROASTRE:
> Que ces noeuds son charmans!
>
> AMÉLITE:
>   Qu'ils flattent ma tendresse!

ZOROASTRE:
  Que je vous aime!

AMÉLITE:
            Doux retour!

ENSEMBLE:
  Tout mon ame est l'amour.
  Il l'enchaîne à jamais; qu'il l'enflâme sans cesse!

[ZOROASTRE: How charming these knots are! AMÉLITE: How they soothe my tenderness! ZOROASTRE: How I love you! AMÉLITE: Sweet return! ENSEMBLE: My entire soul is love. (Love) enchains it forever; it enflames it without ceasing! (*Z livret 1756*, 73–74).]

If the first version of *Zoroastre* attempted to create a radically new form of tragédie en musique in the manner described by Kintzler, as Paolo Russo has noted the second more closely resembled the traditional *comédie larmoyante*, its heroine subjected to continual peril precisely because she loved so deeply.[22] Along the way to the 1756 version, Cahusac abandoned the notion of making act two into a single, ongoing divertissement. Without act two to counterbalance it, however, act four looks like a miscalculation. Cahusac's poetic revisions had allowed the opera to follow a traditional story line, placing divertissement in its familiar and subordinate role.

That at least some audience members were sensitive to the trivialization of the 1749 story is evident from the remarks of the baron Friedrich Melchior Grimm. Grimm lambasted Cahusac's efforts in 1756, not for their poor versification but for the way the poet had succumbed to the very traits that had usually placed the worth of any tragédie en musique in question:

> There is another genre of spectacle even more worthy of censure, because it is founded on a *merveilleux* so flat, so boring, and so ridiculous that there is not enough in it to amuse children. Quinault knew to mask the deformity of this genre with sweet and natural verses, by ideas sometimes sublime and nearly always felicitous. One of his successors, M. de Cahusac, has well understood the secret of reestablishing the insipidity and extravagance of the genre in all its force: a genius, enemy of our ears, who has given in to the rare and hideous talent of amassing nonsense in polished verses, in spite of Apollo and Minerva. The Académie royale de musique has bored us all winter long with a certain *Zoroastre* by this poet, the least of whose magical virtues is in making one sleep standing up.[23]

Whereas his response in 1749 had consisted mainly of recording the occasional epigram, Grimm here engaged in a fundamental questioning of *Zoroastre*'s generic attributes. The tragédie en musique was in itself a far-from-perfect genre, and through his unawareness of its dangers, Cahusac had made it even worse. By "merveilleux," Grimm seems to have intended something more than what we usually understand by the expression, that is, the special effects characteristic of French operatic staging. In particular, his citation of Quinault's sublime ideas and skill in hiding deformities hints at a more serious structural flaw: the preposterous, chimerical stories that had set conservatives like Saint-Évremond, Boileau, and Voltaire on edge from the beginning. In his criticism of Cahusac, Grimm did not limit his remarks to the poet's divertissements but instead addressed the ways in which Cahusac had failed to make the most unwieldy aspects of the story plausible. Grimm went on in this vein to attack the tropes of light and dark that had so pleased the poet, arguing that they were in this instance grotesque. Cahusac had freely mixed day and night within each act, and thus he had had to include some additional alternations between light and dark in order to allow the piece to conclude appropriately in the light of day. Since Grimm complains about the poet's "inability to count to five [acts]," he may have intended with this complaint to underscore the lack of uniform contrast between acts two and four in the 1756 version, which resulted in more alternations between contrasting moods than had appeared in the earlier version.[24] At any rate, the writer makes it clear that even in its watered-down form the 1756 *Zoroastre* had not successfully made the leap to narration through divertissement, but instead remained mired in the much older issue of how divertissement should balance out drama. By way of conclusion, Grimm reassured his readers in rather old-fashioned terms that the proper way to compose lyric tragedies was by imitating nature. The curious trajectory of Grimm's responses to *Zoroastre*, from bemused in 1749 to openly derisive in 1756, suggests that without the high-mindedness of the earlier version the work did not hold together at all. It had degenerated into entertainment of the lowest kind.

More striking even than the audience's responses is the emergence in the 1756 *Zoroastre* of a familiar pattern of reaction to them. Once again, in the initial version of a work Rameau attempted to alter the ontological status of the lyric tragedy, only to give way to public concerns in the second version. The ambivalence that was affecting him musically in the mid-1740s found its counterpart in the very shape of the 1756 drama. The Ramiste Pierre-Louis d'Aquin de Chateau-Lyon made it clear that dissatisfaction with the 1749 *Zoroastre* had caused the authors to begin revising the work almost immediately after its premiere: "It is to jealousy that the magnificent opera *Zoroastre* was sacrificed. Are the actors not ill whenever they wish [to show their disapproval]? Let us hope to see this rather celebrated tragedy again soon in all its brilliance. It is said to be further embellished by corrections that the illustrious author has judged appropriate to make in it."[25] By now the drill would have been a familiar one for the composer. Far from "embellishing" his work, as Chateau-Lyon implies, he had chosen in conjunction with his poet to strip it of its precious novelties and to replace them with elements already familiar to opera audiences.

Without challenging Kintzler's basic premise, which I consider important for my own argument regarding Rameau's attitude in the 1750s, I would note that by focusing on the first versions of Rameau's works, she has concocted a reductive view of Cahusac's and *Zoroastre*'s importance. In her version of events, poet and composer set out in 1749 to become precisely what the public had believed them to be all along, entertainers devoted to divertissements. This presents us with a quandary, for her emphasis results in depicting their most innovative ideas as decidedly unambitious, as ultimately blind to the literary values that still informed the tragedy. It does not begin to address such issues as why poet and composer thought the public would be pleased by continual divertissement or why they avoided tried-and-true plot devices when so much was at stake. Nor does it deal with the immediate public pressure they felt to rewrite *Zoroastre*. By the mid-1740s Rameau knew first-hand how audiences were likely to greet the oxymoronic notion of entertaining tragedy, and if doubts persisted, the reception accorded his lighter works in the 1740s should have laid them to rest. The public did not desire the surplus entertainment Rameau and Cahusac offered them in 1749. What allowed Cahusac to complement Rameau in the 1749 *Zoroastre* was not that he too believed in spectacle, but rather that he believed in dance, which, like music, could bear meanings relevant to the drama. Poet and composer assumed they could establish nonverbal forms of signification as a core operatic practice and that one carefully staged work wholly devoted to this end might assure their success. They entered into the 1749 *Zoroastre* project because of their conviction that they could do more than entertain: music and dance could communicate necessary information to the audience and convince it of the opera's worth. This alone would have made such a project worth the gamble. The semiotics of the nonverbal, in turn, receded in the 1756 revival, precisely because audience members could imagine neither dance nor music as anything other than features *supplemental* to the success of a tragédie en musique.

In Rameau's case, the conviction that music could guide large stretches of operatic narrative was one he had held for most of his career, and, as we have seen, there is little reason to believe that he had not considered its consequences prior to 1749. Important though it was, *Zoroastre* was not the first of Rameau's operas to employ unusual dramaturgy to enhance music's capacity for signification. Experimentation is evident from his earliest tragedies, and these dramaturgical experiments stand in relief when we compare different versions of the same work. Taking revivals into account, we find that in the 1730s *Castor et Pollux* and *Dardanus* foreshadowed the innovations Kintzler attributes to the 1749 *Zoroastre*—grand subjects, emphasis on situations rather than characters, confidence in the dramatic availability of divertissement, and reliance on nonliterary modes of signification—but that these innovations were omitted in the works' revivals. Rameau's collaboration with Cahusac on a tragedy was less the watershed event Kintzler imagines than the culmination of recurring dramaturgical concerns closely associated with Rameau in the minds of his collaborators. The *Zoroastre* of 1749 was not a solution to the composer's longtime problem—how to find a role for music in the lyric tragedy—but evidence of an ever-expanding crisis, in which his assumptions about music's fundamental worth were at stake.

Elements of this trend were apparent already in Rameau's very first opera. In the preface to the 1733 livret of *Hippolyte et Aricie,* Pellegrin pointed with pride to the serious tone of his work, even in comparison to Racine's famous model:

> [I]t is not enough to justify the choice of my subject and the title of my piece; it is infinitely more important to me to make [one] see whether my story is reasonable. I will first avow—without pretending to censure [Racine], who has opened me to this course—that his character Thesée has always appeared to me too credulous and that a son as virtuous as Hippolyte ought not be condemned so lightly on the deposition of a suspicious woman and on the evidence of a sword that could have been unknown to him. I know that a passion as blind as jealousy can carry the greatest errors, but this does not suffice for the theater. The great secret of success [there] is in bringing the spectators to the point of feeling they would do the same as the actors if they found themselves in a similar situation.[26]

Pellegrin wanted to be worthy of his story and its famous literary models, and *Hippolyte* was not unusual among his livrets in this regard. Cuthbert Girdlestone has depicted Pellegrin as a poet and critic whose seriousness or at least sincerity was often inconsistent with his popularity. His earliest livret, *Médée et Jason* (1713), based on well-known spoken tragedies by Pierre Corneille and Bernard Requeleyne de Longepierre, adopted a critical attitude toward its literary sources and contained a surprisingly unromantic ending.[27] Though not devoid of the usual romantic entanglements, his livrets were capable of larger dramatic conflicts as well, and the serious tone of his biblical tragédie en musique, *Jephté,* was believed by contemporaries to have influenced Rameau's operatic career. In 1761 the *Mercure de France* explained that the first production of *Jephté* in 1732 had inspired Rameau to begin composing opera:

> Twenty-five years ago, the music of [*Jephté*] appeared to be in a new and unaccustomed style. A circumstance that the public will perhaps learn with plea-

sure should render this music precious to true connoisseurs. By the celebrated Rameau's admission, it was the occasional cause of the masterpieces with which [Rameau] has enriched our lyric theater. This great man heard *Jephté*; the noble and distinguished character of this work struck him at points [as] apparently analogous to the virile fecundity of his genius. At this moment he conceived that our dramatic music was susceptible to a new force and new beauties. He formulated the project of composing some; he dared to be a creator. He agrees no less than that *Jephté* procured *Hippolyte et Aricie*.[28]

The second act of *Hippolyte* is especially striking for the way it leaves behind the love scenes of act one to follow Thésée's underworld quest to save his friend, Pirithoüs. Although the plot here followed the operatic propensity for spectacular settings and supernatural beings—it could be no more than mentioned in Racine's *Phèdre* without violating unity of place— it also served a noble theme: not *amour* but *amitié,* the loyalty one individual owes another. At the same time, because it was tangential to the larger story, little dialogue was necessary. By act two, scene three, divertissement emerges in Pluton's monologue, "Qu'à servier mon courroux tout l'Enfer se prépare," and the remainder of the act is devoted to choruses, an infernal dance, and, of course, the famous trios for the furies. Drama and music here worked hand in hand and, for the most part, successfully.

Immediately following, however, in act three, scene one, the aspirations of poet and composer came into direct conflict with assumptions about genre. As noted in chapter 3, the earliest version of this scene stresses Phèdre's guilt in the introspective monologue "Cruelle mère des amours." The scene also documents the problems that arise when opera places too much emphasis on tragic emotion. About the time of the work's premiere, Pellegrin and Rameau replaced "Cruelle mère" with the more romantic "Espoir, unique bien d'une fatale flamme," and by 1742, they replaced this piece yet again with the equally romantic recitative "Mes destins sont changez." Phèdre's significance in the story thus withered first from tragedy to love and then from monologue to recitative. Such subtle shifts in dramatic emphasis also occurred in the love scenes. In the 1733 version's meeting in act one, scene two, between Hippolyte and Aricie, Hippolyte's language is full of outrage about unjust laws and infelicitous situations, while in the 1742 version he commits himself wholly to the task of wooing Aricie. Similarly, in their "1733 meeting" in act four, scene two, they spend much of their time discussing Phèdre's plans and their own political situation, while in 1742 they discuss the future of their relationship. The 1733 *Hippolyte et Aricie* is thus a remarkable first opera in more than one sense. Although neither Pellegrin nor Rameau may have been giving expression in it to a comprehensive reform agenda, the work introduces key issues for Rameau's development: the potential for more serious story-telling in the lyric tragedy, the potential of music as a narrative device, and the difficulties these innovations present for performers and audience members.

In light of these circumstances, it is not surprising that Rameau's next collaborator, Voltaire, was dealing with similar problems about the same time. As we saw in chapter 2, in his spoken tragedy *Zaire* (1732) Voltaire responded to the repeated criticism that his tragedies ignored the romantic interests deemed necessary to French theater, and his livret for Rameau's *Samson* returned to the issue with a scenario in which love was not the resolution of the story but its central problem. He wrote to Rameau in 1733 about the character Dalila, "An opera heroine who is not at all amorous will perhaps not be accepted. While my detractors say my work is impious, the parterre will find it too wise and too severe. They will be disheartened at seeing love treated only as a seduction in a theater where it is always consecrated as a virtue."[29] Again in 1736 Voltaire wrote of a work in which love was avoided in the first two acts: "It will be beautiful to have two acts sustained in the temple of Quinault without love-affair jargon. I maintain that to treat love with the respect it merits is not to use it lavishly and make it appear as an absolute master. Nothing is so cold as when it is unnecessary."[30] In Voltaire's version of *Samson,* the gods of the Philistines are not Baal and Dagon but Venus and Adonis. He explained why in the *avertissement* to the 1746 edition: "The names of Venus and Adonis find a more natural place in this tragedy than would be believed at first: it is in effect on their own terrain that the action occurs."[31] Voltaire gives the protagonist Samson a choice between love and duty, and when Samson succumbs to Dalila's temptations, he likewise succumbs to the values represented by the gods Voltaire had substituted. His reward is blindness and humiliation at the hands of the Philistines. At the end of the opera when he redeems himself by destroying their temple, he not only takes vengeance on the gods who tempted him to betrayal but also pointedly defies the very gods who ruled the lyric tragedy. He destroys Quinault's temple as well.

Nevertheless, mood alone does not account for the dramaturgical plan adopted in *Samson*; equally important was Voltaire's decision to regulate the musical excesses that had threatened to overwhelm *Hippolyte et Aricie*. He did this by providing clearly defined points in the story where music could take over, effectively augmenting the divertissements and musical events within each act. Thus in November, 1733, his friend Formont wrote to Cideville, "Our friend [Voltaire] is making an opera entitled *Samson* for Rameau. . . . and since what pleases in [Rameau's] operas are [duos,] trios, choruses, character airs, and so on, [Voltaire] will put only a little recitative [into it] and attempt to provide the musician occasions for exercising his particular kind of talent."[32] In December, 1735, Voltaire himself wrote, "Here is all the interest I know in an opera: a beautiful, well-varied spectacle, some brilliant divertissements, lots of airs, a little recitative, short acts. . . . I wish *Samson* to be in a new style, no more than one recitative scene per act, no confidantes, no verbiage."[33] In seeing Rameau as a composer who emphasized dramatically static musical events at the expense of recitative scenes, Voltaire was in complete agreement with his contemporaries, but where others saw a defect, Voltaire saw a potential virtue. Rameau's dazzling musical compositions provided an excitement and entertainment that would compensate for the absence of love themes, and this in turn would allow the audience to focus its attention on what mattered most to Voltaire, his more serious narratives. What is especially striking about Voltaire's scheme is that he conceived it in direct response to hearing Rameau for the first time—and possibly in reaction to the construction of act two of *Hippolyte*. In the summer of 1733, just months before *Hippolyte*'s premiere, he had attempted a tragic livret entitled *Tanis et Zélide*, which bore no trace of this innovative dramaturgy; after attending the *Hippolyte* premiere the following October, he could think of little else. Rameau's music had lent shape and focus to his larger project for theatrical reform.

If Voltaire's plans for *Samson* remained unfulfilled, Rameau's next tragedy, *Castor et Pollux*, took up the standard and delivered a reasonable facsimile of them in performance.[34] The 1737 opera opens with a tableau of despair that would not have been lost on Gluck when he later set about composing *Orfeo ed Euridice*: a major character has died prior to the beginning of the opera, and the first act begins with a chorus of mourning, "Que tout gémisse."[35] Phébé discovers Télaïre rushing in sorrow to Castor's tomb. An exchange between them informs us that Castor has died defending Sparta from Lincée and that Castor's immortal twin, Pollux, is presently battling the murderer offstage. We learn that Phébé loves Pollux, but fears his love of glory is such that she cannot obtain his love in return. Stage action halts again in scene three, this time for Télaïre's famous monologue "Tristes apprêts," after which the fourth scene opens with news of Pollux's victory, leading to a celebratory divertissement. In the final scene Pollux enters triumphantly to proclaim his victory. Caught up in the glory of the moment, he announces his love for Télaïre. She brings the celebration to a halt by demanding that he put love aside and petition his father, Jupiter, for Castor's return. At this point, the opera's principal theme emerges. Pollux must measure the depth of his loyalty to his brother—his sense of *amitié*—against his love of *gloire*—the temptation to marry Télaïre and rule in his brother's place. In the course of the opera he undergoes a series of tests in which other characters attempt to seduce, cajole, or bully him into abandoning his quest and choosing the immediate rewards of *gloire* over the claims of *amitié*. These tests become the focal points for the drama, creating isolated and intense recitative scenes surrounded by the trappings of divertissement: choruses, songs, set-pieces, instrumental music, and dances.

A more conventional lyric tragedy would have been disposed toward the satisfactory reunion of the lovers, rather than toward Pollux's moral victory. The 1737 *Castor* instead emphasizes his dilemma and relies on static tableaux to establish moods. As Girdlestone points out in his study of the genre, it stands alone in placing fraternal devotion above more popular passions such as jealousy and revenge,[36] and if contemporary commentaries are any indication, audiences shared that judgment. The review in the *Mercure de France* identified the issue of the drama as Pollux's dilemma but regarded him as caught in a simple conflict between fraternal devotion and jealousy: "[In the fifth act] Pollux sees his brother with Télaïre without being jealous of him; he has triumphed over his love to deliver himself completely to the bond that unites him with Castor."[37] The reviewer failed to identify Pollux's relationship with Castor as the more important theme. A passage from *Le Pour et contre* was even more emphatic, treating the character Phébé as superfluous to the story:

> In the style of opera, two lovers are needed for two heroes: the difficulty is therefore only in justifying the love of Phébé by some supposition and rendering her at least as necessary to the denouement as Télaïre, who is not [all that necessary] herself. I would have made Phébé into the daughter of Pluto; I would have supposed the two princesses linked to the two brothers by some arrangement [made by] their parents. . . . Pollux, in love with Télaïre from the beginning, would be the victim of politics and loyalty until the death of his brother, which would have freed him to make his true sentiments known. In appearing unfaithful, he would have made it known that he was not inconstant. Phébé, far from living in such good mutual understanding with Télaïre, would have treated her openly as a beloved rival.[38]

Open jealousy, fear of infidelity, infelicitous betrothals: these suggested improvements turn the work away from its grand themes toward the familiar terrain of the tragédie en musique by introducing characters with whom audience members could identify. They are just the clichés that the poet Bernard had avoided. Phébé and Télaïre could in the 1737 *Castor* be deemed superfluous only because as characters they failed to supply the anticipated amorous intrigues.

The 1754 revival of *Castor et Pollux* might as well have taken its cues from the review in *Le Pour et contre,* for it replaced the earlier version with a conventional lyric tragedy: the theme was now the separation and eventual reunion of the lovers Castor and Télaïre, and the newly written first act provided a traditional exposition, outlining their relationship and the cause of their separation in a series of recitative scenes. The act opens with a scene in which Phébé and her confidante Cléone discuss the approaching wedding of Pollux and Télaïre. Phébé loves Pollux's brother Castor and expresses anger that Castor has abandoned her because he loves her sister, Télaïre. Fearing that Pollux will give up Télaïre out of regard for his brother, Phébé explains that she has used her magic powers to incite Lincée to attack Sparta and kidnap Télaïre. The second scene consists of a monologue for Télaïre; she expresses regret over her impending marriage to Pollux because she does not love him. (From this point on in the act, the level of activity onstage increases scene by scene.) Castor enters for scene three. Télaïre tells him that in light of their feelings for each other it is inappropriate for him to visit her alone; he replies that Pollux knows of his feelings and has given him permission. He informs her that he is leaving Sparta. Pollux enters at the beginning of scene four, asking Castor to stay and telling the lovers that he has overheard their conversation. He will let them marry. The new arrangements are announced in scene five, and a celebratory divertissement ensues. The divertissement is interrupted at the beginning of scene six by the entrance of a Spartan announcing that Lincée is attacking the city, and Castor leaves to join in Sparta's defense. The Spartan observes that Phébé appears to be guiding Lincée's actions. Battle music follows, a voice cries out that Castor has fallen, and a chorus calls upon Pollux to avenge his brother. The remainder of the opera now deals with the obstacles Pollux must overcome to ensure his brother's safe return to Télaïre: he must kill Lincée in battle, he must induce his father Jupiter not to oppose his journey to the underworld, and he must persuade Castor to accept the gift of immortality while he remains behind in Pluto's realm. His own dilemmas have dissipated so that he can reunite the separated lovers, and his behavior now conforms to the traditional values of the tragédie en musique.

Thus, about the time of the *Samson* project and the first version of *Castor et Pollux*, Rameau became directly involved in a departure from the dramaturgical conventions of the tragédie en musique. He had inspired Voltaire with *Hippolyte et Aricie*, and at the very least he played a pivotal role in shifting Voltaire's values from *Samson* onto *Castor*. The public, initially uninformed as to the identity of the *Castor* poet, included in its speculations about his identity not only Voltaire himself but most of his and Rameau's mutual acquaintances: La Pouplinière, Thieriot, Jean-Jacques Le Franc de Pompignan, and the real author, Bernard. It is easy to imagine a group of individuals privately putting Voltaire's principles into practice when he himself had declined to do so, and such a plan was discussed and even proposed to Voltaire.[39] But whatever the circumstances of its creation, this new dramaturgy anticipated the experiments of the 1749 *Zoroastre* by as much as sixteen years.

I am interested here not so much in the historical precedence of the earliest dramaturgical experiments involving Rameau as in tracking the curious evolution of his relationship with collaborators and public. The 1730s represent a truly daring period in his operatic career in which he reflected on, inspired, participated in, and helped develop a shift in the ontological status of the tragédie en musique. He was party to the creation not simply of a new ordering of the tragedy's formal features but of a radically different connection between work and audience based on high drama and musical characterization. Yet this connection proved refractory. Composer and poet may have hoped audience members would view the work as edifying, but the public was more inclined to see it as entertaining and, in some cases, fatuous. What Rameau had not anticipated was the public's attachment to familiar generic values and its inability to make the leap that *Castor* required of it. What they heard in performance was not an improved tragedy assisted by striking music, any more than what they heard in Rameau's music was the voice of nature; rather, they heard a story overwhelmed by music, with artifices that were the work of an individual who placed himself above nature. Before *Castor,* Rameau had been a problematic but interesting composer. After it he became the composer single-handedly responsible for all the problems facing the lyric tragedy. In this respect, it is not coincidental that *Castor* initiated the most intense phase of anti-Rameau rhetoric. He may have wished audiences to treat his transformation of genre as a new way of attending to performances, but the historical outcome was instead a volatile new critical language.

In this setting, Rameau's next tragedy inevitably assumed an important role: the 1739 *Dardanus* was the opportunity either to invest again in the dramaturgical principles that had informed *Samson* and *Castor* or to abandon them in favor of something more recognizable as lyric tragedy. It should come as no surprise that the specter of *Samson* haunted this work as well, or that Voltaire was involved in its creation. The poet Charles-Antoine Le Clerc de La Bruère sent the older writer an early version of his livret, and Voltaire responded with criticism.[40] The resulting livret moved awkwardly between high drama and frivolity, combining love with serious political intrigue. The central romantic issue was the love of the Phrygian princess Iphise for Dardanus, the sworn enemy of her people. If the opera did not openly cultivate the grand themes of *Castor, Samson,* or the second act of *Hippolyte,* it also did not give itself over wholly to the erotic subtext of its prologue (see chapter 3).

Notably, the first act of *Dardanus* stresses Iphise's moral crisis. The poetry of her monologue in act one, scene one, "Cesse, cruel Amour, de regner sur mon ame," differs little in content from Aricie's opening monologue, but the following scenes draw attention to Iphise's growing separation from her family and country. When in scene three she worries over Dardanus's safety, her father, the Phrygian king Teucer, and her suitor, Antenor, bring home the brutal realities of her political situation:

> Manes plaintifs, tristes Victimes,
> Nous jurons d'immoler votre fatal Vainqueur.
> Dieux, qui nous écoutez, qui punissez les crimes;
> C'est vous, qu'atteste ici nôtre juste fureur.

[Plaintive spirits, sad victims, we promise to slay your fatal vanquisher. Gods, who hear us, who punish crimes, it is you who witness here our righteous furor (*D livret 1739*, 4).]

Only in the second act do the lovers actually meet and engage in the kind of amorous chitchat found in act one, scene two, of *Hippolyte*. Love has not been abandoned but displaced. (In a characteristic critical response, Desfontaines regarded act two as the best part of the livret.)[41] The beginning of *Dardanus*, at least, encourages us to treat the work seriously. In addition, the *deus ex machina* in act five forces us to reevaluate the intentions behind the seemingly frivolous dispute that occurred in the prologue between Amour and Jalousie. In act five, scene two, Teucer is unwilling to accept Dardanus's claims on his daughter until Vénus descends to the stage in the final scene and admonishes him to accept his situation:

> Teucer, bannissez pour jamais
> La vengeance et la haine:
> Pour arrêter ses traits,
> Du haut des cieux Venus amene
> Et l'Hymen & la Paix.

[Teucer, banish forever vengeance and hatred: to halt their outbursts, from on high Vénus brings Hymen and Peace (*D livret 1739*, 39).]

Teucer gives in, in spite of himself. Here at the end of the opera we find the reason for Rameau's surprisingly dramatic setting of Vénus's "Troubles cruels, soupçons injurieux" in the 1739 prologue, the scene in which Vénus ordered the forces of Jalousie to adopt more delicate attitudes (see example 3.7a). Though the prologue had hardly warranted Rameau's elaborate setting, "Troubles cruels" set up parallels with act five, scene two. At the end of the opera Vénus once again intervenes, and in setting things right, she implies that Teucer's hatred is ignobly born of his jealousy for Dardanus.

Criticism of La Bruère's 1739 livret did not stress the work's high-minded theme but its overdependence on spectacular devices like Vénus's entrance, especially in the final three acts. Émile Dacier reported on examples from anonymous *nouvelles à la main* of the day (used to circumvent censorship) that attacked the opera's "extravagant situations" and "contradictions" and reduced the fourth-act *sommeil* to a child's lullaby. The marquis d'Argenson, less interested in *bons mots,* was more direct in his criticism. He began with some free association on the value of the work—"qualities and defaults of our moderns, people of intellect and little judgment; pleasant details, silliness in the whole, some charming verses"—and then went right to the point: "[t]he subject is a potpourri of supernatural [*merveilleux*] incidents that do not go together, the sort where all interest is banished."[42] Modern scholars have agreed, including Girdlestone who called the livret "a fairy story with Greek names."[43] The story moves with little compunction from a misguided celebration of Iphise's betrothal to Antenor to the announcement that a monster ravages the countryside, from Dardanus's *sommeil* scene to a battle with the monster and on to a final celebration inspired by Vénus. Whatever clever plot twists La Bruère may have introduced, he relied heavily on *les merveilleux* to tell his story; as a result, the final acts were little more than a series of divertissements. The *nouvelles à la main* reported that members of the orchestra were so busy that they hardly had time to sneeze, and they dubbed the work "the opera of Maundy Thursday" because it ostensibly possessed only one dramatic scene.[44] Within two weeks of its premiere, poet and composer were already promising the public revisions of the offending acts, though in the end these would not be unveiled until the 1744 revival.[45] Thus, to some extent the first *Dardanus* followed the pattern of the 1737 *Castor,* adumbrating serious issues while expanding the role of divertissement to contain the composer's musical ideas. Yet whatever the good intentions of poet and composer, for the public *Dardanus* inevitably reflected the more common assumption that Rameau's operas were about music at the expense of poetry and drama.

The 1744 revival of *Dardanus* was a comprehensive project, its final three acts almost completely new in the revision (the title page of the livret proclaimed it a "nouvelle édition"). La Bruère had purged the work of both *sommeil* and monster and made Vénus's appearance in act five nothing more than a cause for celebration. The real change, however, came in the staging. Where the 1739 work had careened from musical event to musical event, the 1744 version emphasized discourse. The author added five full pages of dialogue, more including the rewritten scenes, and in this way reinstated the dramatic rather than musical content as the primary focus. In act three of the revision Iphise moves into the background to make room for Teucer's and Antenor's confidant, Arcas; in act four the wizard Isménor (who had previously vanished after the second act), Iphise, and the wounded Antenor in turn each visit Dardanus's prison cell to converse with him; and in act five Teucer and Dardanus work through their differences without divine assistance. A 1739 wag may have been quite serious when he observed of the opera's revisions that "the more it is shortened, the more it grows."[46] In a gesture reminiscent of the 1736 print of *Les Indes galantes*, this complicated reassemblage of parts was dealt with by calling the printed score of 1744 a "nouvelle tragédie mise en musique par M. Rameau," and one could well argue that this means more than "newly composed." The 1744 was different in kind from the 1739 work.

The 1749 *Zoroastre* is less a case of Rameau's coming into his own than his last-ditch effort to convince audiences that music could add narrative content to serious drama. Its grand themes, lavish staging, and extended passages of music hold a hint of desperation. The work followed a now-familiar pattern in which the first versions of Rameau's lyric tragedies were outfitted not only with elaborate musical trappings but also with complex and serious dramaturgy, only to have those novelties removed in subsequent productions. Though we now may well regard these changes as improvements, in Rameau's day they had constituted neither improvements nor adjustments: each revival sounded over again the death of beliefs Rameau evidently cherished, the idea that the tragédie en musique could transform itself, the notion that music could bear meaning, the hope that a dying genre could be saved.

But what of the composer's role implicit throughout these experiments? He was the connecting figure, the constant in this narrative of hesitations and reassembled parts, and his audiences openly identified him with a tragedy in which music, dance, and diversion reduced plots to ephemera. Yet we must question where he actually stood, the precarious position from which he operated Archimedes's lever to move the operatic world. Was he coincidentally the vehicle for Pellegrin's aspirations, Voltaire's agenda, and Cahusac's theorizing or did he play a larger part in the reformation of this ontology?

It seems unlikely that the single-minded musician of the 1720s thought much about such matters. To be sure, he was already imagining theoretical connections between music and text when he asked La Motte for a livret in 1727, but the poet would have been an unlikely candidate for opera reform, his literary heyday having ended several decades earlier. Further, if the sprawling dramaturgy of *Hippolyte* is at times suggestive of reforms later attempted, as in its second act, this hardly constitutes a comprehensive plan of reform. By all accounts Pellegrin scarcely knew what he was getting into when he agreed to work with Rameau. A well-known story has it that he required the inexperienced composer to provide a promissory note of 500 livres against the work's possible failure (which he tore up upon first hearing it).[47] Nevertheless, Pellegrin's efforts at seriousness in *Jephté* and *Hippolyte* may have been influential. They provided Rameau with a taste for high-minded story-telling even as they addressed the mounting audience concerns of the 1730s: the perceived frivolity of tragic livrets and apparent decline of the tragédie en musique as a genre. Pellegrin introduced the composer to his audience at a time when both composer and audience were eager for change.

For Rameau, the shifts occurring in his career after the *Hippolyte* premiere were great indeed. They included more than a secure living situation and increased popularity; the introductions to thinkers and literary lions that followed must have seemed a validation of his most cherished theoretical notions. To have encountered Voltaire when the poet's own thinking on tragic staging was undergoing revision was not only timely for Rameau's next project, *Samson,* but of fundamental importance to the formation of his remaining tragedies in the 1730s. Although there is no direct evidence that Voltaire influenced the writing of *Castor et Pollux,* the poet Bernard was an admired friend of Voltaire's, and one who appeared throughout Voltaire's correspondence during the 1730s. The poet for *Dardanus,* La Bruère, was another writer who had sought out Voltaire's opinion of his livret. At the very least, Voltaire's acquaintances knew of Rameau's next two tragic projects after *Samson,* and Rameau, as a marginal figure within that charmed circle, may have felt some obligation or inspiration to maintain Voltaire's dramaturgy in his next projects. The notion of serious stories, simply told and complemented by extravagant musical divertissements, informed the first versions of his remaining tragedies.

Some hint of Rameau's own involvement in these dramaturgical considerations may be evident also in the composer's unusual choices for poets in the years following the *Samson* project. Though he could have picked from among writers with at least some of Voltaire's standing and Pellegrin's success record, he instead selected minor and, in most cases, inexperienced writers. Contemporaries were fascinated by these choices, and opinions regarding the composer's decisions circulated through the rumor mills of Paris. Some believed the composer, motivated by greed, sought out inexpensive poets, a view that may have extended back to *Samson.* Rameau had requested of Voltaire the poet's portion of the profits for that project, and Voltaire had responded with characteristic elegance: "I would like to be able to abandon to you the entire payment for this opera, and I would believe you still rather poorly paid, but having promised the half owed me to a man of letters who is in need, I beg you to divide it with him."[48] Rameau's request was not necessarily out of line—Voltaire regularly shared his proceeds with less fortunate friends—but it may have indicated temerity, since he was broaching the topic with a famous author in a partnership scarcely a month old. A pattern quickly emerged in Rameau criticism. According to this line of reasoning, the composer not only chose bad poets, but did so for the worst possible reasons, in order to reap the lion's share of the profits. Simon-Henri Dubuisson, for example, made this assumption in his remarks on the opéra-ballet *Les Fêtes d'Hébé* (1739): "Although

Monsieurs [Antoine-Gautier de] Montdorge, [Alexandre-Jean-Joseph] Le Riche [de La Pouplinière], and Bernard had worked on the poem for *Talents*, they were not able to succeed in making a passable work of it. Do you not pity Rameau? Does he not appear to you unfortunate? What? Always bad words? He merits his fate. Since *Les Indes galantes*, he has explained that he would no longer work except on poems whose authors surrendered their remuneration to him, and you rightly sense that this avarice will reduce him generally to what is most miserable in this genre."[49] Still, this may have been rumor pure and simple. Collé, who complained bitterly about Rameau's livrets from 1748 until the composer's death, worked with the composer on the pastorale héroïque *Daphnis et Eglé* (1753) without mentioning such an arrangement, though he reported on Rameau's request for a pension from the *prévôt des marchands*.[50] Whatever the case may have been, such speculations provided Rameau's critics with an explanation for the least understood aspect of his work, the relationship between music and poetry. It allowed them to assume that poetry did not matter to the composer. Another plausible interpretation, however, is that after first approaching La Motte and then working with Pellegrin and Voltaire, Rameau came to value inexperienced poets not least for their compliance. They would have been more willing than more experienced poets to follow a musician's lead, more willing to try alternatives. They were, in short, ideal collaborators. As Kintzler quite rightly suggests, Rameau found in Cahusac someone who appreciated musical events, understood the potential of nonverbal communication, and went along with his ideas. It is quite likely he found him because he had been searching for him a long time.

In the end, Rameau's collaboration with Cahusac signaled failure rather than success, because the very notion of seeking out a like-minded poet was foreign to Rameau's critics. Such an act assumed that poetry could be matched to music instead of vice versa, and from a critical standpoint, its results would necessarily have formed the obverse of the generic ideal: whereas the tragédie en musique was about poetry, Rameau's tragedies were about music. He sought out poets who would let his music underscore their serious stories, and in underscoring their stories with music, he proved to his detractors that he held music in higher esteem. If theoretical validation was indeed what Rameau looked for in his poets, then it was a poor strategy to follow, for its effect was to intensify the double bind in which he already found himself. Like the idea of using music to interpret poetry, in the end the idea of extending the dramatic importance of divertissements did not and could never value poetry in a recognizable way. By binding his musical innovations to conservative literary tastes, Rameau once more presented his viewers with an impossible figure of genre and thereby ensured the failure of his ideas, if not his career.

Responses to *Dardanus* record this failure. Desfontaines, for example, took the composer to task for not concealing the poetry's faults with his music: "I will not deny that this poem is feeble in some places. The illustrious artist charged with dressing [these places] up in the dazzling finery of his music has not this time been able to hide [them] with the customary magic of his enchanting art. Could it be that by an excess of complaisance and a desire to be too natural he has ceased to be Rameau?"[51] The marquis d'Argenson was of the opinion that *Dardanus* failed because Rameau's priorities were misplaced: "The music is similarly [uninteresting, because] the musician has prided himself in better perfecting his recitative."[52] The message was simple. Music's function in a Rameau tragedy was to overwhelm poetry, not reveal it, and in choosing to represent himself otherwise in *Dardanus* the composer appeared foolish and misguided. Whatever the impetus for the dramaturgical innovations associated with Rameau's tragedies, his supporters and detractors alike continued to see in them plans for furthering music at the expense of poetry.

In the end, the dramaturgical innovations of *Zoroastre* echoed Rameau's earlier successes and failures. The telling work in this story is not the 1749 opera, with its promises of an unmediated poetic and musical meaning, but its 1756 double, where ambivalence and retrenchment inevitably followed. If the early 1750s mark a turning point in Rameau's career, it is a hollow one in which he was to see fewer works performed and never regain the success he had enjoyed in the late 1740s. And if he still presided over the ontological slippages of the tragédie en musique—from Lullian entertainment to serious tragedy and on to musical diversion—he was ultimately guiding it into oblivion. From this point on, he failed to have any new tragedies staged; his final effort, *Les Boréades* remained untried by audiences and untested by criticism. In effect, he himself had replaced his works as the object of criticism.

CHAPTER 5

In the Mirror

EVEN NOW the temptation is strong to slip into narrative in which Rameau becomes a kind of twentieth-century success story: the ambitious composer who refuses to let *Les Indes galantes* languish in an unflattering and inaccurate form, who sets out to reinvent the tragédie en musique in *Hippolyte et Aricie,* who refines works perhaps as much as seventeen years after conceiving them, who pursues a conservative and old-fashioned ideological agenda in the name of reform. Rameau did all these things, and he did them in a manner familiar to us from narratives of later composers. He exerted his will over an *oeuvre*; he defined his style in a self-conscious manner. If we wanted to pursue this view of Rameau, we could find substantial support for it also in the writings of his contemporaries, who so often remind us of the necessity of familiarizing oneself with Rameau's music before fully appreciating it. Much as in modern analytical formulations, the content of the work is something to be uncovered or unveiled through an intimate knowledge, a familiarity that goes beyond the obvious detail: Rameau is a great composer, but it takes time to discover his greatness. We also find heroic depictions of Rameau by his successors as they looked back on his career. For example, Jean-Benjamin de Laborde, writing in 1780, portrayed him as the intrepid artist who persevered in the face of adversity: "Jealousy kindled hatred, resulting in discord to overwhelm Rameau. But the man of genius scorned the envious and responded to them only with new masterpieces, which finally forced them into silence. The revival of *Castor et Pollux* won every vote. There has never been a success to compare to it, because it met with no contradiction. More than one hundred performances in a row could not diminish the pleasure all Paris experienced in hearing this beautiful opera, which spoke simultaneously to the soul, the heart, the intellect, the eyes, the ears, and the imagination."[1]

Yet Laborde's description threatens to overwhelm us, leaving not a coherent view of the composer but rather an incoherent and chimerical list of his music's effects on the beholder. Understanding here treads perilously near its opposite. Likewise, the victory Laborde ascribes to the composer seems fainthearted at best. The *Castor* revival may have been an irrefutable success, but Rameau had little new to look forward to: stagings of a handful of minor works, usually at court; more revivals of *Hippolyte, Castor, Dardanus,* and *Zoroastre*; and the possible staging of his final tragedy, *Les Boréades.* At the very peak of his reputation, that portion of his output being performed actually waned. And even if he had continued to dominate the stage as he had in the late 1740s, one must ask at what price. As we have seen, he succeeded in the revivals of the 1750s only by effacing some of his most sophisticated ideas.

Yet the wish for descriptive analogies, like our fear of monsters, is powerful, and we are far from exhausting the strategies that might pull Rameau and his music together into the figure of a historical author. There is possibly something of Harold Bloom's "revisionary ratio" in Rameau's behavior toward his past and the past of French opera. From *Hippolyte et Aricie* (1733) through *Zoroastre* (1749), we might say, the composer revisited the primal scene of his own instruction in the composition of opera, the Lullian model that had suffused operatic discourse since the late seventeenth century. And in true Bloomian fashion Rameau did so not through servile imitation but through a complex, refractory interpretation of Lully. Rameau simultaneously preserved his strong precursor by promoting a conservative view of the semiotic relationship between text and music and effaced him by elaborating this relationship as a theoretical and practical edifice in which the familiar composer Lully was no longer recognizable.[2] Further, in becoming a strong composer in his own right, beginning with the *Dardanus* revival of 1744, Rameau also performed the ultimate Bloomian rite of liquidating the precursor altogether. His final revisions bear not only little musical resemblance to Lully's tragédie en musique but also little resemblance in terms of formal design, dramaturgy, or pacing.[3]

But though I believe my description does capture important tensions at work in Rameau's tragedies, I would modify its telos slightly. Bloom's theoretical model is more suitable for the nineteenth-century English poets it was designed to trace than for the meandering, less well-defined goals of an eighteenth-century musician, especially one who wanted also to be a theorist. While Rameau's fumbling, ambivalent relationship with the past captures something of Bloom's primal scene of instruction, Rameau could no more aspire to a coherent operatic style than he could to a coherent, lasting theory of music. He was striving toward an end he could not fully imagine: neither a style nor a theory per se—these were, after all, later inventions—but rather a congruence between his ideas about music and his actual practice. He desired empirical validation of his ideas. His relationship with Lully, though certainly grounded in a knowledge of the earlier composer's works, was largely based on the earlier composer's reputation. Lully was a vantage point from which to view his own accomplishments.

A figure loomed large between Rameau and Lully, one that interfered with whatever intergenerational conflicts the later composer underwent and prevented the likes of Bloom's primal scene from occurring to full effect. That figure was the operagoing public. To succeed, Rameau had to engage not only the past of French opera but something more complex as well, a simulacrum of past ideas as gleaned from the criticism and epigrams of his own historical present. The French public took its critical role seriously. There is in its criticism not simply a wealth of opinion but an ownership of it and a pride in its possession. In Rameau's case, the public took its cues from the composer's unwillingness to trade fully in familiar operatic values, and it answered him with an ambivalence of its own: wild success, in terms of the number of performances, coupled with pervasive critical disfavor.

An apt model for the formation of Rameau as a historical subject in the end, rather than the heroic struggles of Bloom's poets, might be Jacques Lacan's model for the formation of children's personalities. For Lacan, the crucial moment in a child's development comes when the child attempts to pull together its own monstrous *corps morcelé*—an agglomeration of needs, drives, functions, and uncontrollable body parts—into a coherent human entity like those it sees around it. To do so, the child seeks to locate this stability in an imaginary, mirror-like process of reflection, grasping its sense of self by envisioning how others see it.[4] For Rameau, the public was that mirror, its critical vicissitudes both the key and the challenge to his task of creating a coherent compositional persona. We might say he looked outward from the stage of the Opéra into the audience, seeking to find there validation for his ideas. Thus, the persistent conflation of the composer and his work in the minds of the public forms an important if accidental insight into Rameau. He would have liked to be another Lully and to have dominated theoretical and practical musical discourses, and undoubtedly he believed in some sort of self-destiny: perhaps not in a modern sense, but in a remarkably personal sense, he believed in the rightness and timeliness of his ideas. If he could only get the formula right, so his thinking seems to have gone, his works would intercede on his behalf and speak for him.

Yet what Rameau perceived in looking out from this metaphorical stage never worked entirely because his attempts at composing his persona were breached by the public's inability to follow his theoretical arguments and compositional agendas. There was at the core of Rameau's work a hollowness or void, filled to the point of bursting with ideas and stunning effects but ultimately incomprehensible to the people it was designed to impress. In composing an elegy for his teacher Chabanon had understood this and dismissed those audience members who still thrilled to word painting. At the time of Rameau's death, alas, the *Mercure* still fell into just this category. In its obituary, it felt no compunction in withdrawing with one hand what it had offered with the other:

> In the use [Rameau] has made [of music], one can scarcely contest the force and beauty of harmony, the superior genius in several symphonies, in choruses, in the pieces of measured song. Nearly all of the *airs de danse* of this musician are so striking and distinguished that in Italy and all countries where only Ital-

ian opera is known, it is principally the airs of this French musician that are employed for ballets. But for an exquisite taste in the just and sublime expression of the words, for an art as wise as ingenious in nearly all choruses and in a great number of symphonies, seemingly employing little means under an august veil of simplicity, who could refuse the immortal Lully the justice that the great Rameau rendered him verbally whenever the occasion presented itself?[5]

Indeed, the commentator was willing to regard Rameau's success as something of a historical fluke: "Since the deviations of a new fashion have rendered [Rameau's] music simpler to our ears, and consequently more analogous to the original genre of our opera, it seems to have become more precious to the public. It is therefore incontestable that it is not at all by a taste for sentiment, but by a passing caprice that this fashion shares our attention and even (let us say it, blushing) obtains a kind of preference."[6] However entertaining it might have been, Rameau's work represented the failure of the generic contract between composer and public, the failure of the circuit through which artist and audience communicated. What the public could not recognize, it could not understand. In Rameau and his work, we encounter the seams and sutures of the composer's imaginary construction, written and overwritten with the symbolic values of images, projects, doubts, and ideas. Some originated with the composer, some with his audience.

This is why the monsters in Rameau's art are so important. They are the figure of Rameau himself as perceived by his audiences, and they signal as well the failure of his meaning, the failure of communication. Rameau's audiences experienced his operas as different in kind from his predecessors', first of all, because they heard them as pieces of music, but also because they heard them as pieces in the other sense of the word, as poorly assembled fragments of opera itself. The most telling phrase in Jean-Baptiste Rousseau's poem about Rameau, surely the most-cited example of Lulliste writing, is the one referring to Rameau's "heterogeneous art":

> Distillateurs d'accords baroques
> Dont tant d'idiots sont férus,
> Chez les Thraces et les Uscoques
> Portez vos opéras bourrus.
> Malgré votre art hétérogène,
> Lulli de la lyrique scène
> Est toujours l'unique soutien;
> Fuyez, laissez-lui son partage
> Et n'écorchez pas davantage
> Les oreilles des gens de bien.

[Venter of grotesque harmonies, with which so many imbeciles are smitten, take your surly operas among savage tribes. In spite of your heterogeneous art, Lully is always the sole support of the lyrical scene. Flee! Leave him his part, scorch no more the ears of good people.][7]

Like the monster that defeated Hippolyte or the one that Dardanus conquered, Rameau and his works disrupted the social order and signaled a descent into savagery. In its social implications, Rousseau's epigram was not so distant from Voltaire's description of the sphinx in *Oedipe*:

> Né parmi des rochers, au pied du Cithéron,
> Ce monstre à voix humaine, aigle, femme, et lion,
> De la nature entière exécrable assemblage,
> Unissait contre nous l'artifice à la rage.

[Born among the rocks at the base of Cythera, this monster—in voice human, an eagle, woman, and lion, the execrable assemblage of all of nature—united artifice and rage against us (*OCV*, 2:62).]

With his feckless and wildly successful upending of the balance between music and poetry, Rameau posed more of a threat than he seems at first to have realized. Logically, his responses to these encounters with the public—his constant recrafting of theories, works, and ontologies—could do no more than exacerbate the situation.

The silence surrounding Rameau's final opera *Les Boréades* is therefore an engaging one. It is a silence created not by the absence of meaning but rather by a surfeit. As was the case with the 1736 print of *Les Indes galantes,* it is a silence made noisy by the echoes of the competing values, possible interpretations, and potential explanations that informed Rameau's every decision as an opera composer. Unperformed, scarcely even rehearsed at the time of the composer's death, *Les Boréades* never faced the critical tests of the French operagoing public. Indeed, if Sylvie Bouissou is correct in her assertion that the work was rehearsed only twice in 1763 for possible performance at Choisy, *Les Boréades* might never have faced public scrutiny at all.[8] Instead, it would have remained sealed off from the public by royal decree, a private entertainment known about Paris only by word of mouth. True scrutiny of the work would have required a staging open to criticism, a staging in Paris at the Académie royale de musique, and by the early 1750s Rameau was no longer on very good terms with that institution. Had *Les Boréades* been performed in Paris, one wonders whether critics would have even bothered to invoke the tragédie en musique as a model. The time when tragedies enjoyed successful premieres was long past, taste no longer had much to do with the original texts of Lully and Quinault, and even the original versions of Rameau's operas were distant memories. The notion of experiencing *Les Boréades* as part of the tradition that had defined Rameau's early career would have seemed quaint, almost naive. And without performances of *Les Boréades* there could be no revivals or revisions. There would have been no chance for Rameau to weigh his theoretical ideals against public perceptions, no opportunity to gainsay his initial compositional efforts with second thoughts.

By virtue of being sealed off in this manner from Rameau's other works, *Les Boréades* opens up the possibility of understanding the composer's momentous decisions from the mid-1740s through the early 1750s. Untouched by public scrutiny, performers' whims, or the composer's own concessions, it appears to offer us the zero degree of Rameau's music, a pure and unblemished account of his compositional values. For this reason, the choices he made should be informative. For example, he might have returned to the dramaturgical plan derived from Voltaire. Although by this time he had every indication that audiences would not receive it well, he had staked the entirety of his career on returning to this mise-en-scène for every premiere after *Hippolyte et Aricie,* only to avoid it in subsequent revivals. He faced similar decisions in setting the poetry of *Les Boréades*. He could have returned one last time to his representational strategies of the 1730s, moved on to the more equivocal settings of the mid-1740s revivals, or engaged the simpler musical paradigm first broached in the revivals of *Castor* and *Zoroastre. Les Boréades* was either the place for a full transformation of Rameau's earlier values into something that assuaged audience concerns or the opportunity to repeat his own ideas once more in the hope of finally making his case before the public.

Future assessments of *Les Boréades* will depend to a large extent on Bouissou's summary evaluation in her book on this work. There she rejects Cuthbert Girdlestone's assessment that "[a] Rameau opera . . . tends to be a collection of pieces of beautiful and often great music, more or less loosely linked together,"[9] and instead makes the case for a heroic narrative of the conclusion of Rameau's career. Seizing on Catherine Kintzler's characterization of the 1749 version of *Zoroastre* as the definitive achievement in Rameau's development and on the likelihood that Cahusac provided the livret for *Les Boréades,* Bouissou argues that *Les Boréades* is the culmination of the composer's musical ideas, the point where he achieves the fullness of musical representation he had sought since 1733. Invoking older views of the operas of Berg, Wagner, Verdi, and Mozart, she argues that Rameau's final lyric tragedy is guided by a large-scale, encompassing form, a carefully crafted blend of musical and dramatic effects designed to present the composer's ideas in the best possible light. Accordingly, she divides this story of the wooing of Alphise into three musical and dramatic phases. She characterizes the first three acts, largely in A major, as dominated by Alphise's suitors—the north wind Borée's noisy sons, Calisis and Borilée—and especially by the use of counterpoint in their accompaniments and the prominent melismatic singing and perfect fourths in their vocal parts. The second phase centers around Borée's anger when he learns that Alphise has rejected his sons. Extending from the third act into the fourth, the tonal center of this phase shifts to C major, and stormy repeated notes and a characteristic dotted rhythm emerge as important musical figures. In the final phase, the characters experience the consequences of Borée's anger. This crucial stage, in which the story's issues are resolved, maintains the rapid-fire accompanimental figures of the second phase but colors them through a modal shift from C major to C minor. The whole makes for a gradual increase in dramatic tension peaking somewhere in the fourth act.[10]

Bouissou's observations seem reasonable enough applied to a composer as musically calculating as Rameau was, but one wonders at her almost old-fashioned need to couch them in terms of unity and coherence. At the time she was writing her book, Carolyn Abbate, Roger Parker, and James Webster were all lodging important arguments against unity as a guiding principle in eighteenth-century opera.[11] Further, by leveling her own argument for unity against Girdlestone's, Bouissou suggests something of an unspoken primal scene for *Les Boréades*. She ignores Masson's rather more vehement assessment of this work in particular: "From what one can judge by the manuscripts, this work is extremely uneven. The livret, without a doubt by Cahusac, appears to be rather inferior to those of Rameau's other lyric tragedies. The music presents some ill-matched curiosities: it collects, in a sometimes laborious manner, pieces very different in style and of a no doubt diverse provenance."[12] One person's masterpiece is another's monster. Bouissou's omission of Masson is glaring: it is the difference between yet another heroic narrative of the composer's life and a view informed by the aging composer's growing uncertainty over how to convince audiences. She ignores the confusion that had already begun to mark Rameau's compositional decisions by the mid-1740s. By the late 1750s and early 1760s, Rameau's earliest works were being stripped of his most cherished scenes as they entered their third and fourth revivals. By the 1760s, the composer himself appeared to his contemporaries to have given up: "In 1763, after the first performance of *Castor* at Fontainebleau, . . . [Rameau] told [someone the following] regarding novelties that people wished he would add to his opera *Castor et Pollux*: 'My friend, I have more taste than previously, but I no longer have any genius at all.'"[13] *Les Boréades* is the composer's final word on the tragédie en musique. At some point in the 1750s Rameau brought at least two decades of experience to its composition, and it is likely, whatever genius it may or may not possess, that it continues to reflect his need to assemble and reassemble the *disjecta membra* of his operatic ontology.

Turning to the matter of dramaturgy, we find the composer once again choosing repetition over development. The individual acts of *Les Boréades* replicate Voltaire's inversion of the balance between drama and divertisse-ment, distinguishing between plot and musical events and emphasizing musical events to a greater extent than plot. Nevertheless, the effect in *Les Boréades* is quite different from that of Rameau's earlier tragedies because the story is one of the simplest yet attempted in a tragédie en musique.

In conformity with Voltaire's plan, the dramatic scenes of *Les Boréades* amount to isolated passages of narrative set within a continuous web of monologues, choruses, ariettes, and dance music.[14] Act one, scenes one through three, present the longest continuous series of dialogues in the opera. Alphise, queen of Bactria, confides to Semire that though she is re-quired to marry a descendent of Borée, she loves neither Borilée nor Ca-lisis but instead the mysterious Abaris, rumored to be of royal descent. Bo-rilée and Calisis enter and pressure her to decide between them. The divertissement follows. In act two, scenes two and three are similarly de-voted to drama. Adamas, high priest of Apollo, enters reflecting on Abaris's circumstances. Until Abaris proves worthy of his lineage, he is to remain unaware that he is the son of Apollo and a nymph descended from the line of Borée. Already in this scene the orchestra intrudes, in the ariette-like "Lorsque la lumière féconde" and the accompanied air "Ce n'est qu'en volant à la gloire," and hearing the former tempts one to believe the di-vertissement has begun. Abaris informs Adamas of his feelings. Alphise then enters in scene two, and the two characters confess their mutual love in dialogue recitative. During the following divertissement, players enact the story of Borée's abduction of the nymph Orithée. While the second-act encounter between Abaris and Alphise is undoubtedly important, the scene itself proves redundant because the would-be lovers rehearse the same emotions again in act three, scene two. There, after a substantial di-vertissement in which Amour presents Alphise with a magic arrow, scene four brings Alphise's renunciation of her crown: she would rather spend her days with Abaris than rule Bactria. She presents him with Amour's magic arrow, and in the final instrumental piece of act three she is abducted by the outraged Borée.

It is worth pausing at this point to note the expansiveness of this story. The events taking place in the first three acts—the woman admits to lov-ing the man, the man admits to loving the woman, they confess their feel-ings and anger a god—had all transpired within the first act of *Hippolyte et Aricie*. Similarly, by act four of *Castor* (1737 version), Pollux had already encountered his own crisis and was preparing to enter the underworld, and in *Dardanus* (1739 version) the main character had already been impris-oned for loving an enemy. In *Les Boréades*, however, the principal crisis, though long foreseen, has only just emerged. It is no longer a moral dilemma of the kind that drove Pollux or Iphise, but a question of right and wrong conducted in terms familiar from *Zoroastre* (as Kintzler rightly points out).[15] The remainder of the narrative continues in this manner. In act four, scene three, Adamas asks Abaris to protect the Bactrians and to save Alphise. When Abaris in turn asks what chance he, a mere mortal, has against a god, Adamas urges him in an accompanied air to abandon his love of Alphise for the greater good of all. Abaris considers killing himself with Amour's arrow, but Adamas informs him it is just the weapon he needs. In act five, Abaris calls upon Apollo to speed him to Alphise's side so he can rescue her. Given this restrained approach to storytelling, little room is left for the dénouement. It must unfold quickly in act five, scenes two and four, amid the trappings of divertissement in scenes one, three, and five, in a narrative space smaller even than those provided for the preceding acts.

Divertissement thus dominates this story: the temptations of Calisis's troupe of Plaisirs and Graces in act one, the premonitory staging of the abduction of Orithée by Borée in act two, the arrival of Amour and abduction of Alphise in act three, the sorrows of the Bactrians and celebration of Abaris's courage in act four, the depiction of Borée's kingdom and the final celebration in act five. For the audiences that might have seen *Les Boréades,* these spectacles taken together could conceivably have wiped the story away altogether, removing the battle between right and wrong entirely and leaving behind little more than a conventional love story. And in doing so, the divertissements would have reenacted the critical distinction between drama and music that had influenced Rameau's mature tragedies, once more placing him in the double bind that characterized his career. However much he cared for poetry, his conception of its place in the tragedy was guided fundamentally by a musical understanding, and whether his audiences could perceive the subtleties of his music, they correctly saw his emphasis on music as ill-formed and ill-informed by conventional standards.

If in its dramaturgy *Les Boréades* signals the return of Rameau's earlier dramaturgical principles, in its text setting it fulfills the transformation of text-setting procedures that he had begun in the early 1750s. Gone are the relays and recursions of the early tragedies, the *Nouveau système,* and the *Observations.* In their place the composer offers something audiences could have heard and appreciated, the simple musical anchors of the *Castor* and *Zoroastre* revivals. The best way to observe this shift in attitude is to consider a situation from *Les Boréades* in which Rameau used a musical technique similar to one found in *Hippolyte et Aricie* (1733). In spite of the similarities, the semiotic results in *Les Boréades* were rather different, which gives some indication of how fully Rameau's attitude had changed.

In his first lyric tragedy, it will be recalled, Rameau opened the story with the monologue "Temple sacré, séjour tranquille," in which Aricie expressed her anguish at being called to a chaste religious duty when in fact she was deeply in love. As we saw in example 2.1, the composer responded to the dramatic situation with subtle, even obscure references in her ac-

companiment to the lament tetrachord. While Aricie describes the trappings of the cult of Diane and their role in her life, the tetrachord remains
in the background; then, when her true feelings emerge, the tetrachord
also emerges through a change in accompaniment, harmonization, and orchestration. The effect is one of dramatic information having emerged
from the musical background.

Compare this passage with "Charmes trop dangereux, malheureuse tendresse," from act two, scene one, of *Les Boréades,* shown in example 5.1.[16]
Abaris begins this act in a position similar to Aricie's. He must suppress his
love for the queen whom he cannot hope to marry and recommit himself
to the religious duties of his youth:

> Charmes trop dangereux, malheureuse tendresse,
>> Faut-il vous combatre sans cesse,
>> Et vous voir triompher toujours;
> A ce Temple Adamas consacra ma jeunesse,
> Et du Dieu que j'y sers j'implore le secours,
>> Il voit sans pitié ma foiblesse,
> Au pied de ses autels le trouble qui me presse
>> Semble s'accroitre tous les jours.

[Charms too dangerous, unfortunate tenderness, is it necessary to combat you
and see you ever triumph? Adamas consecrated my youth to this temple, and
I beg the god I serve there for aid. He sees my weakness without pity. At the
foot of his altar the trouble that weighs upon me seems to grow each day.][17]

Rameau chose to set Abaris's words—"Charmes trop dangereux"—once
more to a descending tetrachord. As in "Temple sacré," he uses the device
not as a ground bass per se, but rather as a reference to the kinds of pieces
that contained ground basses. It is a gesture designed to color these particular words through an association with the lament. Yet in spite of this similarity with act one, scene one, of *Hippolyte,* "Charmes trop dangereux" reveals
none of the earlier monologue's complexity. There is no attempt to have the
music refer either forward or backward to other musical passages, no attempt
to recreate the dramatic logic of the poetry in musical terms. The music here
is little more than a label, conveying to the audience in direct terms the character's emotional state. Its relationship is with the words alone.

Much the same can be said of the scenes of dialogue in *Les Boréades.* Notably in the first three acts, one encounters harmonically simple recitative;
short, simple airs; and nimble use of orchestral accompaniment. In the
strictest sense, the scenes can be called expressive, but the composer has
again redefined musical expressivity in terms rather different from his earliest experiments. Take for example the scene between Abaris and Alphise
in act three, scene two, shown in example 5.2.[18] This is the scene in which

Example 5.1. "Charmes trop dangereux, malheureuse tendresse," *Les Boréades,* act 2, scene 1, mm. 11–19

they admit to being in love. It begins with Abaris expressing doubt about their ability to carry through with the love they had confided to each other in the preceding act:

> Mes Rivaux ont pour eux leur naissance et la loi,
> Vous allez m'immoler aux droits du rang suprême,
> Vôtre peuple animé par Adamas lui même
> Vient en foule à vos pieds vous demander un Roi.

[My rivals have their birth and the law on their side. You are going to sacrifice me to the rights of supreme rank. Your people, urged on by Adamas himself, come in crowds to your feet to ask of you a king.][19]

A series of short airs follow. Abaris assumes that all is over in "Je vous perds, je le sens à ma douleur mortelle" (I lose you, I feel it in my mortal sadness), Alphise reassures him in "Je ne vis que pour vous, ma tendresse est extrême" (I see only you, my tenderness is extreme), and Abaris responds with delight that "Que d'un objet aimé L'Empire est Enchanteur" (For an object of love the world is an enchantment). (Only the first of these three airs is shown in example 5.2.) Rameau's musical setting is simpler even than Lully's in "Enfin il est en ma puissance." In keeping with the theme of elevated social rank in Abaris's opening speech, the C-minor passage moves immediately from a half cadence (m. 3) to a strong half cadence in G major (m. 5) and on to cadences in G major (mm. 7, 9). One could attempt an interpretation similar to Rameau's interpretation of "Enfin," but without Lully's subtle tonicizations of successive harmonic areas, it is difficult to make the case for a recursive reference here to C minor. Aside from a short circle-of-fifths progression in mm. 16–18—at Abaris's remark, "J'ai vû luire à mes yeux l'aurore la plus belle" (I have seen the most beautiful dawn glisten before my eyes)—C minor is never folded, bent, or prodded in such a way as to make a case for anything more musically sophisticated than an anchor text. As though to ensure such a straightforward interpretation, the key relationships between the following airs are the simplest imaginable. Both Abaris's despair and Alphise's reassurance are cast securely in C minor, with E-flat major as a medial key. In his moment of joy, Abaris shifts modally from C minor to C major. Nor do more expressive gestures contribute much in the way of sophistication. The chromatic alterations at "Le jour plus sombre" (m. 19) represent precisely the kind of progression for which Chabanon exhibited so little patience, painting text rather than emotion. This music does not intepret. It labels.

Les Boréades thus effects something new in Rameau's ontology of the tragédie en musique. It combines features drawn from the first versions of his earlier tragedies—specifically, from Voltaire's dramaturgy—with the simpler text setting of their revivals. If, as Bouissou and Kintzler would

Example 5.2. *Les Boréades,* act 3, scene 2, mm. 1–21

Example 5.2, *continued*

seem to agree, the ultimate purpose of Rameau's pokings and proddings was to create a more dramatic musical event, then by the standards of his time he miscalculated once again. Earlier audiences may have complained over the musical busy-ness of the composer's monologues and dialogues, but at least that busy-ness had attracted their attention for good or ill to the opera's poetry. Here, as he conformed once more to the expectation that his tragedies were about divertissements, the modest story and un-complicated text setting threaten to vanish altogether under the weight of a massive musical architecture located in the divertissements. Inarticulate music had triumphed, and this could be regarded only as a failure. As Grimm had noted in connection with the 1756 revival of *Zoroastre,* Qui-nault's talent had lain in concealing the preposterous underpinnings of the divertissement; Rameau's and Cahusac's lay instead in calling attention to them.

Les Boréades, then, is not so far from the 1736 print of *Les Indes galantes* as one might first think. The *Les Indes* print bore its scars openly. Critical response resulted in a cutting away of its drama and a reshuffling of what remained. *Les Boréades,* too, bore scars, though in a less obvious manner. Like its predecessor, it cut away recitative and turned attention to the ostensibly pure musical event. As with *Les Indes,* the motivation behind this process was an attempt to communicate with an audience, to render to the audience what it expected. However, the composer also sought to render what the audience wanted, which was not always the same as its expectation. For whatever reasons, audiences desired the very entertainments that they criticized in Rameau's works. The composer could communicate with them only by abandoning the literary values they claimed to admire. *Les Boréades* was thus overwritten with three decades of critical commentary, and its pristine, unperformed state does not prevent it from becoming Rameau's ultimate revival. No matter how he chose to act, Rameau and his tragedies could not help but be monstrous.

We can hear the music of *Les Boréades.* Though it was not enshrined among the problematic editions of the *Oeuvres complètes,* there is a recording and a facsimile (as well as a dissertation). The minutia of performance practice may sometimes escape us; we may not care for tone, tuning, or execution in a given version; we may not be able to imagine the work in all its detail, but the music itself is available, and in some sense we can hear it.

It is when we wish to understand what we hear that we run into problems, for surely this is part of the listener's task, to wonder about what he or she hears. We wonder why a seventy-year-old composer took up the mantle of a then defunct genre. We wonder how (or even whether) an audience anticipated his last creation: with curiosity? enthusiasm? trepidation? We wonder why, after the composer's death, the opera remained unperformed, even though it had been rehearsed a year earlier. The strangely anachronistic decision to rehearse a new tragédie en musique fourteen years after the premiere of Rameau's previous tragedy is part of the listener's fare as well, for audiences created texts from their musical experiences. They anticipated, speculated, enjoyed, and reviled what they heard, just as we do. Music—at least, this music—is not about and was never really about the notes, *pace* La Motte. In the composer's time it was about values, behaviors, and beliefs. It was about successes and failures, intrigues and coincidences, pleasing and displeasing. It was—and is—about the people who listened to it, fought over it, thought about it, and took pleasure in it. It was about what is still most difficult to understand, human behavior. When we hear music we enjoy, we want to know or at least to imagine how and why a composer used particular ideas in particular ways.

In this instance, however, I am not thinking of just any music or performance. I'm thinking about a performance of *Les Boréades* I can only hear and an audience I can only watch. I'm thinking of an imaginary performance from the eighteenth century, attended by the inmates of a local insane asylum. The theater is old and dark. Part of a private residence, it has clearly seen better days. It is dark and dingy. Candles gutter in its drafts. I cannot see the stage, the singers, or the dancers. I can hear the music only in heavily edited snippets, and desiring to understand it, I must seize it in whatever manner I can. Taking the only means at my disposal, I peer into the crowd, searching its faces, noting its behaviors, and reading significance into every smile, twitch, and grimace. Of course, I do not understand everything there is to know about the performance or even the audience members. But this audience responds intensely and in a variety of ways—obliviousness, tears, sexual abandon, misbehavior, shouting—and I am set the task of fitting what I know of this performance together with the responses it evokes.

This performance is not one I have invented. It occurred as one of several vignettes forming the 1988 film *Aria,* a series of short episodes in which various directors staged opera excerpts. The *Les Boréades* segment was directed by Robert Altman, and it was, typically, among those most vilified and despised by reviewers. For example, Michael Walsh treated it as a meaningless bit of visualization, writing, "Altman's *Les Boréades* has a promising premise: How would an 18th-century audience composed entirely of the lame, the daft, and the lewd behave at a performance of Rameau? But beyond gathering the extras from his 1986 *Rake's Progress* in Paris and letting them flash their bums at each other, he does nothing with it; even Rameau isn't this boring."[20] Similarly, a less attentive Richard Corliss saw in it an opportunity for visual silliness: "Robert Altman had the inspiration to show a restless 17th-century audience at Rameau's *Les Boréades,* then neglected to develop his night-at-the-opera sketch with any coherence."[21] One wonders whether some of this cool reception was because among the sections of *Aria,* the *Les Boréades* segment was devoted the least to the usual trappings of opera and especially to those of Italian opera: poignant sentiments, struggling sopranos, uninhibited displays of passion, and more or less ordinary lives thrown onto a stage. Certainly, there is nothing unusual for Altman about this staging of *Les Boréades.* As in a number of his films, the beholder is distracted from a central, guiding narrative—in this case the opera performance, heard only as a soundtrack—by a frenzy of detailed activities occurring at the story's margins, here the behaviors of an audience of mad men and women, which in turn threaten to unseat the central narrative and take its place.

As Walsh noted, a number of reviewers complained about Altman's derivation of this vignette from an earlier project. Crowded scenes of madness, chiaroscuro lighting effects, and a general feeling of mayhem were prominent features also in his stagings of Stravinsky's *The Rake's Progress,* first in Ann Arbor, Michigan (1982), and then in Paris and Lille (1986).[22] For the director to recycle them once again was considered by his critics to reveal a sad want of imagination. The problem with this interpretation, of course, is that it ignores the intertextuality of creative acts. Artists have always reused themes, motives, images, and ideas from earlier works. There is a sense in which examples I have borrowed from Rameau's works perform more or less the same function, and there are many more I could have chosen from. The rejection of Altman's *Les Boréades* staging on the grounds that he derived it from his staging of *The Rake's Progress* misses an important point in not seeing it as a commentary on the earlier work. In Altman's production of the Stravinsky work, the mad men and women stood, squatted, and gamboled about the peripheries of the stage, observing firsthand the same events as actual audience members might. Both the virtual audience of mad people and the real audience witnessed the central story as acted and sung by the principal actors. This should have underscored an important difference in the *Aria* segment. In Altman's later staging we see *only* the audience.

What that production of *The Rake's Progress* did not possess was a striking spatial metaphor for the critical process of history. It did not refer to an earlier creation. It did not seek to reinterpret or reconsider an earlier production as the *Aria* segment did. I take this distinction to be significant to a director in a way that it would not be for a critic or an audience member. Much of a director's time is spent imagining what audiences will see. To create an effective film, a director takes control of his audience's visual and auditory experience, much as the principal actors in Altman's *The Rake's Progress* control the narrative space for the virtual, mad audience as well as for actual audience members. Inevitably, however, some of a director's time will be spent in the more historical act of understanding the responses of past audiences. At this point, he or she becomes concerned with comprehending the earlier audiences' pleasures, devotions, quibbles, and rejections. The *Les Boréades* segment in *Aria* might thus be thought of more practically as Altman's critical reflection on past work, in this case *The Rake's Progress*. The actual artwork, *Les Boréades*, disappears from sight, to be replaced by a virtual audience's understanding of a work that is no longer fully present. In this particular case, the director asks the real audience viewing the film to make sense of *Les Boréades* by viewing only the unintelligible reactions of his virtual audience. In much the same way, one can easily imagine the director attempting to make sense of his critics, trying to see and hear what they saw and heard by observing them rather than the films and stagings they commented on. Issues on the periphery of the film experience overtake the central narrative and displace it.

However one may feel personally about Altman's use of *Les Boréades*, I take it to be a powerful allegory for the experiences of Rameau that I have traced. Rameau's career is the career of someone who constantly looked back, someone who, even as he was creating new works, reflected on his past works and tried to sort out their reception. However recalcitrant or ornery Rameau was—and contemporary accounts hardly recorded him as warm or ingratiating—he devoted much time to trying to understand his audiences. He listened to criticism and attempted to weave the opinions into a form compatible with his own theories and ideas. He was, as Thomas Christensen has noted with reference to the theoretical writings, an individual unusually willing to make over himself by making over his ideas.[23] And to accomplish this task, he had little more at his disposal than Altman had: the work, its fragments hovering in the back of his mind, and his senses, cast outward from the stage into the theater, where sat the individuals he could never quite discern and the criticism he could never altogether fathom. Pulling his impressions together, he began the new opera or, more tellingly, began to recompose the old one. His repetitions, revisions, and revivals operated not only on a musical level but also on a largely symbolic or representational one. His music recorded his encounters with the public.

I take Altman's staging of *Les Boréades* as the basis for a second, equally profound allegory, that of music historians and critics trying to uncover past events. We can always hear the music. Perhaps it is fragmentary, perhaps there is not enough of it, perhaps we do not sufficiently understand how to perform it, and perhaps we do not know what it means. But, as Carl Dahlhaus pointed out some years ago, we always begin with the music.[24] What follows, as Dahlhaus also pointed out, is less precise, but sooner or later it involves imagining what it was like to hear that music—to observe that spectacle—through the ears and eyes of another, grasping it through the texts others made of it: documents, treatises, or reviews. In this imaging, we repeat the composer's actions. We compose the music over in our minds. We too look out into the darkened theater, hoping to understand something we cannot see but can only hear. We search for understanding. The composer is a helpful individual, but he is no different from the other members of the audience. Never confiding, never revealing his intentions, Rameau sits in the audience among those who watch, perceive, and respond. He is one more mind, one more authority, one more sign, whose chief value is in drawing together the works that bear his name.

Notes

Preface

1. Carl Dahlhaus, *Foundations of Music History,* trans. J. B. Robinson (Cambridge: Cambridge University Press, 1983), 45.

2. Louis Laloy, *Rameau,* 3d ed. Les Maîtres de la musique. (Paris: Félix Alcan, 1919), 1.

3. Michel Foucault, "What Is an Author?" trans. Josué V. Harari, in *The Foucault Reader,* ed. Paul Rabinow (New York: Pantheon, 1984), 105–8. Cf., Dahlhaus, *Foundations of Music History,* 44–53, the chapter entitled "Does Music History Have a 'Subject'?"

4. Roland Barthes, "The Death of the Author," in *Image Music Text,* trans. Stephen Heath (New York: Hill and Wang, 1977), 143.

5. Alexander Nehamas, "Writer, Text, Work, Author," in *Literature and the Question of Philosophy,* ed. Anthony J. Cascardi (Baltimore: Johns Hopkins University Press, 1987), 277. In making this argument, Nehamas is in effect relying on the relationship between notions of *meaning* and *intention.* Meaning is difficult to grasp apart from an assumed intention to mean something, just as intention is difficult to grasp apart from the assumption that an artwork has meaning. On the problematic relationship between the categories *meaning* and *intention,* see the essays in W. J. T. Mitchell, ed., *Against Theory: Literary Studies and the New Pragmatism* (Chicago: University of Chicago Press, 1985).

6. Laloy, *Rameau,* 3–4.

7. Lionel de La Laurencie, *Rameau* (Paris: Librairie Renouard, 1926).

8. See Cuthbert Girdlestone, Albert Cohen, and Mary Cyr, "Rameau, Jean-Philippe," *The New Grove Dictionary of Music and Musicians,* ed. Stanley Sadie, 6th ed., 20 vols. (New York: Macmillan, 1980), 15:559–73; Graham Sadler and Albert Cohen, "Jean-Philippe Rameau," in *The New Grove French Baroque Masters: Lully, Charpentier, Lalande, Couperin, Rameau* (New York: W. W. Norton, 1986), 207–308; and Sylvie Bouissou, *Jean-Philippe Rameau:* Les Boréades *ou la tragédie oubliée* (Paris: Méridiens Klincksieck, 1992).

9. Paul-Marie Masson, *L'Opéra de Rameau* (Paris: Henri Laurens, 1930), 1.

10. Ibid.

11. See, for example, Guido Adler, "Style-Criticism," trans. Oliver Strunk, *The Musical Quarterly* 20 (1934): 172–76, and, more generally, idem, *Der Stil in der Musik* (Leipzig: Breitkopf und Härtel, 1929; reprint, Wiesbaden: Dr. Martin Sändig oHG, 1973).

12. I borrow this notion from Svetlana Alpers, "Is Art History?" *Daedalus* 106 (Summer 1977): 1–13.

Chapter 1
Monstrous Opera

1. "Le Public ayant paru moins satisfait des Scenes des INDES GALANTES, que du reste de l'Ouvrage, je n'ai pas cru devoir appeler de son Jugement; & c'est pour cette raison que je ne lui présente ici que les Symphonies entremêlées des Airs chantans, Ariettes, Récitatifs mesurez, Duo, Trio, Quatuor & Choeurs, tant du Prologue, que des trois premieres Entrées, qui font en tout plus de Quatre-vingt Morceaux détachés, dont j'ai formé quatre grands Concerts en différens Tons: les Symphonies y sont même ordonnées en Piéces de Clavecin, & les Agrémens y sont conformes à ceux de mes autres Piéces de Clavecin, sans que cela puisse empêcher de les joüer sur d'autres Instrumens, puisqu'il n'y a qu'à y prendre toûjours les plus hautes Notes pour le Dessus, & les plus basses pour la Basse: Ce qui s'y trouvera trop haut pour le Violoncello, pourra y être porté une Octave plus bas." For a transcription of the title page associated with the print used in the present study, see the bibliography. The preface to *Les Indes galantes* is transcribed in full in Charles Malherbe's preface to Jean-Philippe Rameau, *Les Indes galantes*, rev. ed., ed. Paul Dukas, *OC*, 7:lxxxiv–lxxxv.

2. A table of the redistributed contents is provided by Malherbe in *OC*, 7:lxxxiii–lxxxiv.

3. See *Einzeldrucke vor 1800*, 12 vols., Répertoire international des sources musicales, A / 1 (Kassel: Bärenreiter, 1971–1992), entries B 2160 and C 740.

4. Louis Laloy, *Rameau*, 3d ed., Les Maîtres de la musique (Paris: Félix Alcan, 1919), 47–49; Graham Sadler and Albert Cohen, "Jean-Philippe Rameau," in *The New Grove French Baroque Masters: Lully, Charpentier, Lalande, Couperin, Rameau* (New York: W. W. Norton, 1986), 207–308.

5. These values have been viewed in scholarship from the vantage point of the gradual rise in importance of instrumental music in eighteenth-century discourse about music. For treatments of this subject specific to France, see Maria Rika Maniates, "'Sonate, que me veux-tu?' The Enigma of French Musical Aesthetics in the 18th Century," *Current Musicology* 9 (1969): 117–40, and John Neubauer, *The Emancipation of Music from Language: Departure from Mimesis in Eighteenth-Century Aesthetics* (New Haven: Yale University Press, 1986).

6. "Une seule édition parut, et encore sous une forme si incomplète, si bizarre même, qu'on aurait peine à constater dans l'histoire de l'Opéra le retour du même fait: pareil exemple est rare, en effet, et peut-être unique en son genre" (*OC*, 7:lxxxii).

7. "Comme on n'a point encore entendu la Nouvelle Entrée des Sauvages que j'ajoûte ici aux trois premieres, je me suis hasardé de la donner complette: Heureux si le succès répond à mes soins!" (*OC*, 7:lxxxiv–lxxxv.)

8. It is listed as such in Sadler and Cohen, "Jean-Philippe Rameau," 293.

9. Jonathan Culler, *Ferdinand de Saussure*, rev. ed. (Ithaca: Cornell University Press, 1976), 15–16. Svetlana Alpers, "Is Art History?" *Daedalus* 106 (Summer 1977): 1–13.

10. Cuthbert Girdlestone reports that the abbé de Saint-Pierre invented a chair to joggle (*se tremousse*) as a form of exercise (*Jean-Philippe Rameau: His Life and Work*, rev. ed. [New York: Dover, 1969], 349, n.1. (Cf., the original French, n. 11.)

11. "J'allai hier à l'Opera. Ce n'est pas la peine de rien dire des paroles. La Musique est une Magie perpétuelle, la Nature n'y a aucune part. Rien de si scabreux & de si raboteux: c'est un chemin, où l'on cahotte sans cesse. Le Musicien dispense d'acheter le fauteüil de l'Abbé de S. Pierre. L'excellent *Tremoussoir* que cet Opera, dont les airs seroient très-propres à ébranler les nerfs engourdis d'un paralytique! Que ces secousses violentes sont differentes du doux ebranlement que sçavent operer Campra, des Touches, Monteclair, Mouret, &c. L'inintelligibilité, le galimatias, le néologisme veulent donc passer du discours dans la Musique; c'en est trop. Je suis tiraillé, écorché, disloqué par cette diabolique Sonate des *Fêtes Indiennes* . . . " (Pierre-François-Guyot Desfontaines, *Observations sur les écrits modernes* 2 [3 September 1735]: 238; reprint, 34 vols. in 4 [Geneva: Slatkine, 1967], 1:156). The letter is cited in *OC,* 7: lvi; Paul-Marie Masson, "Lullistes et Ramistes, 1733–1752," *L'Année musicale* 1 (1911): 192; Girdlestone, *Jean-Philippe Rameau,* 349; Sadler and Cohen, "Jean-Philippe Rameau," 219.

12. On the particular vehemence of criticism directed at Rameau in 1737, see Charles Dill, "The Reception of Rameau's *Castor et Pollux* in 1737 and 1754" (Ph.D. diss., Princeton University, 1989), 33–74, and Graham Sadler, "Patrons and Pasquinades: Rameau in the 1730s," *Journal of the Royal Musical Association* 113 (1988): 314–37.

13. Leslie Ellen Brown, "Departures from Lullian Convention in the *Tragédie lyrique* of the *Préramiste* Era," *"Recherches" sur la musique française classique* 22 (1984): 59–78.

14. The literature dealing with aspects of this facet of French aesthetics is extensive. See Paul-Marie Masson, "Musique italienne et musique française. La première querelle," *Rivista musicale italiana* 19 (1912), 519–45; idem, "La Musique italienne en France pendant le premier tiers du xviiie siècle," in *Mélanges de philologie, d'histoire et de littérature offerts à Henri Hauvette* (Paris: Les Presses françaises, 1934; reprint, Geneva: Slatkine, 1972), 353–65; Georges Snyders, *Le Goût musical en France aux xviie et xviiie siècles,* Études de psychologie et de philosophie, 18 (Paris: J. Vrin, 1968); Maniates, "Sonate, que me veux-tu?" 117–40; Georgia Cowart, *The Origins of Modern Musical Criticism: French and Italian Music 1600–1750,* Studies in Musicology, 38 (Ann Arbor: UMI Research Press, 1981); Neubauer, *The Emancipation of Music*; Belinda Cannone, *Philosophies de la musique, 1752–1789,* Théorie et critique à l'âge classique, 4 (Paris: Klincksieck, 1990). Catherine Kintzler's *Poétique de l'opéra français de Corneille à Rousseau* (n.p.: Minerve, 1991) is in some ways an extended meditation on this issue as it pertains to French opera. Also relevant are Gloria Flaherty, *Opera in the Development of German Critical Thought* (Princeton: Princeton University Press, 1978) and Bellamy Hosler, *Changing Aesthetic Views of Instrumental Music in 18th-Century Germany,* Studies in Musicology, 42 (Ann Arbor: UMI Research Press, 1981).

15. Masson wrote on both of these subjects. See Paul-Marie Masson, "Le 'Ballet héroïque,'" *La Revue musicale* 9 (1928): 132–54; idem, "Musique italienne et musique française," 519–45; and idem, "La Musique italienne en France," 353–65. On the development of the opéra-ballet, see also James R. Anthony, "The French Opera-Ballet in the Early 18th Century: Problems of Definition and Classification," *Journal of the American Musicological Society* 18 (1965): 197–206.

16. "La mauvaise humeur de l'Auteur de cette Lettre n'empêchera pas le Pub-

lic de regarder M. Rameau comme un des plus grands Musiciens de notre siécle. Le plus solide reproche qu'on peut faire à sa Musique, est que l'oreille françoise n'y est pas encore assez accoutumée. Mais combien de gens encore aujourd'hui ne peuvent goûter les Sonates de Corelli & de Vivaldi, dont néanmoins tous les connoisseurs sont un si grand cas?" (Desfontaines, *Observations* 2 [3 September 1735]: 239 [reprint, 1:156]).

17. On the latter topic and its relation to musical issues, see Cowart, *The Origins,* 27–48.

18. For earlier critical accusations made on the basis of overly learned music, see the "Dissertation sur la musique italienne & françoise," *Mercure de France* (November 1713): 3–62. For examples of earlier epigramatic criticism, see Antonia Louise Banducci, "'Tancrède' by Antoine Danchet and André Campra: Performance History and Reception (1702–1764)" (Ph.D. diss., Washington University, 1990), and Jérôme de La Gorce, *L'Opéra à Paris au temps de Louis XIV. Histoire d'un théâtre,* (Paris: Éditions Desjonquères, 1992).

19. "Les Indes galantes, en 1735, paroissoient d'une difficulté insurmontable; le gros des spectateurs sortoit en déclamant contre une musique surchargée de doubles croches, dont on ne pouvoit rien retenir. Six mois après, tous les airs depuis l'ouverture jusqu'à la derniere gavote, furent parodiés & sûs de tout le monde. A la reprise de 1751, notre parterre chantoit *brillant soleil,* &c. avec autant de facilité que nos peres psalmodioient *Armide est encore plus aimable;* &c." (*Encyclopédie, ou Dictionnaire raisonné des sciences, des arts et des métiers . . . ,* ed., Denis Diderot and Jean le Rond d'Alembert, 28 vols. [Paris: various publishers, 1751–1772]; fascimile in 5 vols. [New York: Pergamon Press, 1969], 6:318).

20. "Enfin ces symphonies qui nous semblent si belles, quand elles sont employées comme l'imitation d'un certain bruit, nous paroîtroient insipides, elles nous paroîtroient mauvaises, si l'on les employoit comme l'imitation d'un autre bruit. La symphonie de l'Opera d'Issé dont je viens de parler, sembleroit ridicule, si l'on la mettoit à la place de celle du tombeau d'Amadis. Ces morceaux de musique qui nous émeuvent si sensiblement, quand ils font une partie de l'action théâtrale, plairoient même médiocrement, si l'on les faisoit entendre comme des *Sonates,* ou des morceaux de symphonies détachés, à une personne qui ne les auroit jamais entendues à l'Opera, & qui en jugeroit par conséquent sans connoître leur plus grand mérite; c'est-à-dire, le rapport qu'elles ont avec l'action, ou, pour parler ainsi, elles jouent un rôle" (Jean-Baptiste Dubos, *Réflexions critiques sur la poësie et sur la peinture,* 7th ed., 3 vols. [Paris: Pissot, 1770; facsimile, Geneva: Slatkine, 1967], 1:483–84).

21. The point is more important than it may first seem if we remember that the semantic dimension in music continues to present difficulties for modern analysts. For a good summary of the problems it creates, see Harold S. Powers, "Language Models and Musical Analysis," *Ethnomusicology* 24 (1980): 1–2 and, more generally, 1–9.

22. Jeffrey Kallberg, "The Rhetoric of Genre: Chopin's Nocturne in G Minor," *Nineteenth Century Music* 11 (Spring 1988): 243 and, more generally, 243–46.

23. "Suivez, pour la trouver, Théocrite et Virgile: / Que leurs tendres écrits, par les Grâces dictés, / Ne quittent point vos mains, jour et nuit feuilletés. / Seuls, dans leurs doctes vers, ils pourront vous apprendre / Par quel art sans bassesse un

auteur peut descendre" (Nicolas Boileau-Despréaux, *Oeuvres,* ed. Georges Mongrédien [Paris: Garnier frères, 1961], 166).

24. See, for example, Charles Dill, "Music, Beauty, and the Paradox of Rationalism," in *French Musical Thought, 1600–1800,* ed. Georgia Cowart, Studies in Music, 105 (Ann Arbor and London: UMI Research Press, 1989), 197–210.

25. "Il n'y a personne à qui il ne soit permis d'y prendre quelque goût: & comme sans être poëte on peut très-bien sentir la différence qu'il y a de Virgile qui peint la nature, à Lucain qui fait montre d'esprit; on peut sans être musicien sentir les vraies beautés de la musique, & juger sainement du mérite des musiciens. Mais ne risquons ni de leur attribuer aucune méprise, ni de vouloir donner à l'un aucune préférence sur un autre, qu'à l'aide d'une régle lumineuse qui soit avouée des musiciens mêmes, & qui décide de la juste valeur de leur méthode" ([Noël-Antoine Pluche], *Le Spectacle de la nature, ou Entretiens sur les particularités de l'histoire naturelle,* rev. ed., 9 vols. [Paris: Frères Estienne, 1755], 7:97–98).

26. See Sima Godfrey, ed., *The Anxiety of Anticipation,* Yale French Studies, 66 (New Haven: Yale University Press, 1984), her preface to the volume, iii–ix, and her essay "The Anxiety of Anticipation: Ulterior Motives in French Poetry," 1–26.

27. Évrard Titon du Tillet, *Description du parnasse françois, exécuté en bronze, suivie d'une liste alphabetique des poëtes, & des musiciens rassemblés sur ce monument* (Paris: La veuve Ribou, Pierre Prault, La veuve Pissot, 1727), 3.

28. The most important surveys of Lullian opera in this respect continue to be Lois Rosow, "Lully's *Armide* at the Paris Opéra: A Performance History: 1686–1766" (Ph.D. diss., Brandeis University, 1981), and Herbert Schneider, *Die Rezeption der Opern Lullys im Frankreich des Ancien régime,* Mainzer Studien zur Musikwissenschaft, 16 (Tutzing: Hans Schneider, 1982).

29. "Animal qui est né avec des parties beaucoup plus grandes, ou beaucoup plus petites que naturellement elles ne doivent être. Animal qui est né avec plus de parties que la nature n'en demande" (Pierre Richelet, *Dictionnaire françois, contenant les mots et les choses, plusieurs nouvelles remarques sur la langue françoise: ses expressions propres, figurées & burlesques, la prononciation des mots les plus difficiles, le genre des noms, le regime des verbes: avec les termes les plus connus des arts et des sciences,* 2 vols. [Geneva: Jean Herman Widerhold, 1685], 2:39); "Animal qui a une conformation contraire à l'ordre de la nature" (*Le Dictionnaire de l'Académie françoise,* 2 vols. [Paris: Jean-Baptiste Coignard, 1694], 2:83).

30. "Animal qui naît avec une conformation contraire à l'ordre de la nature, c'est-à-dire avec une structure de parties très-différentes de celles qui caractérisent l'espece des animaux dont il sort. Il y a bien de sortes de *monstres* par rapport à leurs structures. . . .

"S'il n'y avoit qu'une différence légere & superficielle, si l'objet ne frappoit pas avec étonnement, on ne donneroit pas le nom de *monstre* à l'animal où elle se trouveroit" (*Encyclopédie,* 10:671).

31. Aristotle, *Generation of Animals,* trans. A.L. Peck, The Loeb Classical Library (Cambridge: Harvard University Press, 1953), IV, iii, 401.

32. *Horace on the Art of Poetry,* ed. Edward Henry Blakeney (Freeport: Books for Libraries Press, 1928), 41.

33. "Cette diversité a un fonds bien vaste dans la poésie héroïque: les entreprises de guerre, les traitez de paix, les ambassades, les négociations, les voyages, les em-

barquemens, les conseils, les délibérations, les bâtimens de palais et de villes, les passions, les reconnaissances impréveues, les révolutions surprenantes et inopinées, et les différentes images de tout ce qui se passe dans la vie des Grands peuvent y estre employées, pourvu qu'elles aillent au mesme but. Sans cet ordre les figures les plus belles deviennent monstrueuses et semblables à ces extravagances qu'Horace traitte de ridicules, au commencement de sa *Poétique*" (René Rapin, *Les Reflexions sur la poetique de ce temps et sur les ouvrages des poètes anciens et modernes,* ed. E. T. Dubois [Paris: F. Muquet, 1675; reprint, Geneva: Droz, 1970], 77).

34. Michel Foucault, *The Order of Things: An Archaeology of the Human Sciences* (New York: Vintage Books, 1973), xviii; see his chapter on classification in the eighteenth century, 125–65. See also Barbara Maria Stafford, *Body Criticism: Imaging the Unseen in Enlightenment Art and Medicine* (Cambridge: The MIT Press, 1991), especially 210–79.

35. "Les Opera ne sont qu'un fatras monstrueux" ([Pierre de Villiers,] "Epitre III. A un Homme qui estimoit de mauvais ouvrages, & sur tout les tragédies de l'opera," *Poesies de D* V***,* rev. ed. [Paris: Jacques Collombat, 1728], 297 [see also 305, 308]); "La regles de la Scène au caprice immolées / Par des traits monstrueux s'y trouvent violées" and " . . . fuyez loin de nous, monstres de l'Italie" ([Jean de Serré de Rieux,] *Les Dons des enfans de Latone: La Musique et la Chasse du cerf, poëmes dédiés au roy* [Paris: Pierre Prault, Jean Desaint, Jacques Guerin, 1734], 104); "Il s'ensuit delà qu'un bel Opera n'est jamais qu'un beau Monstre" (*Le Pour et contre* 2 [1733], 319), reprinted in Steve Larken, ed., *Studies on Voltaire and the Eighteenth Century* 309–310 [1993–1994] 333); "L'Opéra fut traité de monstre, de folie Italienne; à peine voulut-on lui permettre d'être un Concert agréable" and "L'Opéra est un monstre qui n'a ni proportion ni vrai semblance" ([Gabriel Bonnot de Mably,] *Lettres a madame la marquise de P . . . sur l'opera* [Paris: Didot, 1741; facsimile, New York: AMS Press, 1978], ix–x and 3, respectively); " . . . que l'Opera est un Spectacle monstrueux" and "Mais quel monstre qu'une Tragédie mise en Musique d'un bout à l'autre?" ([Toussaint Rémond de Saint-Mard,] *Reflexions sur l'opera* [The Hague: Jean Neaulme, 1741; facsimile, Geneva: Minkoff, 1972], 1–2 and 12, respectively); "M. de F. dit qu'on s'en passe sans peine dans les Opera: mais il n'en a dû rien conclure pour la Tragédie. Un Opera est toujours un mauvais Poëme, & le plus bel Ouvrage de ce genre n'est qu'un monstre" (*Jugemens sur quelques ouvrages nouveaux* 1 [1744], 263). The original passage in Fontenelle reads, in part: "Si les sujets sont susceptibles de cette perfection, à la bonne heure; sinon, il faut ne s'en écarter que le moins qu'il est possible, et se consoler de ne la pouvoir attraper, sur ce qu'elle n'est pas en elle-même fort importante. Ne nous passons-nous pas sans peine de l'unité de lieu dans tous les opéra, et de l'unité de temps, j'entends l'unité exacte, dans presque toutes les tragédies?" (Bernard Le Bovier de Fontenelle, *Réflexions sur la poétique* [1742], *Oeuvres complètes,* 3 [Paris, 1818; facsimile, Geneva: Slatkine, 1968], 26). "J'aimerais peut-être mieux l'opéra, si on n'avait pas trouvé le secret d'en faire un monstre qui me revolte" (*OCV,* 21:202).

36. "Il naître de vous un garçon. / Il vivra pour vanger son pere, / Pour faire aux Muses double outrage. / Car outre sa rauque Chanson, / D'escrire, il lui prendra la rage. / J'entends, je vois l'Anthropage / Col d'Autruch, sourcil froncé, / Cuirejaune, et de poinl hérissé, Nez creux, vray masque de Satire, / Bouche pour

mordre, et non pour rire, / Teste pointu, et cour Menton, / Jambes seches comme Ecriton" ("Chansonnier Maurepas," *F-Pn,* français 12634: 141–45). See also the appendix in Sadler, "Patrons and Pasquinades," 335, lines 36–47.

37. On eighteenth-century views of satire in this manner, see Stafford, *Body Criticism,* 176.

38. These particular examples are drawn from the "Dissertation sur la musique," 27–28, and Pluche, *La Spectacle de la nature,* 104.

39. See Sebastien de Brossard, *Dictionaire de musique, contenant une explication des termes grecs, latins, italiens, & françois, les plus usitez dans la musique,* 2d ed. (Paris: Christophe Ballard, 1705; reprint, ed. Harald Heckmann, Hilversum: Frits Knuf, 1965), 14, 231, 249, and Michel Corette, *L'École d'Orphée* (Paris, 1738), available in Carol Reglin Farrar, "Seven String Instrument Treatises of Michel Corette: Translation with Commentary" (Ph.D. diss., University of North Texas, 1978), 62.

40. [Louis-César-François de La Baume Le Blanc La Vallière], *Ballets, opera, et autres ouvrages lyriques, par ordre chronologique depuis leur origine; avec une table alphabetique des ouvrages et des auteurs* (Paris: Cl.-J. Baptiste Bauche, 1760; reprint, London: H. Baron, 1967), 174.

41. Godfrey, "The Anxiety of Anticipation," 1–20, and Kallberg, "The Rhetoric of Genre," 243–44.

42. Anthony, "The French Opera-Ballet in the Early 18th Century," 198. See also Masson, "Le 'Ballet héroïque,'" 132–54.

43. On the statistical dominance of the opéra-ballet, see Robert Fajon, *L'Opéra à Paris du roi soleil à Louis le Bien-aimé* (Geneva: Slatkine, 1984), 70–71.

44. I draw the distinction between *topographical* and *economical* from Sigmund Freud, "The Unconscious," *The Standard Edition of the Complete Psychological Works of Sigmund Freud,* gen. ed. James Strachey, 24 vols. (London: Hogarth Press and the Institute of Psycho-Analysis, 1953–75), 14:166–204.

45. " . . . car la danse est, comme vous sçavez, l'ame d'un Ballet, & moins il est chargé de paroles, plus il y a d'apparence qu'il réüssira" ([Nicolas Boindin], *Lettres historiques sur tous les spectacles de Paris,* 2 vols. (Paris: Pierre Prault, 1719), 2:129.

46. "On convint pourtant que le Poëme est bien écrit, on y auroit souhaité de l'intérêt, mais il n'est pas aisé, aux Auteurs mêmes qui on travaillé le plus pour ce Théatre, d'en mettre beaucoup dans un Ballet. Ce genre de pièce . . . semble plûtôt fait pour l'esprit, que pour le coeur; & d'ailleurs les Danses en composent les deux tiers" (François and Claude Parfaict, "Histoire de l'Académie royale de musique depuis son établissement jusqu'à présent," 2 vols., *F-Pn,* nouvelles acquisitions françaises 6532, 2:86).

47. "Voilà donc à peu près tout ce qui constitue le Ballet: une petite intrigue, peu de récitatif, des Ariettes, beaucoup de danses . . . " (Saint-Mard, *Reflexions sur l'opera,* 95).

48. "La tragédie ne devient agréable au spectateur, que parce qu'il devient luy-mesme sensible à tout ce qu'on luy représente, qu'il entre dans tous les différens sentimens des acteurs, qu'il s'intéresse dans leurs avantures, qu'il craint, et qu'il espère, qu'il s'afflige, et qu'il se réjouit avec eux. Le théâtre est froid et languissant, dès qu'il cesse de produire ces mouvemens dans l'âme de ceux qui y assistent. Mais comme de toutes les passions la crainte et la pitié sont celles qui font de plus grandes

impressions sur le coeur de l'homme, par la disposition naturelle qu'il a à s'épou-
vanter et à s'attendrir: Aristote les a choisies entre les autres, pour toucher davantage les esprits, par ces sentimens tendres qu'elles causent, quand le coeur s'en laisse
pénétrer" (Rapin, *Reflexions sur la poetique de ce temps,* 99).

49. "Permis d'être fou à celui qui a fait l'acte des Incas" (D3029, *CWV,* 93:172).
I will follow the numbering of Voltaire's letters employed in *CWV.*

50. Girdlestone, *Jean-Philippe Rameau,* 330; Masson, "Le 'Ballet héroïque,'"
137–38; Sylvie Bouissou, brochure notes in Jean-Philippe Rameau, *Les Indes
galantes,* Harmonia mundi France 901367.69.

51. Masson, "Le 'Ballet héroïque,'" 137–38.

52. "*Zoroastre* ne conclud donc pas davantage contre la nécessité des bons
Poëmes, dans les Opéras tragiques, que les *Indes galantes* ne doivent favoriser l'in-
différence des Musiciens pour les paroles, dans les Opéra Ballets. Quelque applaudi
qu'ait été celui-ci dans son origine, on sçait combien sa fortune a été différente dans
les reprises. En observant, d'après les événemens, tous les ouvrages de ce genre, on
trouvera qu'il n'en est aucun, de ceux dont la Musique fait le seul mérite, qui ait
soutenu l'épreuve des retours sur le Théâtre; au lieu que l'on pourroit en citer beaucoup d'autres, qui, à la faveur des Poëmes, ont obtenu grâce & l'obtiennent encore
pour cette *petite* Musique, ainsi que la qualifient les prétendus connoisseurs, qui af-
fectent toujours, par vanité personelle, de déprise le genre national" (*Mercure de
France* [February 1761], 97–98).

53. "Il est plus connu pour sa fécondité que pour son talent. *Faiseur* dans toute
l'acception du mot, il fit représenter des pieces à la plupart des théâtres" (*Grand
dictionnaire universel du xixᵉ siècle,* 17 vols., ed. Pierre Larousse [Paris: Administration du grand dictionnaire universel, 1866–1879; reprint, Geneva: Slatkine,
1982], 8:898.

54. Example 1.1 is based on *LIG,* 154–55.

55. "On cite le *Bémol* en signe de molesse, de foiblesse, &c . . ." (Rameau, *OSN,*
54, *CTW,* 3:293).

56. "On cite le *Diéze,* ou le *Béquare* en signe de force, de joye . . ." (ibid.). See
also 59–61 (*CTW,* 3:196–97).

57. I draw this recursive image of musical experience from David Lewin, "Music
Theory, Phenomenology, and Modes of Perception," *Music Perception* 3 (Summer
1986): 327–92.

58. Michel-Paul-Guy de Chabanon, "Chabanon's Éloge de M. Rameau," trans.
Edward R. Reilly, *Studies in Music from the University of Western Ontario* 8 (1983):
6–7.

59. "L'Opera n'est point un monstre, quoique les gens de mauvaise humeur
soutiennent que l'assemblage de tant de parties ne sçauroient former qu'un tout
monstrueux. Ce sentiment ne peut exister que faute d'avoir envisagé ce spectacle
du point de vue d'où tous les gens sans passion doivent le regarder. Il seroit un
monstre en effet, si toutes les parties qui le composent se cédoient réciproquement
le droit de la prééminence pour briller chacune en particulier, sans égard marqué
pour l'objet principal qui les réunit. Mais si au contraire on envisage la Musique
comme l'Art qui constitue l'essence de ce spectacle, & les autres Arts qu'on y em-
ploie, comme subordonnés à celui-ci, & n'étant que des moyens dont on se sert
pour le faire briller dans toute ses parties, alors le caractere monstrueux de ce spec-

tacle disparoîtra, & l'on ne verra plus qu'un tout formé par des parties qui con-
coureront à la perfection d'un seul & unique objet . . ." ([Marc-Antoine Laugier,]
Sentiment d'un harmoniphile sur différents ouvrages de musique, ed. A. J. Labbet
and A. Léris [Amsterdam: Jombert, Duchesne, Lambert, 1756; facsimile, Geneva:
Minkoff, 1972], 50).

Chapter 2
Different Tragedies

1. "L'Opera de *Thézée* est sur la scène depuis le 29 de novembre. Il est vêtu et
décoré magnifiquement. On ne peut rien ajouter à la beauté de l'exécution, et je
doute que dans aucun temps elle ait été aussi parfaite. Thevenard y fait Egée avec
applaudissement, quoyque sa voix soit presque éteinte. Mlle Antier joue le rôle de
Medée a la grande manière. Tribou, et Mlle Pelissier, sans avoir une grande voix,
font pleurer l'auditoire aux scènes d'Eglé et de Thezée. On n'a pas plus de talent,
qu'en ont ces deux acteurs. Malgré l'éloge unanime qu'on donne à l'opéra, les representations depuis quinze jours sont extrémement foibles. Il n'y a plus de gout;
les choses nobles ne font plus d'impression. Les dames qui sont la boussole des
spectacles ne donnent aucun signe de sensibilité aux beautés touchantes. Les graces
de la musique sont perdües; on ne connoit que celles de la danse qui ne sont pas,
a beaucoup pres, suffisantes pour nous soutenir. *Alceste* reussît mediocrement,
l'hiver dernier, et seroit tombé sans le secours d'un pas de deux qui attira tout Paris.
Le pis du pis est qu'il n'y a point d'esperance que le gout se relève, a moins que le
Roy n'en prenne pour l'Opera" (André Tessier, "Correspondance d'André Cardinal des Touches et du Prince Antoine 1er de Monaco [suite]," *La Revue musicale*
8 [February 1927], 115).

2. " . . . mais depuis quelques années Lulli commence à devenir ancien" (Yves-
Marie André, *Essai sur le beau,* rev. ed. [Paris: Ferra ainé, 1818], 167). "Nous n'en
parlons point d'un nouveau musicien qui semble partager tout Paris" (ibid., 165).

3. "On a trouvé la Musique de cet Opéra un peu difficile à exécuter, mais par
l'habileté des Simphonistes et des autres Musiciens, la difficulté n'en a pas empêché
l'exécution. . . . Le Musicien a forcé les plus séveres critiques à convenir que dans
son premier Ouvrage Lyrique. Ii [*sic*] a donné une Musique mâle et harmonieuse;
d'un caractere neuf; nous voudrions en pouvoir donner un Extrait, comme nous
faisons du Poëme, et faire sentir ce qu'elle a de sçavant pour l'expression dans les
Airs caracterisez, les Tableaux, les intentions heureuses et soutenuës, comme le
Choeur et la Chasse du 4e Acte; l'Entrée des Amours au Prologue; le Choeur et la
Simphonie du Tonerre; la Gavotte parodiée que chante la Delle Petitpas au 1er Acte;
les Enfers du 2e Acte, l'Image effrayante de la Furie avec Thesée et le Choeur, &c.
Au 3me Acte, le Monologue de Thesée, son invocation à Neptune, le Frémissement
des Flots. Le Monologue de Phedre dâns l'Acte suivant. Celui d'Aricie, dans le 5e
la Bergerie, &c." (*Mercure de France* [October 1733], 2248–49).

4. "Nous voicy arrivons au premier Ouvrage Lyrique d'un Musicien, qui
méprisant, ou peut être ne pouvant d'assujetir à composer dans le gout de ceux qui
l'ont précédé, a voulu nous faire voir que la science profonde, peut, dans cet art,
suppléer au Génié, & aux talens naturels, & attirer même des admirateurs, & des
partisans: Et prenant une route nouvelle, qui luy est particuliere, il entreprit d'être

dans son genre, ce que Lully est dans le sien" (François and Claude Parfaict, "Histoire de l'Académie royale de musique depuis son établissement jusqu'à présent," 2 vols., *F-Pn*, nouvelles acquisitions françaises 6532: 67).

5. "C'est ici l'époque de la révolution qui se fit dans la Musique & de ses nouveaux progrès en France. M. RAMEAU doit en être & en sera probablement regardé comme l'auteur & la principale cause. La partie du Public qui ne juge & ne se décide que par impression, fut d'abord étonnée d'une Musique bien plus chargée & plus fertile en images, que l'on n'avoit coutume d'en entendre au Théâtre. On goûta néanmoins ce nouveau genre, & l'on finit par l'applaudir. Le desir avide de la nouveauté, le mérite réel de l'ouvrage & jusqu'à la contrariété des opinions, tout concourut au succès de cette première production d'un grand Musicien, sur le compt duquel les sentimens se sont depuis réunis à l'admiration" ("Essai d'eloge historique de feu M. Rameau, compositeur de la musique du cabinet du roi, pensionnaire de sa majesté & de l'Académie royale de musique," *Mercure de France* [October 1764], 187–88).

6. Michel-Paul-Guy de Chabanon, "Chabanon's Éloge de M. Rameau," trans. Edward R. Reilly, *Studies in Music from the University of Western Ontario* 8 (1983), 6.

7. "L'Ouvrage a grossi sous la main par l'application qu'on a crû devoir faire de l'Idée générale aux differentes espéces de *Beautez,* qui ont parû meriter le plus d'attention. Pour tirer de leurs vrais Principes les raisons qu'on rend des Beautez de la Musique, une longue Digression Physique a été nécessaire; c'est ce qui a rendu le dernier Chapitre beaucoup plus long que les autres. Si les Principes qu'on y pose sont vrais, & que les conséquences qu'on en tite [sic] éclaircissent le sujet, qu'on y traite, ce Chapitre pourra ne pas déplaire" (Jean-Pierre de Crousaz, *Traité du beau* [Amsterdam: François l'Honoré, 1715, *8]).

8. "Il y a peu de sujets surquoi les Hommes soient plus partagez que sur celui de la Musique. S'il y en a qu'elle enchante, il s'en trouve aussi qui ne la peuvent soufrir; elle calme l'inquietude des uns, elle en fait naître dans les autres; on en voit chez qui elle répand l'allegresse, & on en voit qu'elle rend sombres & reveurs. Parmi ceux qui l'aiment, quelle diversité de goûts ne se rencontre-t-il pas? Le Peuple veut des Vaudevilles & des airs à danser; mais pour ce qui est des ouvertures, des Chacones & d'autres airs de cette force, il n'y aperçoit que du bruit. Les Nations mêmes se trouvent partagées sur la preférence, qu'on doit donner aux differentes especes de Musique. Si nos principes nous conduisent à découvrir du réel au milieu de tant de diversités, qui tiennent, ce semble, de la bizarrerie, ce sera une nouvelle preuve de leur justesse" (Crousaz, *Traité du beau,* 171–72).

9. Charles Dill, "Music, Beauty, and the Paradox of Rationalism," in *French Musical Thought, 1600–1800,* ed. Georgia Cowart, Studies in Music, 105 (Ann Arbor: UMI Research Press, 1989), 197–210.

10. Jean-Baptiste Dubos, *Réflexions critiques sur la poësie et sur la peinture,* 7th ed., 3 vols. (Paris: Pissot, 1727; facsimile, Geneva: Slatkine, 1967).

11. "L'esprit ne pouvant concevoir un Héros qui chante, s'attache à celui qui fait chanter, et on ne sauroit nier qu'aux représentations du Palais Royal, on ne songe cent fois plus à Baptiste, qu'à Thesée ni à Cadmus" (Charles de Saint-Denis, Seigneur de Saint-Évremond, "Sur les opéras," *Oeuvres en prose,* 11 vols., ed. René Ternois [Paris: Marcel Didier, 1966], 3:152–53).

12. "Eh, allons donc, Mr. le Comte, interrompit le Chevalier, étalés bien vôtre Saint Evremont. Mais en un mot, il n'est point naturel, si vous voulés, que tout ce qu'on met en chant soit chanté. Cela n'est point vrai-semblable en soi même, j'y consens: mais cela est devenu vrai-semblable & naturel par l'usage. Le Musicien doit suposer que cela l'est, & agir sur ce pié là: de la même maniere qu'un Poëte traite les sujets de la Fable, comme s'ils étoient véritablement historiques. On sçait bien que tous ces faits de l'antiquité fabuleuse sont faux: mais ils se sont établis, on les passe pour vrais en Poësie, & un Auteur qui prend dans la Fable un sujet de Tragédie, n'est pas moins obligé à y garder exactement les moeurs, les caracteres & les bienseances, que s'il l'avoit pris dans l'Histoire la plus autentique. C'est ainsi qu'en doit user le Muscien. Il lui est permis, il lui est ordonné de croire qu'il n'y a rien que de naturel, & rien qui ne doive être naturellement exprimé dans ce qu'il met en Musique: & même il faut qu'il s'efforce d'exprimer le plus naturellement les choses les moins naturelles, afin de leur donner une espece de vrai-semblance par la naïveté de son chant, & de faire oublier, s'il se peut, à des spectateurs aussi délicats que Mr. de S. Evremont, que c'est forcer la nature & la vrai-semblance que de chanter ces sortes de choses" (Jean-Laurent Le Cerf de la Viéville, *Comparaison de la musique italienne et de la musique françoise*, 2d ed., 3 vols. [Brussels: François Foppens, 1705; facsimile, Geneva: Minkoff, 1972], 1:30–31).

13. "Qu'il arrive un Dieu, un Enchanteur, une Fée: Qu'on nous tourne la tête avec un peu de merveilleux, nous dispensons de cette vraisemblance, qui nous est si chere . . ." ([Toussaint Rémond de Saint-Mard,] *Reflexions sur l'opera* [The Hague: Jean Neaulme, 1741; facsimile, Geneva: Minkoff, 1972], 13–14).

14. "Ces Etres chimériques dont le Spectateur n'a pas d'idée bien précise, laissent la liberté au Musicien de leur donner un langage plus musical. Il est assez naturel de leur prêter des sentimens plus impétueux, & le Poëte même n'est point obligé d'assujettir ses Héros aux bienséances essentielles dans une action où n'introduit que des hommes. Atys & Roland poussent leur fureur à un excès qui auroit été ridicule sur un autre Théâtre, & l'on n'est point choqué que Renaud soit enivré des charmes d'Armide, & qu'il oublie sa gloire" ([Gabriel Bonnot de Mably,] *Lettres a madame la marquise de P . . . sur l'opera* [Paris: Didot, 1741; facsimile, New York: AMS Press, 1978], 49–50).

15. "L'Opera est un Poëme dramatique mis en Musique, & pour qu'il soit bon, il suffit qu'il représente une action intéressante" (ibid., 39).

16. "Mais comme il y a dans l'Epopée deux sortes de grands: le Merveilleux & l'Héroïque; il peut y avoir aussi deux espèces de Tragédie, l'une héroïque, qu'on appelle simplement Tragédie, l'autre merveilleuse, qu'on a nommée Spectacle Lyrique ou Opera. Le merveilleux est exclus de la première espèce, parce que ce sont des hommes qui agissent en hommes; au lieu que dans la seconde, les Dieux agissant en Dieux, avec tout l'appareil d'une puissance surnaturelle; ce qui ne seroit point merveilleux, cesseroit en quelque sorte d'être vraisemblable" ([Charles Batteux,] *Les Beaux arts reduits a un même principe* [Paris: Durand, 1747; facsimile, n.p.: Johnson Reprint, 1970], 219). See Catherine Kintzler, *Poétique de l'opéra français de Corneille à Rousseau* (n.p.: Minerve, 1991), 197–244.

17. Batteux, *Les Beaux arts reduits a un même principe,* 220–21.

18. "Les Dieux, les premiers Héros dont la Fable nous donne des idées si poëtiques & si élevées, l'Olimpe, les Enfers, l'Empire des Mers, les Métamorphoses

miraculeuses, l'Amour, la Vengeance, la Haine, toutes les passions personnifiées, les Elémens en mouvement, la Nature entiere animée fournissoient dèslors au génie du Poëte & du Musicien mille tableaux variés, & la matiere inépuisable du plus brillant Spectacle" (Louis de Cahusac, *La Danse ancienne et moderne ou Traité historique de la danse*, 3 vols. [The Hague: Jean Neaulme, 1754], 3:65–66).

19. See for example Paul-Marie Masson, "Lullistes et Ramistes, 1733–1752," *L'Année musicale* 1 (1911), 205–6, and Catherine Kintzler, *Jean-Philippe Rameau: Splendeur et naufrage de l'esthétique du plaisir à l'âge classique* (Paris: Le Sycomore, 1983), 104–5. More generally, see Kintzler's discussion of some of the passages discussed here, pp. 104–110.

20. "L'opéra est un spectacle aussi bizarre que magnifique, où les yeux et les oreilles sont plus satisfaits que l'esprit, où l'asservissement à la musique rend nécessaires les fautes les plus ridicules, où il faut chanter des ariettes dans la destruction d'une ville, et danser autour d'un tombeau; où l'on voit le palais de Pluton et celui du Soleil; des dieux, des démons, des magiciens, des prestiges, des monstres, des palais formés et détruits en un clin d'oeil. On tolère ces extravagances, on les aime même, parce qu'on est là dans le pays des fées; et, pourvu qu'il y ait du spectacle, de belles danses, une belle musique, quelques scènes intéressantes, on est content. Il serait aussi ridicule d'exiger dans *Alceste* l'unité d'action, de lieu et de temps, que de vouloir introduire des danses et des démons dans *Cinna* et dans *Rodogune*" (Voltaire, "Préface de l'édition de 1730," *OCV*, 2:52).

21. "On vous aura sûrement mandé ce que c'est que Rameau et les différentes opinions qui divisent le public sur sa musique. Les uns la trouvent divine et au dessus de Lully, les autres la trouvent fort travaillée, mais point agréable et point diversifiée. Je suis je l'avoue des derniers. J'aime cent fois mieux Issé que l'on joue à présent" (D689, *CWV*, 86:436).

22. "J'assistay hier à la première représentation de l'opéra d'Aricie et d'Hipolite. Les paroles sont de l'abbé Pellegrin, et dignes de l'abbé Pellegrin. La musique est d'un nommé Ramau, homme qui a le malheur de savoir plus de musique que Lully. C'est un pédant en musique. Il est exact, et ennuyeux" (D611, *CWV*, 86:403).

23. "Notre ami fait un nouvel opéra intitulé Sansom [*sic*] pour Rameau pour Lequel il s'est Rengoué après avoir été si dégoûté" (D682, *CWV*, 86:430); "Savez vous bien que pendant ma maladie j'ay fait l'opéra de Samson Pour Ramau?" (D686, *CWV*, 86:434).

24. "C'est une leçon publique plus instructive, que la philosophie: parce qu'elle instruit l'esprit par les sens, et quelle rectifie les passions par les passions mesmes, en calmant par leur émotion le trouble qu'elles excitent dans le coeur. Aristote qui reconnut deux défauts importans à régler dans l'homme, l'orgueil et la dureté, trouva le remède à ces deux défauts dans la tragédie. Car elle rend l'homme modeste, en luy représentant des Grands humiliez: et elle le rend sensible et pitoyable en luy faisant voir sur le théâtre les étranges accidens de la vie et les disgrâces imprévues, ausquelles sont sujettes les personnes les plus importantes" ([René Rapin,] *Reflexions sur la poetique de ce temps, et sur les ouvrages des poètes anciens & modernes*, ed. E. T. Dubois [Paris: F. Muguet, 1675; reprint, Geneva: Droz, 1970], 97).

25. "La tragédie moderne roule sur d'autres principes: peut-estre que le génie de notre nation ne pourroit pas aisément soutenir une action sur le théâtre par le

seul mouvement de la terreur et de la pitié. Ce sont des machines, qui ne peuvent se remuer comme il faut, que par de grands sentimens et par de grandes expressions, dont nous ne sommes pas tout à fait si capables que les Grecs. Peut-estre que notre nation, qui est naturellement galante, a esté obligée par la nécessité de son caractère à se faire un système nouveau de tragédie, pour s'accommoder à son humeur" (ibid., 103).

26. "Rien ne me paroist aussi d'un plus petit sens que de s'amuser à badiner, par des tendresses frivoles, lorsqu'on peut estre admirable par tout le merveilleux des grands sentimens et des grands spectacles" (ibid., 105).

27. "Pour la tragédie, je dois commencer en déclarant que je ne souhaite point qu'on perfectionne les spectacles, où l'on ne représente les passions corrompues que pour les allumer. Nous avons vu que Platon et les sages législateurs du paganisme rejettoient loin de toute république bien policée les fables et les instruments de musique qui pouvoient amollir une nation par le goût de la volupté. Quelle devroit donc être la sévérité des nations chrétiennes contre les spectacles contagieux? Loin de vouloir qu'on perfectionne de tels spectacles, je ressens une véritable joye de ce qu'ils sont chez nous imparfaits en leur genre. Nos poètes les ont rendu languissants, fades et doucereux comme les romans. On n'y parle que de feux, de chaînes, de tourments. On y veut mourir en se portant bien. Une personne très imparfaite est nommée un soleil, ou tout au moins une aurore. Ses yeux sont deux astres. Tous les termes sont outrez et rien ne montre une vraye passion. Tant mieux; la foiblesse du poison diminue le mal. Mais il me semble qu'on pourroit donner aux tragédies une merveilleuse force, suivant les idées très philosophiques de l'antiquité, sans y mêler cet amour volage et déréglé qui fait tant de ravages" (François de la Mothe Fénelon, *Lettre a l'académie,* ed. Ernesta Caldarini [Geneva: Droz, 1970], 89–90).

28. Rapin, *Reflexions sur la poetique de ce temps,* 100–2; Fénelon, *Lettre a l'académie,* 91–95.

29. "Lettres écrites en 1719 qui contiennent la critique de l'*Oedipe* de Sophocle, de celui de Corneille, et de celui de l'auteur," *OCV,* 2:11–46.

30. "Lorsqu'en 1718 il fut question de représenter le seul *Oedipe* qui soit resté depuis au théâtre, les comédiens exigèrent quelques scènes où l'amour ne fût pas oublié; . . . il fallut en passer par ce que les acteurs exigeaient; il fallut s'asservir à l'abus le plus méprisable" (*Commentaires sur Corneille, CWV,* 55:820).

31. Trusten Wheeler Russell, *Voltaire, Dryden, and Heroic Tragedy* (New York: Columbia University Press, 1946). Also see Norbert Sclippa, *La Loi du père et les droits du coeur: Essai sur les tragédies de Voltaire,* Histoire des idées et critique littéraire, 326 (Geneva: Droz, 1993).

32. "Une passion véritablement tragique, regardée comme une faiblesse, et combattue par des remords. Il faut, ou que l'amour conduise aux malheurs et aux crimes, pour faire voir combien il est dangereux; ou que la vertu en triomphe, pour montrer qu'il n'est pas invincible; sans cela, ce n'est plus qu'un amour d'églogue ou de comédie" (Voltaire, "Discours sur la tragédie," *OCV,* 2:324).

33. "La véritable tragédie est l'école de la vertu; et la seule différence qui soit entre le théâtre épuré et les livres de morale, c'est que l'instruction se trouve dans la tragédie toute en action, c'est qu'elle y est intéressante, et qu'elle se montre relevée des charmes d'un art qui ne fut inventé autrefois que pour instruire la terre

et pour bénir le ciel, et qui, par cette raison, fut appelé le langage des dieux" (Voltaire, *Dissertation sur la tragédie ancienne et moderne, OCV,* 4:505).

34. "J'ai cru même que le meilleur moyen d'oublier la tragédie d'Ériphyle était d'en faire une autre. Tout le monde me reproche ici que je ne mets pas d'amour dans mes pièces. Ils en auront cette fois-ci, je vous jure, et ce ne sera pas de la galanterie. Je veux qu'il n'y ait rien de si turc, de si chrétien, de si amoureux, de si tendre, de si furieux que ce que je versifie à présent pour leur plaire" (D494, *CWV,* 86:195).

35. "On a rejoué icy Zaire. Il y avoit honnêtement du monde et cela fut assez bien reçu à ce qu'on m'a dit. Il n'en est pas de même de Biblis et de son frère Caunus, mais on y va quoy qu'on en dise du mal. L'opera est un rendezvous public où l'on s'assemble à de certains jours sans savoir pourquoy. C'est une maison où tout le monde va quoy qu'on dise du mal du maître et qu'il soit ennuyeux. Il faut au contraire bien des efforts pour attirer le monde à la comédie, et je voi presque toujours que le plus grand succez d'une bonne tragédie n'aproche pas celuy d'un opera médiocre" (D536, *CWV,* 86:250).

36. Kintzler mistakenly assumes that Voltaire had by this time been commissioned, probably by La Pouplinière, to write the livret for *Samson* (*Jean-Philippe Rameau,* 110). Given the tone of comments by Voltaire and his friends, cited previously, as well as his own mention of the *Tanis* livret in a July letter (D635, *CWV,* 86:364), this seems unlikely.

37. "L'opéra de Rameau a Beaucoup Repris faveur et comme ce qui plait dans son opéra sont Les [? duo,] trio, Cheurs, airs de caractère &ct, il ne mettra dans son opéra que très peu de Récitatif, et tâchera de ménager au musicien Les occasions d'exercer La sorte de talent qu'il a" (D682, *CWV,* 86:430).

38. On the *Samson* collaboration, see Cuthbert Girdlestone, "Voltaire, Rameau et Samson," *"Recherches" sur la musique française classique* 6 (1966): 133–43; Charles Dill, "Creative Process in Rameau's *Castor et Pollux,*" in *The Creative Process,* Studies in the History of Music, 3 (New York: Broude Brothers, 1992), 93–106; and Kintzler, *Jean-Philippe Rameau,* 110–22.

39. "Voylà tout L'intérest que je connois dans un opera. Un bau spectacle bien varié, des fêtes brillantes, baucoup d'airs, peu de récitatif, des actes courts, c'est là ce qui me plait. Une pièce ne peut être véritablement touchante que dans la rue des fossez s^t Germain. Phaeton, le plus bel opera de Lully, est le moins intéressant" (D971, *CWV,* 87:294).

40. "Le noms de Vénus et d'Adonis trouvent dans cette tragédie une place plus naturel qu'on ne le croirait d'abord: c'est en effet sur leurs terres que l'action se passe" (*OCV,* 3:4).

41. Michel Poizat, *The Angel's Cry: Beyond the Pleasure Principle in Opera,* trans. Arthur Denner (Ithaca: Cornell University Press, 1992); Carolyn Abbate, *Unsung Voices: Opera and Musical Narrative in the Nineteenth Century* (Princeton: Princeton University Press, 1991).

42. "Qui dit un savant Musicien, entend ordinairement par-là un homme à qui rien n'échappe dans les différentes combinaisons des notes; mais on le croit en même temps tellement absorbé dans ces combinaisons, qu'il y sacrifie tout, le bon sens, le sentiment, l'esprit & la raison. Or ce n'est là qu'un Musicien de l'école, école où il n'est question que de notes, & rien de plus; de sorte qu'on a raison pour lors de lui

préférer un Musicien qui se pique moins de science que de goût. Cependant celui-ci, dont le goût n'est formé que par des comparaisons à la portée de ses sensations, ne peut tout au plus exceller que dans de certains genres, je veux dire dans les genres relatifs à son tempérament. Est-il naturellement tendre? il exprime bien la tendresse: son caractère est-il vif, enjoué, badin, &c.? sa musique y répond pour lors; mais sortez-le de ces caractères qui lui sont naturels, vous ne le reconnoissez plus. D'ailleurs comme il tire tout de son imagination, sans aucun secours de l'art, par ses rapports avec les expressions, il s'use à la fin. Dans son premier feu, il étoit tout brillant; mais ce feu se consume à mesure qu'il veut le rallumer, & l'on ne trouve plus chez lui que des redites ou des platitudes. Il seroit donc à souhaiter qu'il se trouvât pour le théâtre un Musicien qui étudiât la nature avant que de la peindre, & qui par sa science sçût faire le choix des couleurs & des nuances dont son esprit & son goût lui auroient fait sentir le rapport avec les expressions nécessaires" ("Lettre de M. Rameau à M. Houdart de La Motte, de l'Académie françoise, pour lui demander des paroles d'opéra. A Paris, 25 octobre 1727," *Mercure de France* [March 1765], 37–38).

43. Jean-Philippe Rameau, *Treatise on Harmony,* trans. Philip Gossett (New York: Dover, 1971), 177–78. For the original French, see *CTW,* 1:191–92. The idea is not new with Rameau; indeed, it is surprisingly old-fashioned (see, for example, Charles Masson, *Nouveau traité des regles pour la composition de la musique,* 2d ed. [Paris, 1699; facsimile, New York: Da Capo, 1967], 26–28). As we will see, Rameau breaks from this tradition in his theorizing about this seemingly practical information.

44. "De méme qu'un discours est ordinairement composé de plusieurs Phrases; de même aussi une Piece de Musique est ordinairement composée de plusieurs *Modulations,* qu'on peut regarder comme autant de *Phrases Harmoniques*" (*NS,* 40–41; *CTW,* 2:50–51).

45. On Rameau's tendency to depend on both of the traditional meanings of *modulation*—as the composing out of music within a key and as changing from one key to another—see E. Cynthia Verba, "Rameau's Views on Modulation and Their Background in French Theory," *Journal of the American Musicological Society* 31 (1978), 467–79, especially 470–72.

46. Significantly, Jean le Rond d'Alembert includes the monologue as a "leçon de composition aux Commençans," complete with Rameau's added staff of fundamental bass, in *Elemens de musique, theorique et pratique, suivant les principes de M. Rameau* (Paris: David l'aîné, Le Breton, Durand, 1752; reprint, Monuments of Music and Music Literature in Facsimile, 2/19, New York: Broude Brothers, 1966), 164.

47. "Si ces Phrases ont peu de rapport entr'elles, on tâche de leur donner des *Modulations* proportionnées, &c. . . . Il y a encor un choix à entre les *Cadences,* conformément au Sens des paroles" (*NS,* 41; *CTW,* 2:51).

48. In using the expression *syntagmatic,* I borrow from the notion of syntagm or syntagma as used in linguistics to describe the purely linear or metonymic dimension of language and its relationships. As Ferdinand de Saussure observed with regard to linguistics: "In its place in a syntagma, any unit acquires its value simply in opposition to what precedes, or to what follows, or to both" (*Course in General Linguistics,* ed. Charles Bally and Albert Sechehaye, trans. Roy Harris [London: Duckworth, 1983], 121).

49. "S'il n'est pas absolument impossible de déterminer les Chants, & les *Modulations* en consequence, qui conviendroient le mieux aux expressions les plus marquées, c'est d'ailleurs une entreprise qui demanderoit peut-être plus que la vie d'un seul homme" (*NS,* 43; *CTW,* 2:53). Like Descartes, Rameau was unwilling to formulate a theory of musical expression not because he denied its existence, but because the sheer range of possibilities lay beyond rational comprehension. See Charles Dill, "Music, Beauty, and the Paradox of Rationalism,"197–210.

50. Rameau was quite taken with this mode of demonstration and also used it in his *Erreurs sur la musique dans l'Encyclopédie* (Paris: Sebastien Jorry, 1755), pp. 53–56; *CTW,* 5:223–25. He mentions the same method of proof in a letter to the abbé François Arnaud (see Julien Tiersot, "Lettres inédites de Rameau," *La Revue musicale* 16 [1935], 18–19).

51. Kintzler, *Jean-Philippe Rameau,* 99–133.

52. I take the distinction between denotation and connotation as used here from the earlier writings of Roland Barthes. We may choose from many examples the following passage as exemplary: "Connotation is a secondary meaning, whose signifier is itself constituted by a sign or system of primary signification, which is denotation: if E is the expression, C the content, and R the relation of the two which establishes the sign, the formula for the connotation is: (ERC) R C" (Roland Barthes, *S / Z,* trans. Richard Miller [New York: Hill and Wang, 1974], 7).

53. See especially Barthes's essay, "Rhetoric of the Image," recently reprinted in *The Responsibility of Forms: Critical Essays on Music, Art, and Representation,* trans. Richard Howard (New York: Hill and Wang, 1985), 27–30. Something similar to this model has been proposed by writers on eighteenth-century French musical aesthetics. In these instances the authors have not connected the idea to specific musical practices of composers, and it is not always possible to tell whether their theoretical models are intended to be applied to actual practice in any substantive way. See, for example, Jean-Jacques Robrieux, "Jean-Philippe Rameau et l'opinion philosophique en France au dix-huitième siècle," *Studies on Voltaire and the Eighteenth Century* 238 (1985), 308–9, where something like it is used to describe French musical aesthetics in general, and Catherine Kintzler, *Jean-Philippe Rameau,* 124–32, where a similar model is applied to Rameau's recitative.

54. "On fait sonner ici l'Harmonie avant la Mélodie qui en est produite, pour qu'elle inspire au Chanteur le sentiment dont il doit être affecté indépendamment des paroles: sentiment qui frappera tout homme sans prévention, qui voudra bien se livrer aux purs effets de la Nature" (*OSN,* 99; *CTW,* 3:316).

55. Lawrence Kramer, *Music as Cultural Practice, 1800–1900* (Berkeley: University of California Press, 1990), 1–20.

56. The transcription is based on *H score 1733,* 2.

57. "Supposé qu'on mette des paroles en Musique, il faut y considerer pour lors le rapport qu'ont entr'elles les Phrases du discours qu'expriment ces paroles, & tâcher d'y conformer, le plus qu'il est possible, le rapport des *Modulations.*

"Si l'on veut qu'une Phrase ait beaucoup de rapport à celle qui la précede ou qui luy succede, on ne doit pas manquer de donner à ces deux Phrases les *Modulations* les plus relatives; & par la même raison, si ces Phrases ont peu de rapport entr'elles, on tâche de leur donner des *Modulations* proportionnées, &c." (*NS,* 41; *CTW,* 51).

58. For a different analysis of this monologue that also considers the relation-

ship between singer and accompaniment, see Cuthbert Girdlestone, *Jean-Philippe Rameau: His Life and Work*, rev. ed. (New York: Dover, 1969), 132–34.

59. James R. Anthony, *French Baroque Music from Beaujoyeulx to Rameau*, rev. ed. (New York: W. W. Norton, 1978), 86.

60. ATYS. / TRAGEDIE. / MISE EN MUSIQUE. / *Par Feu M^r. De Lully Esc^er. Con^er. / Secretaire du Roy, Maison, Couronne / de France et de ses Finances, et Surjntendant / de la Musique de Sa Majesté.* / SECONDE EDITION. / Gravée par H. de Baussen. / A PARIS. / *A l'Entrée de la Porte de l'Academie Royale / de Musique au Palais Royal, / ruë S^t. Honoré.* / M. DCC IX / *Avec Privilege du Roy.* [(Facsimile, Béziers: Société de musicologie de Languedoc, 1987), 52.]

61. A connection nicely made through instrumental coloration in William Christie's recording of *Atys* (Harmonia mundi France 901257.59).

Chapter 3
Rameau's Twins

1. Paul-Marie Masson, "L'Opéra au xviiie siècle. Les premières représentations du 'Dardanus' de Rameau (novembre–décembre 1739)," *La Revue musicale* 2 (April 1903): 167–73.

2. Graham Sadler points out that the redating of Voltaire's letters from the 1730s places Rameau's employment by La Pouplinière after the premiere of *Hippolyte* (Sadler and Albert Cohen, "Jean-Philippe Rameau," in *The New Grove French Baroque Masters: Lully, Charpentier, Lalande, Couperin, Rameau* [New York: W. W. Norton, 1986], 221, and Graham Sadler, "Patrons and Pasquinades: Rameau in the 1730s," *Journal of the Royal Musical Association* 113 [1988]: 314–24).

3. A detailed study of this brief but important exchange has yet to be made, but see J. T. de Booy, "Denis Diderot: Ecrits inconnus de jeunesse," 2 vols., *Studies on Voltaire and the Eighteenth Century* 119–20 (1974), 119:341–963.

4. See Herbert Schneider, *Die Rezeption der Opern Lullys im Frankreich des Ancien régime*, Mainzer Studien zur Musikwissenschaft, 16 (Tutzing: Hans Schneider, 1982), 75–122, and Lois Rosow, "Lully's *Armide* at the Paris Opéra: A Performance History: 1686–1766" (Ph.D. diss., Brandeis University, 1981), 340–435.

5. The most important study of Rameau's analysis of "Enfin" is E. Cynthia Verba, "The Development of Rameau's Thoughts on Modulation and Chromatics," *Journal of the American Musicological Society* 26 (1973): 69–91. See also the discussions by Eugène Borrel, *L'Interprétation de la musique française (de Lully à la révolution)* (Paris: Félix Alcan, 1934), 196–210; idem, *Jean-Baptiste Lully*, Euterpe, 7 (Paris: La Colombe, 1949), 37–47; Jean-Claude Malgoire in Catherine Kintzler and Jean-Claude Malgoire, eds., *Jean-Philippe Rameau. Musique raisonée* (N.p.: Stock, 1980), 201–15; Fritz Reckow, "'Cacher l'Art par l'Art même.' Jean-Baptiste Lullys 'Armide'-Monolog und die 'Kunst des Verbergens,'" *Analysen. Beiträge zu einer Problemgeschichte des Komponierens. Festschrift für Hans Heinrich Eggebrecht zum 65. Geburtstag,* Beiheft zum Archiv für Musikwissenschaft, 23 (Stuttgart: F. Steiner, 1984), 128–57.

6. I have previously made this argument in "Rameau Reading Lully: Meaning and System in Rameau's Recitative Tradition," *Cambridge Opera Journal* 6 (March 1994): 1–17.

7. This is especially suggestive because it points up our tendency, like Rameau's, to privilege music in the analysis of opera. See Carolyn Abbate, "Analysis," *The New Grove Dictionary of Opera,* ed. Stanley Sadie, 4 vols. (London: Macmillan, 1992), 1:116–20.

8. Allan R. Keiler, "Music as Metalanguage: Rameau's Fundamental Bass," in *Music Theory: Special Topics,* ed. Richmond Browne (New York: Academic Press, 1981), 83–100.

9. "Je remarque d'abord que M. Rameau l'a cité avec raison en exemple d'une modulation exacte & très-bien liée: mais cet éloge appliqué au morceau dont il s'agit, devient une véritable satyre, & M. Rameau lui-même se seroit bien gardé de mériter une semblable louange en pareil cas: car que peut-on concevoir de plus mal conçu que cette régularité scolastique dans une scene où l'emportement, la tendresse & le contraste des passions opposées mettent l'Actrice & les Spectateurs dans la plus vive agitation?" (*LSL,* 79–80; *QDB,* 1:751–52).

10. "Armide furieuse vient poignarder son ennemi. A son aspect, elle hésite, elle se laisse attendrir, le poignard lui tombe des mains; elle oublie tous ses projets de vengeance, & n'oublie pas un seul instant sa modulation. Les réticences, les interruptions, les transitions intellectuelles que le Poëte offroit au Musicien n'ont pas été une seule fois saisies par celui-ci" (*LSL,* 80; *QDB,* 1:752).

11. *OSN,* 70; *CTW,* 3:301. A facsimile of this print can also be found in *QDB,* 3:1731–1885.

12. There is intentional irony in Rameau's argument, for Rousseau himself had commented in the *Encyclopédie* article on the cadence, "CADENCE, . . . *en terme de chant,* . . . se fait ordinairement sur la pénultieme note d'une phrase musicale, d'où sans doute il a pris le nom de *cadence.* Quoique ce mot soit ici très-mal adapté, & qu'il ait été condamné par la plûpart de ceux qui ont écrit sur cette matiere, il a cependant tout-à-fait prévalu; c'est le seul dont on se serve aujourd'hui à Paris en ce sens, & il est inutile de disputer contre l'usage" (*Encyclopédie, ou Dictionnaire raisonné des sciences, des arts et des métiers,* ed., Denis Diderot and Jean le Rond d'Alembert, 28 vols. [Paris: various publishers, 1751–1772], facsimile in 5 vols. [New York: Pergamon Press, 1969], 2:515).

13. "*Tril* justement semblable à celui des Trompettes dans les Chants de Victoire" (*OSN,* 70; *CTW,* 3:301). More generally, see *OSN,* 70–71, especially notes (*k*) and (*l*) (*CTW,* 3:301–2). The notion of the cadence as a *repos absolu* was part of Rameau's theoretical vocabulary as well; see, for example, *Démonstration du principe de l'harmonie* (Paris: Durand, Pissot, 1750), 36–38; *CTW,* 3:184–85.

14. "Un Auteur, qui me fait la grace d'adopter mes Principes, n'ignore pas sans doute l'intime rapport déja cité entre le *Mode majeur* & le *mineur,* il n'ignore pas, non plus, que celui-ci doit son origine au premier, qu'il en dépend, & que s'il a la molesse en partage, l'autre au contraire est mâle, vigoreux" (*OSN,* 74; *CTW,* 3:303).

15. "Eviter tout repos dès le début jusqu'à la fin du deuxiéme vers, pour y faire sentir la liaison du sens, puisque la même *Tonique* subsiste jusqu'à l'hémistiche du deuxiéme, où elle passe à une autre *Tonique,* voilà déja beaucoup; mais employer d'abord le *Mode mineur,* pour que sa molesse opposée à la vigueur du *Majeur* y ajoûte un nouvel aiguillon, & la redouble, pour ainsi dire, dans le moment que ce *Majeur* va terminer un repos absolu, sur ces mots, *ce superbe Vainqueur,* voilà le grand coup de Maître" (*OSN,* 74–75; *CTW,* 3:303–4).

16. "Les mots de *charme* & de *sommeil* ont été pour le Musicien un piége inévitable; il a oublié la fureur d'Armide, pour faire ici un petit somme, dont il se réveillera au mot *percer*" (*LSL*, 82; *QDB*, 1:754).

17. "... fait souhaiter un nouveau repos sur la *Tonique* qui doit la suivre: de sorte qu'on sent par-là qu'Armide a encore quelque chose à dire" (*OSN*, 80; *CTW*, 3:306).

18. "Le monologue débute par le *Ton mineur* de *mi*, & passe à son *majeur* relatif à la tierce, qui est celui de *sol*, pour donner plus de force aux épithètes dont Armide caractérise son héros; de-là, pour faire sentir sa réflexion sur l'accident qui le met en sa possession, *Le charme du sommeil le livre à ma vengeance*, vient immédiatement *sol dièse*, qui donne justement le *Ton* de la quarte du *régnant*, savoir le *mineur* de *la*; puis se livrant à son transport, c'est par ce *Ton régnant* qu'elle exprime, *Je vais percer son invincible coeur*. On sent tous les effets de cette belle modulation, sans en savoir la cause, même sans s'en être jamais occupé: quelle est heureuse!" (Jean-Philippe Rameau, *Code de musique pratique* [Paris: De l'Imprimerie royale, 1760], 168–69; *CTW*, 4:192–93). Cited in Paul-Marie Masson, *L'Opéra de Rameau* (Paris: Henri Laurens, 1930), 164.

19. Masson, *L'Opéra de Rameau*, 173–76. I would, with some small reservations, include the commentaries of Borrel, Malgoire, and Reckow (see n. 5) in the same category as Masson.

20. "On appelle *moduler* l'art de conduire un chant & son harmonie, tant dans un même *Ton*, que d'un *Ton* à un autre" (Rameau, *Code de musique pratique*, 135; *CTW*, 4:159). See Masson's remarks in *L'Opéra de Rameau*, 480 and 480 n. 1.

21. "De la Modulation en général," "Du rapport des *Tons*, de leur entrelacement, de la longueur de leurs phrases conséquemment à leurs rapports, du moment de leur début, & de la marche fondamentale," "Notes d'ornement ou de goût, où l'on traite encore de la Modulation," "De la Composition à plusieurs parties," "De l'Expression" (Rameau, *Code de musique pratique*, 135, 138, 151, 159, 165; *CTW*, 4:159, 162, 175, 183, 189).

22. Transcription based on *C score 1737*, 142–43.

23. "Premièrement, la déclaration d'amour que vous m'avez donnée pour la troisième Scène du second Acte ne va pas. Tout le monde la trouve jolie. . . . Elle fut admirée d'un chacun; il faut lui rendre justice de ce côté-là; mais une déclaration doit toujours finir par une cadence soutenue, et il n'y a pas moyen avec votre syllabe; il m'en faut une qui finisse, par exemple, par *Prendre*. Je serai à mon aise pour placer ma cadence là-dessus; au nom de Dieu, des syllabes heureuses et je réponds de tout.

"On me conseille de finir le troisième Acte par un Quatuor, il me faut des paroles: mais il ne faut qu'aucun vers tienne à l'autre, pour que je fasse fuguer mes quatre parties" (Antoine-Gautier de Montdorge, *Réflexions d'un peintre sur l'opéra* [The Hague: Pierre Gosse, 1743], 22–26, cited in François Moureau, "Les Poètes de Rameau," *JPR*, 72).

24. "On a reproché à M. Rameau de ne point entendre le Récitatif; il me paraît même que quelques-uns de ses amis n'osant au commencement le justifier de ce côté-là, ont mieux aimé avancer que tout le monde peut faire un Récitatif, que de soutenir la bonté du sien. Il est pourtant bien constaté qu'il n'y a rien de si difficile au monde que de faire le Récitatif" (*Lettre de M. Grimm sur Omphale* [1752], 9; facsimile in *QDB*, 1:11).

25. Aside from Rameau's appendix, the principal source on the early alterations made for *Hippolyte et Aricie* is the review in the *Mercure de France* 25 (October 1733): 2233–49. See also Graham Sadler, "Rameau, Pellegrin and the Opéra: The Revisions of 'Hippolyte et Aricie' during Its First Season," *The Musical Times* 124 (September 1983): 533–37 and Thomas R. Green, "Early Rameau Sources: Studies in the Origins and Dating of the Operas and Other Musical Works," 3 vols. (Ph.D. diss., Brandeis University, 1992), 2:553–59.

26. See also Cuthbert Girdlestone's comments on these versions of act three, scene one, in *Jean-Philippe Rameau: His Life and Work*, rev. ed. (New York: Dover, 1969), 155–57, 176–79.

27. A definitive statement on the complex evolution of act three, scene one, must await a critical edition. At present, the most thorough treatment remains Malherbe's in *OC*, 6:lxxx, and my comments here reflect his position, which seems plausible.

28. Versification here is reconstructed from the musical manuscript *F-Pn*, Vm² 319: 175. The continued presence of "Cruelle mère" in livrets may indicate that the recitative added in 1742 was not by Pellegrin. In 1742 the abbé was nearing eighty years of age and the end of his life, and the exceptionally unwieldy versification of the new recitative further supports the possibility that another author was involved.

29. *OC*, vol. 6, can be misleading on these scenes, unless one reads carefully. Here the editors reverse their policy of favoring the 1733 version by providing the 1742 musical text in the main body of the edition (56–61) and relegating the 1733 version to the appendix (430–33). (See also pp. lxxv, lxxvii.)

30. Transcriptions based on *H score 1733*, 6, and "Hippolyte et Aricie, Tragedie de Mᴿ. Pellegrin mise en Musique par Mᴿ. Rameau; représentée pour la premiere fois le premier octobre 1733," *F-Pn*, Vm² 319: 4.

31. Here the text of *OC*, vol. 6, is contradictory. On p. lxxv Malherbe claims that the edition uses the 1742 text, relegating the 1733 version to the appendix; on p. lxxxi he claims the opposite. In fact, the edition uses the 1742 version in its main body (pp. 267–70) and places the 1733 version in the appendix (pp. 450–53).

32. Transcriptions based on *H score 1733*, 133–34, and *F-Pn*, Vm² 319: 132.

33. Transcriptions based on *D score 1739*, 1–2, and *D score 1744*, 2.

34. Transcriptions based on *D score 1739*, xviii–xix, and *D score 1744*, xix.

35. Transcriptions based on *C score 1737*, 155–56, and *C score 1754*, 133–34.

36. Jean-Philippe Rameau, *Treatise on Harmony*, trans. Philip Gossett (New York: Dover, 1971), 82. For the original French, see *CTW*, 1:97–98.

37. The ritournelle, along with those portions of the scene omitted from example 3.8b, may be found in *OC*, 8:420–21.

38. Graham Sadler, "A Re-Examination of Rameau's Self-Borrowings," in *Jean-Baptiste Lully and the Music of the French Baroque: Essays in Honor of James R. Anthony*, ed. John Hajdu Heyer (Cambridge: Cambridge University Press, 1989), 259–89; see especially 262–67.

39. Schneider, *Die Rezeption der Opern Lullys im Frankreich des Ancien régime*, 79.

40. Rosow, "Lully's 'Armide' at the Paris Opéra," 398–416. More generally, see Schneider, *Die Rezeption der Opern Lullys im Frankreich des Ancien Régime*, 75–122.

41. Scholars have long recognized in the 1754 revival of *Castor* and the 1756 revival of *Zoroastre* an increased tendency to choose simpler musical parameters in setting texts. See, for example, Graham Sadler, "Rameau's 'Zoroastre': The 1756 Reworking," *The Musical Times* 120 (April 1979): 301–3.

42. Transcriptions based on *C score 1737*, 38–39, and *C score 1754*, 51–52.

43. Sadler, "Rameau's 'Zoroastre,'" 302.

44. Transcription based on "Zoroastre, Opéra, tragédie avec un prologue, par Cahusac, Musique de Rameau. 1749," *F-Po*, A.167ᶜ: 128–29.

45. "Puisqu'il est de fait qu'excepté les *Indes Galantes, les Talens lyriques* & *Zoroastre*, tous les Ouvrages que mit au Théâtre notre illustre Musicien, n'ont jamais eu dans leur nouveauté une affluence de Spectateurs aussi soutenue & aussi continuelle que dans les reprises subséquentes & surtout dans les dernières" ("Essai d'eloge historique de feu M. Rameau, compositeur de la musique du cabinet du roi, pensionnaire de sa majesté & de l'Académie royale de musique," *Mercure de France* [October 1764]: 189–90).

46. This kind of situation has been documented, for example, with respect to *Dardanus*. Of the 1744 revival Paul-Marie Masson commented, "Nous avons très peu de détails sur cette reprise, qui était pourtant en grande partie une création. Il semble bien que le public n'en ait pas saisi l'importance. . . . Le *Mercure de France* se contente de mentionner l'événement, comme une reprise ordinaire, sans aucun commentaire particulier, sans aucune allusion à la version nouvelle. Il renvoie même ses lecteurs au compte rendu qu'il avait donné en 1739, et qui était devenu inutisable!" ("Les Deux versions du 'Dardanus' de Rameau," *Acta musicologica* 26 (1954): 38–39. Malherbe wrote of the 1764 revival, "Lorsque reparut *Dardanus*, après ce long intervalle, quelques gazettes se crurent obligées de raconter à nouveau la pièce, comme si elle était déjà oubliée; et, dans leur empressement à signaler les changements du livret, elles ne se souvenaient guère de l'époque à laquelle ils avaient été effectués; plus d'un critique voulut tenir ainsi pour spéciales à 1760 des modifications qui, nous l'avons démontré plus haut, dataient de 1744" (*OC*, 8:lviii).

Chapter 4
Rameau Mise-en-Scène

1. Thomas Christensen, *Rameau and Musical Thought in the Enlightenment*, Cambridge Studies in Music Theory and Analysis, 4 (Cambridge: Cambridge University Press, 1993). See also Scott Burnham, "Musical and Intellectual Values: Interpreting the History of Tonal Theory," *Current Musicology* 53 (1993): 79–83.

2. See Sigiswald Kuijken's brochure notes to Jean-Philippe Rameau, *Zoroastre* (Harmonia mundi 1C 157) and Paul-Marie Masson, "Les Deux versions du 'Dardanus' de Rameau," *Acta musicologica* 26 (1954): 40–41.

3. Paul-Marie Masson, *L'Opéra de Rameau* (Paris: Henri Laurens, 1930), 98, 109; Graham Sadler and Albert Cohen, "Jean-Philippe Rameau," in *The New Grove French Baroque Masters* (New York: W. W. Norton, 1986), 259; idem, notes to Jean-Philippe Rameau, *Castor et Pollux* (Erato 4509–95311–2); Cuthbert Girdlestone, Albert Cohen, and Mary Cyr, "Rameau, Jean-Philippe," *The New Grove Dictionary of Music and Musicians*, ed. Stanley Sadie, 6th ed., 20 vols. (New York: Macmillan, 1980), 15:565–66.

4. I borrow this notion from recent work by Scott Burnham and intend by it something of Burnham's larger point as well: what are *we* about when we go about observing Rameau? I thank Prof. Burnham for sharing his unpublished paper, "How Music Matters: Poetic Content Revisited."

5. "Un Seigneur Anglois s'étant présenté à la cinquieme représentation de *Zoroastre,* pour avoir place dans les Balcons, dans les Loges, à l'Amphithéâtre, on lui disoit par-tout, que toutes les places étoient retenues. 'Voilà, dit-il, la chose la plus singuliere & la plus étrange que j'ai vu de ma vie. Je n'entre pas dans une maison de Paris, que je n'y entende dire un mal horrible de cet Opéra; & j'y viens quatre fois de suite pour le voir, sans pouvoir y trouver de place. Il n'y a que des François au monde capables de ces contradictions'" ([Jean-Marie-Bernard Clément,] *Anecdotes dramatiques,* 3 vols. [Paris: La veuve Duchesne, 1775], 2:282–83). See also Friedrich Melchior Grimm, *Correspondance littéraire, philosophique et critique par Grimm, Diderot, Raynal, Meister, etc.,* ed. Maurice Tourneux, 16 vols. (Paris: Garnier frères, 1877–1882), 1:390.

6. "La marquise de Pompadour, qui a la surintendance des spectacles, vient de régler que nous n'aurions à l'Opéra que de la musique de Rameau d'ici à deux ans, quelque mécontentement qu'en montre le public. On a renvoyé au magasin l'opéra de *Médée,* déjà tout appris, tout répété. Adieu le bon goût et la bonne musique française!" (René-Louis de Voyer de Paulmy, marquis d'Argenson, *Journal et mémoires du marquis d'Argenson,* ed. Edme-Jacques-Benoit Rathery, 9 vols. [Paris: Madame veuve Jules Renouard, 1859–1867], 5:344). This was not the first time such fears had been expressed. As Émile Dacier noted, audience members responded much the same way in 1739, when performances of *Dardanus* were replaced with performances of Rameau's opéra-ballet *Les Fêtes d'Hébé* ("L'Opéra au xviiie siècle. Les Premières représentations du 'Dardanus' de Rameau [novembre-décembre 1739]," *La Revue musicale* 3 [April 1903]: 169–70).

7. "On prétend que M. d'Argenson, qui a actuellement l'Opéra dans son département, s'est expliqué aux directeurs et leur a signifié qu'il ne vouloit pas qu'on donnât plus d'un opéra de Rameau par an; les partisans de sa musique sont furieux de cet ordre, et publient que ce ministre veut faire tomber l'Opéra, que ce grand génie soutenoit lui seul, dans le dessein de l'ôter aux directeurs actuels, pour le donner à Rebel, Francoeur et Jéliotte, qu'il protège. On ajoute que Rameau est piqué jusqu'au vif, jure de ne plus travailler, et que même il a retiré une tragédie de lui et de Cahusac, qu'il avoit donnée pour cet hiver.

"Je crois tout cela outré, et M. de Boizemont, qui est toujours chez Mme d'Argenson, m'a dit que M. d'Argenson, à la vérité, ne vouloit pas qu'on mit plus de deux opéras de Rameau par année; et que c'étoit afin de ne pas ôter l'émulation aux autres musiciens; mais qu'il ne pensoit, ni de près ni de loin, à *tanner* ces directeurs-ci et à donner l'Opéra à ce triumvirat" (Charles Collé, *Journal et mémoires de Charles Collé sur les hommes de lettres, les ouvrages dramatiques et les événements le plus mémorables du règne de Louis XV (1748–1772),* ed. Honoré Bonhomme, rev. ed., 3 vols [Paris: Firmin Didot frères, 1868], 1:82–83).

8. Ibid., 1:300.

9. Ibid., 1:321.

10. Charles Malherbe, for example, reports that a revival of *Hippolyte et Aricie* slated for the 1751–52 season was abandoned in the middle of preparations: "Une

reprise avait été cependant proposée pour la saison 1751–52, et approuvée offi-
ciellement par une lettre de d'Argenson en date de 'Versailles, 31 may.' On com-
mença même à brosser de nouveaux décors, comme nous le verrons plus loin; mais
le projet n'aboutit pas et la pièce ne reparut que le vendredi 25 février 1757" (*OC*,
6:lxvi).

11. On Rameau's consideration of Voltaire's livret *Pandore*, see Sadler, *The New
Grove French Baroque Masters*, 227, and Thomas R. Green, "Early Rameau Sources:
Studies in the Origins and Dating of the Operas and Other Musical Works," 3 vols.
(Ph.D. diss., Brandeis University, 1992), 2:592–96.

12. On *Linus*, see Sadler, *The New Grove French Baroque Masters*, 231, and
Green, "Early Rameau Sources," 2:680–84. On the dating of the revised versions
of *Zoroastre* and *Castor et Pollux*, see Green, "Early Rameau Sources," 2:684–87.
On the dating of the earliest material for *Les Boréades*, see Green, "Les Fragments
d'opéras dans la partition autographe de *Zéphyre*," *JPR*, 266–68, and idem, "Early
Rameau Sources," 2:675–79. For a different, later dating of initial work on *Les
Boréades* about 1757, see Catherine Kintzler, *Jean-Philippe Rameau: Splendeur et
naufrage de l'esthétique du plaisir à l'âge classique* (Paris: Le Sycomore, 1983),
241–55, and Sylvie Bouissou, *Jean-Philippe Rameau: Les Boréades ou la tragédie
oubliée* (Paris: Méridiens Klincksieck, 1992), 40–41. (The latter source takes note
of Green's article in *JPR*.)

13. Graham Sadler, "Rameau's Last Opera: *Abaris, ou Les Boréades*," *The Musical Times* 116 (April 1975): 327–29; Kintzler, *Jean-Philippe Rameau: Splendeur et
naufrage*, 241–55; Bouissou, *Jean-Philippe Rameau: Les Boréades*, 87–127;
Green, "Early Rameau Sources," 2:675–79.

14. "Peut-être lorsque l'ouvrage sera connu, m'estimerois-je fort heureux qu'on
voulût le laisser sur la tête d'un autre; mais quelque soit alors le jugement du Public, la honte ou l'honneur ne doivent rejaillir que sur moi, & j'attends mon sort
avec un désir constant de reconnoître mes fautes, de les corriger & de plaire" ("Lettre de M. de Cahusac à M. Remond de Sainte Albine, sur les bruits qui courent que
M. de Cahusac n'est point auteur du nouvel opera de *Zoroastre*," *Mercure de France*
[November 1749], 203).

15. Clément, *Anecdotes dramatiques*, 2:284. See also Grimm, *Correspondance
littéraire*, 1:395.

16. "Les paroles sont de l'abbé Pellegrin, et dignes de l'abbé Pellegrin" (D661,
CWV, 86:403).

17. "En offrant sur la Scène Lyrique un Personnage aussi célèbre, on a crû ne
devoir épargner ni recherches, ni soins pour rassembler les traits principaux qui le
distinguent dans l'Histoire Ancienne, & c'est sur ces materiaux qu'on a tracé son
caractere, & le plan de cet Ouvrage. . . .

"Ce Personnage & le contraste qu'il fournit, sont tirez du fonds du sujet même.
Zoroastre eut à combattre & à détruire l'idolâtrie répandue alors dans la Perse, ainsi
que dans presque tout le reste du monde" (*Z livret 1749*, 5–6).

18. "Notre Tragédie & notre Comédie ont une étendue & une durée qui sont
soutenues par les charmes du discours, par la finesse des détails, par la variété des
saillies de l'esprit. L'action se divise en Actes: chaque Acte est partagé en Scènes:
les Scènes amenent successivement les situations: les situations, à leur tour, entre-
tiennent la chaleur, forment le noeud, conduisent au dénouement, & le préparent.

"Telles doivent être, mais avec plus de précision encore, les Tragédies & les Comédies en Danse: je dis, avec plus de précision, parce que le geste est plus précis que le discours. Il faut plusieurs mots, pour exprimer une pensée: un seul mouvement peut peindre plusieurs pensées, & quelquefois la plus forte situation. Il faut donc que l'action théâtrale marche toujours avec la plus grande rapidité, qu'il n'y ait point d'entrée, de figure, de pas inutile. Une bonne Piéce de Théâtre en Danse doit être un Extrait serré d'une excellente Piéce Dramatique écrite" (Louis de Cahusac, *La Danse ancienne et moderne ou Traité historique de la danse*, 3 vols. [The Hague: Jean Neaulme, 1754], 3:149–50).

19. "Le chant si naturel à l'homme, en se développant, a inspiré aux autres hommes qui en ont été frappés, des gestes relatifs aux différens sons dont ce chant étoit composé; le corps alors s'est agité, les bras se sont ouverts ou fermés, les piés ont formé des pas lents ou rapides, les traits du visage ont participé à ces mouvemens divers, tout le corps a répondu par des positions, des ébranlemens, des attitudes aux sons dont l'oreille étoit affectée: ainsi le chant qui étoit l'expression d'un sentiment a fait développer une seconde expression qui étoit dans l'homme qu'on a nommée *danse*. Et voilà ses deux principes primitifs.

"On voit par ce peu de mots que la voix & le geste ne sont pas plus naturels à l'espece humaine, que le chant & la *danse*; & que l'un & l'autre sont, pour ainsi dire, les instrumens de deux arts auxquels ils ont donné lieu" (*Encyclopédie, ou Dictionnaire raisonné des sciences, des arts et des métiers*, ed., Denis Diderot and Jean le Rond d'Alembert, 28 vols. [Paris: various publishers, 1751–1772],; facsimile in 5 vols. [New York: Pergamon Press, 1969], 4:623).

20. "Si le plan général de l'Opéra est bien fait, comme le sont, par exemple, tous ceux de Quinault, chacune des parties qui le composent est relative à l'action principale. Par conséquent pour qu'il soit bien exécuté, il faut que chaque Danse prise séparément s'y rapporte, & fasse ainsi, de maniere ou d'autre, partie de cette action" (Cahusac, *La Danse ancienne et moderne*, 3:126–27).

21. Kintzler, *Jean-Philippe Rameau: Splendeur et naufrage*, 80–94.

22. Paolo Russo, "Les Incertitudes de la tragédie lyrique: *Zoroastre* de Louis de Cahusac," *Revue de musicologie* 75 (1989): 47–64. See also Graham Sadler, "Rameau's 'Zoroastre': The 1756 Reworking," *The Musical Times* 120 (April 1979): 301–3. This is not the first time that the second version of a Rameau opera was associated with a *comédie larmoyante*. Russo seems to be unaware that Cideville playfully associated *Dardanus* with Nivelle de La Chaussée's *L'École des mères* in a 1744 letter, as reported by Masson in "Les Deux versions du 'Dardanus' de Rameau," 39. Jacques Morel, meanwhile, has associated the *comédie larmoyante* with a more historically plausible date, citing the 1733 *Hippolyte et Aricie* (see "*Hippolyte et Aricie* de Rameau et Pellegrin dans l'histoire du mythe de Phèdre," *JPR*, 98–99).

23. "Il est un autre genre de spectacle bien plus digne de censure, puisqu'il est fondé sur un merveilleux si plat, si ennuyeux et si ridicule qu'il n'y a pas de quoi amuser les enfants. Quinault savait masquer la difformité de ce genre par des vers doux et coulants, par des idées quelquefois sublimes, presque toujours heureuses. Un de ses successeurs, M. de Cahusac, à qui un génie, ennemi de nos oreilles, a octroyé à forfait le rare et effroyable talent d'amasser dans des vers raboteux, du non sens, en dépit d'Apollon et de Minerve, a bien su le secret de rétablir l'insipidité et

l'extravagance du genre dans toute sa force. L'Académie royale de musique nous a ennuyés, pendant tout l'hiver, par un certain *Zoroastre* de ce poëte, dont la moindre des vertus magiques est de faire dormir debout" (Grimm, *Correspondance littéraire*, 3:227). The last expression seems to involve an untranslatable pun, based on the expression "un conte à dormir debout," which may be translated as "tall tale" or "old wives' tale."

24. "Et qu'il ne sait pas compter jusqu'à cinq, il s'est si fort embrouillé dans ses calculs que, dans chaque acte, il a été obligé de faire faire [*sic*] nuit et jour deux ou trois fois pour qu'il fît jour à la fin de la pièce" (ibid.). On Grimm's reactions to the 1749 *Zoroastre*, see *Correspondance littéraire*, 1:385, 390, 394–95, 408.

25. "Cest à cette jalousie que le magnifique Opéra de *Zoroastre* a été sacrifié. Les Acteurs ne sont-ils pas malades quand ils le veulent? Esperons, de revoir au plutôt cette célèbre Tragédie dans tout son éclat. On l'a dit encore embellie par des corrections que son illustre Auteur a jugé à propos d'y faire" ([Pierre-Louis d'Aquin de Chateau-Lyon,] *Siecle litteraire de Louis XV ou Lettres sur les hommes celebres*, 2d ed., 2 vols. [Amsterdam: Duchesne, 1754], 1:67–68).

26. "Mais, ce n'est pas assez de justifier le choix de mon Sujet & le titre de ma Piece; il m'importe infiniment davantage de faire voir si ma Fable est raisonnable. J'avoüerai d'abord, sans prétendre censurer l'élegant Auteur qui m'a ouvert cette carriere, que son *Thésée* m'a toûjours paru trop crédule, & qu'un Fils aussi vertueux qu'*Hippolyte* ne devoit pas être condamné si legerement, sur la déposition d'une femme suspecte, & sur l'indice d'une épée qu'on pouvoit avoir prise à son insçu, je sçais qu'une passion aussi aveugle que la jalousie, peut porter à de plus grandes erreurs, mais cela ne suffit pas au Théatre; & le grand secret pour être approuvé, c'est de mettre les Spectateurs au point de sentir, qu'ils feroient de même que les Acteurs, s'ils se trouvoient en pareille situation" (*H livret 1733*, iii–iv).

27. Cuthbert Girdlestone, *La Tragédie en musique (1673–1750) considérée comme genre littéraire* (Geneva: Droz, 1972), 245–67. On Pellegrin's attitudes toward the literary sources of *Médée*, see his "Dissertation sur la tragedie de Médée," *Mercure de France* (January 1729): 152–73. As Jean Duron has pointed out, Pellegrin was looked down on socially in part because he had been forced to make a living writing popular verse (see Jean Duron, "Pellegrin, Abbé Simon-Joseph," *The New Grove Dictionary of Opera*, ed. Stanley Sadie, 4 vols. [London: Macmillan, 1992], 3:939–40).

28. "La Musique de cet Opéra, il y a 25 ans, paroissoit nouvelle & d'un ton auquel on n'étoit pas accoutumé. Une circonstance, que le Public apprendra, peut-être, avec plaisir, doit rendre cette Musique précieuse aux vrais connoisseurs. C'est elle qui, de l'aveu du célèbre M. *Rameau*, a été la cause occasionnelle des chef-d'oeuvres dont il a enrichi notre Théâtre lyrique. Ce grand homme entendit *Jephté*; le caractère noble & distingué de cet ouvrage le frappa, par des points analogues apparemment à la mâle fécondité de son génie. Il conçut dès ce moment, que notre Musique dramatique étoit susceptible d'une nouvelle force & de nouvelles beautés. Il forma le projet d'en composer; il osa être créateur. Il n'en convient pas moins que *Jephté* procura *Hipolite* & *Aricie*" (*Mercure de France* [March 1761]: 153). See also the "Essai d'eloge historique de feu M. Rameau, compositeur de la musique du cabinet du roi, pensionnaire de sa majesté & de l'Académie royale de musique," *Mercure de France* (October 1764): 186–87.

29. "On s'accommodera peut-être mal d'une héroïne d'opéra qui n'est point amoureuse, cependant que mes calomniateurs disent que mon ouvrage est impie, le parterre le trouvera peut-être trop sage et trop sévère, il se rebutera de voir l'amour traité seulement de séduction sur un théâtre où il est toujours consacré comme une vertu" (D690, *CWV,* 86:436).

30. "Il sera beau que deux actes se soutiennent sans jargon d'amourette dans le temple de Quinault. Je maintiens que c'est traiter l'amour avec le respect qu'il mérite que de ne le pas prodiguer et ne le faire paraître que comme un maître absolu. Rien n'est si froid quand il n'est pas nécessaire" (D1003, *CWV,* 87:340. See also D999, *CWV,* 87:332–33, and D1000, *CWV,* 87:333–35).

31. "Les noms de Vénus et d'Adonis trouvent dans cette tragédie une place plus naturelle qu'on ne le croirait d'abord: c'est en effet sur leurs terres que l'action se passe" (*OCV,* 3:4).

32. "Notre ami fait un nouvel opéra intitulé Sansom [sic] pour Rameau. . . . et comme ce qui plait dans son opéra sont Les [? duo,] trio, Cheurs, airs de caractère &tc, il ne mettra dans son opéra que très peu de Récitatif, et tâchera de ménager au musicien Les occasions d'exercer La sorte de talent qu'il a" (D682, *CWV,* 86:430).

33. "Voylà tout L'intérest que je connois dans un opera. Un beau spectacle bien varié, des fêtes brillantes, baucoup d'airs, peu de récitatif, des actes courts. . . . Je veux que le Samson soit dans un goust nouvau, rien qu'une scène de récitatif à chaque acte, point de confident, point de verbiage" (D971, *CWV,* 87:294).

34. In this respect, Cuthbert Girdlestone's comparison of the 1733 *Hippolyte* and the 1737 *Castor,* while failing to acknowledge the pivotal role of *Samson,* is instructive. See *Jean-Philippe Rameau: His Life and Work,* rev. ed. (New York: Dover, 1969), 228–29.

35. On the likelihood that Gluck knew Rameau's work, see Bruce Alan Brown, *Gluck and the French Theatre in Vienna* (New York: Oxford University Press, 1991), 331, 362–63.

36. Girdlestone, *La Tragédie en musique (1673–1750),* 329–30.

37. "Pollux revoit son Frere avec Telaïre, sans en être jaloux; il a triumphé de son amour, pour se livrer tout entier à l'amitié qui l'unit à Castor" (*Mercure de France* [December 1737]: 2669).

38. "En stile d'Opera, pour deux Heros il falloit deux Amantes: la difficulté n'étoit donc qu'à justifier l'amour de Phébé par quelque supposition, & à la rendre du moins aussi nécessaire au dénoument que Telaire, qui ne l'est pas trop ellemême. J'aurois fait de Phébé, la Fille de Pluton; j'aurois supposé les deux Princesses liées aux deux Freres, par quelque promesse de leur Parens . . . Pollux, dans le fond amoureux de Telaire, se seroit fait violence par politique & par amitié, jusqu'à la mort de son Frere, qui lui auroit donné la liberté de faire éclater les vrais sentimens de son coeur. En paroissant infidelle, il auroit fait connoître qu'il n'étoit pas inconstant. Phébé loin de vivre en si bonne intelligence avec Telaire, l'auroit traitée ouvertement comme une Rivale aimée" (*Le Pour et contre* [1737], 319).

39. I have recounted these events in more detail in "Creative Process in Rameau's *Castor et Pollux,*" in *The Creative Process,* Studies in the History of Music, 3 (New York: Broude Brothers, 1992), 102–3.

40. See D1657, *CWV*, 89: 366; D1684, *CWV*, 89:420–21; D1694, *CWV*, 89:443–49.

41. "Le second Acte, heureusement imaginé, n'est composé que de Scénes intéressantes" (Pierre-François-Guyot Desfontaines, *Observations sur les écrits modernes* 20 [19 December 1739], 89; reprint, 34 vols. in 4 [Geneva: Slatkine, 1967], 3:298).

42. "Qualitez et deffauts de nos modernes, gens d'esprit et de peu de jugement; agréments de détails, impertinence dans le total, quelques vers charmants. Le sujet est un pot pourri d'incidents merveilleux qui ne vont pas ensemble, de sort que tout intérest est banni" (René-Louis de Voyer de Paulmy, marquis d'Argenson, "Notices sur les Oeuvres de théâtre," ed. H. Lagrave, *Studies on Voltaire and the Eighteenth Century,* 42–43 [Oxford: The Voltaire Foundation, 1966], 43:482).

43. Girdlestone, *Jean-Philippe Rameau: His Life and Work,* 127. See also Masson, "Les Deux versions du 'Dardanus' de Rameau," 42, and Graham Sadler, "La Bruère, Charles-Antoine Le Clerc de," *The New Grove Dictionary of Opera,* 2:1071–72.

44. Dacier, "L'Opéra au xviiie siècle," 166, 168.

45. On the chronology of these revisions, see *OC,* 10:xxxi–xxxv; Dacier, "L'Opéra au xviiie siècle," 168–73, and Green, "Early Rameau Sources," 2:589–91, 597–99.

46. "Plus on le raccourcit / Et plus il se rallonge" (cited in *OC,* 10:li; Dacier, "L'Opéra au xviiie siècle," 168; and Masson, "Les Deux versions du 'Dardanus' de Rameau," 38).

47. See, for example, the "Essai d'eloge historique de feu M. Rameau," 187.

48. "Je voudrais pouvoir vous abandonner toute la rétribution de cet opéra et je vous croirais encore bien mal payé, mais ayant destiné la moitié de ce qui devait m'en revenir à un homme de lettres qui est dans le besoin, je vous prie de partager avec lui. D'ailleurs, vous êtes l'unique maître de tout" (D690, *CWV,* 86:437).

49. "Quoique MM. Mondorge, Le Riche et Bernard aient travaillé au poème des *Talents,* ils n'ont pu parvenir à en faire un ouvrage passable? Ne plaignez-vous pas Rameau? Ne vous paraît-il pas bien malheureux? Quoi! toujours de mauvaises paroles! il mérite son sort. Depuis les *Indes Galantes,* il s'est expliqué qu'il ne travaillerait plus que sur des poèmes dont les auteurs lui abandonneraient la rétribution, et vous sentez bien que cette avarice le réduira communément à ce qu'il y a de plus misérable en ce genre" (Simon-Henri Dubuisson, *Lettres du Commissaire Dubuisson au Marquis de Caumont, 1735–1741,* ed. Albert Rouxel [Paris: P. Arnould, 1882], 569).

50. Collé, *Journal et mémoires,* 1:321.

51. "Je ne dissimulerai pas que ce poëme est foible par quelques endroits. L'illustre Artiste, chargé de les revêtir de l'éblouïssante parure de sa Musique, n'a pû cette fois-ci, par les prestiges ordinaires de son Art enchanteur, dérober ces défauts. Seroit-ce par un excès de complaisance, & pour vouloir être trop naturel, qu'il auroit une fois cessé d'être Rameau?" (Pierre-François-Guyot Desfontaines, *Observations sur les écrits modernes* 20 [19 December 1739], 90–91; reprint, 3:299).

52. "La musique est de mêsme, le musicien s'est picqué de se perfectioner davantage dans le récitatif" (d'Argenson, "Notices sur les Oeuvres de théâtre," 43:482).

Chapter 5
In the Mirror

1. "La jalousie enflamma la haine, qui eut recours à la discorde pour accabler Rameau: mais l'homme de génie méprisa les envieux, & ne leur répondit que par de nouveaux chefs-d'oeuvre, qui enfin les forcerent à se taire. La reprise de *Castor & Pollux* entraîna tous les suffrages; jamais succès n'a pu être comparé à celui-là, puisqu'il n'éprouva aucune contradiction, & que plus de cent représentations de suite ne purent diminuer le plaisir que tout Paris éprouvait à entendre ce bel opéra, qui parlait à la fois à l'ame, au coeur, à l'esprit, aux yeux, aux oreilles & à l'imagination" ([Jean-Benjamin de Laborde], *Essai sur la musique ancienne et moderne*, 4 vols. [Paris: Ph.-D. Pierres, 1780; facsimile, New York: AMS Press, 1978], 3:465).

2. See, for example, E. Cynthia Verba, "The Development of Rameau's Thoughts on Modulation and Chromatics," *Journal of the American Musicological Society* 26 (1973), 69–91, and Charles Dill, "Rameau Reading Lully: Meaning and System in Rameau's Recitative Tradition," *Cambridge Opera Journal* 6 (March 1994): 1–17.

3. The Bloomian narrative I have in mind here is found in Harold Bloom, *A Map of Misreading* (New York: Oxford University Press, 1975). See especially 41–62.

4. Jacques Lacan, "The Mirror Stage as Formative of the Function of the I as Revealed in the Psychoanalytic Experience," in *Écrits: A Selection*, trans. Alan Sheridan (New York: W. W. Norton, 1977), 1–7.

5. "Dans l'usage qu'il en a fait, on ne sçauroit lui contester les forces & la beauté de l'harmonie, le génie supérieur dans plusieurs symphonies, dans les choeurs, dans les morceaux de chant mesuré. Prèsque tous les airs de Danse de ce Musicien sont si saillans & si caractérisés, qu'en Italie & dans tous les Pays où l'on ne connoit que l'Opéra Italien, ce sont principalement les airs de ce Musicien François qu'on employe pour les Ballets. Mais pour un goût exquis dans la juste & sublime expression des paroles, pour un art aussi sçavant qu'ingénieux dans prèsque tous les Choeurs & dans un grand nombre de symphonies, n'employant que peu de moyens en apparence sous le voile auguste de la simplicité, qui pourroit refuser à l'immortel LULLI la justice que lui rendoit verbalement le grand RAMEAU, toutes les fois que l'occasion s'en présentoit?" ("Essai d'eloge historique de feu M. Rameau," *Mercure de France* [October 1764]: 197–98).

6. "Depuis que les écarts d'une mode nouvelle ont rendu sa musique plus simple à nos oreilles, par conséquent plus analogue au genre originaire de notre Opéra, elle semble être devenue plus précieuse au Public. Il est donc incontestable que ce n'est point par un goût du sentiment, mais par un caprice passager que cette mode partage notre attention, & même (disons-le en rougissant,) obtient une sorte de préférence" (*Mercure de France* [October 1764]: 190).

7. Jean-Baptiste Rousseau, *Correspondance de Jean-Baptiste Rousseau et de Brossette,* ed. Paul Bonnefon, 2 vols. (Paris: Société nouvelle de librairie et d'édition, 1910–1911), 2:281.

8. Bouissou has argued convincingly that the two rehearsals of *Les Boréades* in April, 1763, were probably intended for a later performance at Choisy that never occurred (Sylvie Bouissou, *Jean-Philippe Rameau. Les Boréades ou la tragédie oubliée* [Paris: Méridiens Klincksieck, 1992], 55–84).

9. Cuthbert Girdlestone, *Jean-Philippe Rameau: His Life and Work,* rev. ed. (New York: Dover, 1969), 560.

10. On the unity of *Les Boréades,* see Bouissou, *Jean-Philippe Rameau:* Les Boréades, 169–200.

11. See, for example, Carolyn Abbate and Roger Parker, "Dismembering Mozart," *Cambridge Opera Journal* 2 (July 1990): 187–95, and James Webster, "Mozart's Operas and the Myth of Musical Unity," *Cambridge Opera Journal* 2 (July 1990): 197–218.

12. Paul-Marie Masson, *L'Opéra de Rameau* (Paris: Henri Laurens, 1930), 51–52.

13. "En 1763, après la premiere représentation de *Castor* à Fontainebleau, . . . il dit encore à la même personne, au sujet de quelques nouveautés qu'on avoit voulu lui faire ajouter à son Opéra de *Castor & Pollux: Mon ami, j'ai plus de goût qu'autrefois, mais je n'ai plus de génie du tout*" ([Jean-Marie-Bernard Clément,] *Anecdotes dramatiques,* 3 vols. [Paris: La veuve Duchesne, 1775], 1:179).

14. Bouissou neatly avoids this issue by leaving dance out of consideration, even while acknowledging its relative weight in the overall scheme of the opera: "Quant aux danses, nous n'en traiterons point car elles sont la partie la plus connue, la plus accessible et la plus appréciée de l'oeuvre de Rameau. Les 40 danses des *Boréades*—chiffre élevé relativement à la moyenne des autres tragédies lyriques qui en comprennent 28 pour *Hippolyte et Aricie,* 21 pour *Castor et Pollux,* 36 pour *Dardanus* et 31 pour *Zoroastre*" (Bouissou, *Jean-Philippe Rameau:* Les Boréades, 164).

15. Catherine Kintzler, *Jean-Philippe Rameau: Splendeur et naufrage de l'esthétique du plaisir à l'âge classique* (Paris: Le Sycomore, 1983), 241–55.

16. Jean-Philippe Rameau, *Les Boréades. Tragédie lyrique de Jean-Philippe Rameau (1764).* Facsimilé de la partition originale (Paris: Stil, 1982), 35–36.

17. Ibid., 35–36.

18. Ibid., 88–89.

19. Ibid., 88.

20. Michael Walsh, "Sound Track: 'Aria' Operatunities," *Film Comment* 24 (June 1988): 77.

21. Richard Corliss, "Opera for the Inoperative: Catchy Tunes and Deep Passions Highlight the *Aria* Anthology," *Time* 131 (May 2, 1988), 79.

22. For descriptions of these productions, see Michael Margolin, "Our Critics Abroad: Ann Arbor," *Opera* 34 (March 1983): 298–99, and Charles Pitt, "Our Critics Abroad: Lille," *Opera* 37 (August 1986): 940–41.

23. Thomas Christensen, *Rameau and Musical Thought in the Enlightenment,* Cambridge Studies in Music Theory and Analysis, 4 (Cambridge: Cambridge University Press, 1993).

24. Carl Dahlhaus, *Foundations of Music History,* trans. J. B. Robinson (Cambridge: Cambridge University Press, 1983), see especially 19–33.

Sources Cited

THIS LIST has been divided into four parts: musical sources, livrets, sources originating before 1800, and sources originating after 1800. The distinction drawn between the latter two categories has been pursued as rigorously as possible: if the source originated prior to 1800, it has been so listed, even if it is available in a later edition, reprint, or facsimile.

Musical Sources

ATYS. / TRAGEDIE. / MISE EN MUSIQUE. / *Par Feu M^r. De Lully Esc^{er}.* *Con^{er}.* / *Secretaire du Roy, Maison, Couronne* / *de France et de ses Finances, et* *Surjntendant* / *de la Musique de Sa Majesté.* / SECONDE EDITION. / Gravée par H. de Baussen. / A PARIS. / *A l'Entrée de la Porte de l'Academie* *Royale* / *de Musique au Palais Royal,* / *rüe S^r. Honoré.* / M. DCC IX / *Avec Privilege du Roy.* [Facsimile, Béziers: Société de musicologie de Languedoc, 1987.]

CASTOR ET POLLUX, / TRAGEDIE / MISE EN MUSIQUE / *Par Monsieur* Rameau, / Représentée pour la premiere fois, par l'Académie Royale / de Musique, le 24 Octobre 1737. / *Prix en blanc douze livres.* / SE VEND A PARIS, / Chez{ / PRAULT fils, Quay de Conty, vis-à-vis la descente du Pontneuf, à la Charité, / la veuve BOIVIN, rue Saint Honoré, à la Regle d'or, / M. LECLAIR, rue de Roule, à la Croix d'or, / M. DUVAL, Marchand Papetier, proche l'Opera, / &chez l'AUTEUR, rue des Bons-Enfans. / *Avec Approbation* *& Privilege du Roy.*

CASTOR / ET POLLUX. / TRAGÉDIE. / *Mise en Musique* / PAR M^R. RAMEAU. / *Représentée pour la premiere fois par L'Academie Royale de* *Musique Le 24.* / *Octobre 1737. Refondu, Et remis au Théâtre au Mois de Decembre 1754.* / Prix en blanc 15th. / *Gravée par Le S^r. Hue.* / SE VEND A PARIS / *Chez* { / *L'Auteur Rue des bons Enfans.* / *Et aux adresses ordinaires.* / *A la Porte de l'Opera.* / Avec approbation Et privilege du Roy. / *Imprimée par* *Monthulay.*

DARDANUS, / *TRAGEDIE,* / MISE EN MUSIQUE / PAR M. RAMEAU, / ET REPRESENTÉE POUR LA PREMIERE FOIS, / PAR L'ACADÉMIE ROYALE DE MUSIQUE, / Le dix-neuf Octobre 1739. / *Le Prix, en blanc, 13.* liv. *Et relié,* 15 liv. / A PARIS, / Chez { / L'AUTEUR, RUE DES BONS-EN-FANS, A L'HOTEL D'EFFIAT. / LA VEUVE BOIVIN, RUE S. HONORE', A LA REGLE D'OR. / M. LE CLAIR, RUE DU ROULE, A LA CROIX D'OR. / Me MONET, GRANDE PLACE DE L'HOSTEL DE SOISSONS, A LA LYRE D'OR. / *AVEC APPROBATION ET PRIVILEGE DU ROY.*

DARDANUS, / *NOUVELLE TRAGÉDIE,* / MISE EN MUSIQUE / PAR M. RAMEAU, / ET RÉPRÉSENTÉE POUR LA PREMIERE FOIS, / *PAR L'A-CADÉMIE ROYALE DE MUSIQUE,* / LE 7. AVRIL 1744. / *Le prix, en blanc,*

13. liv. *Et relié,* 15. liv. / A PARIS, / CHEZ { / L'AUTEUR, RUE S. HONORE', A LA REGLE D'OR, / M. LE CLAIR, RUE DU ROULE, A LA CROIX D'OR. / *AVEC APPROBATION ET PRIVILEGE DU ROY.*

HIPPOLITE / *ET* / ARICIE / *Tragedie Mise en Musique* / PAR / M^R. RAMEAU / *Représentée par l'Academie* / *Royale de Musique* / *Le Jeudy Premier Octobre 1733.* / PARTITION IN FOLIO / Gravé par De Gland / *Prix en blanc 18th.* / *et 21th.* *Reliée.* / A PARIS / Chez { / *L'Hauteur Rue du Chantre* / *Le S^r. Boivin M^d. Rüe S^r. Honoré à la Regle d'Or.* / *Le S^r. Le Clerc M^d. Rüe du Roule à la Croix d'Or.* / *Avec Privilegé du Roy* / *Imprimé par Montulé.*

LES INDES GALANTES, / *BALLET,* / RÉDUIT A QUATRE GRANDS CONCERTS: / AVEC UNE NOUVELLE ENTRE'E COMPLETTE. / *Par Monsieur RAMEAU.* / Le Prix en blanc douze livres. / SE VEND A PARIS, / Chez { / M. BOIVIN, rüe Saint Honoré, à la Regle d'Or. / M. LECLAIR, rue du Roulle, à la Croix d'Or. / L'AUTEUR, rüe des Bons Enfans, à l'Hôtel d'Effiat. / *AVEC PRIVILEGE DU ROI.*

Rameau, Jean-Philippe. *Les Boréades. Tragédie lyrique de Jean-Philippe Rameau (1764).* Facsimilé de la partition originale. Paris: Stil, 1982.

_____. "Hippolyte et Aricie, Tragedie de M^r. Pellegrin mise en Musique par M^r. Rameau; représentée pour la premiere fois le premier octobre 1733." *F-Pn,* Vm² 319.

_____. *Oeuvres complètes.* 18 vols. Edited by Camille Saint-Saëns et al. Paris: A. Durand et fils, 1895–1924. Reprint, New York: Broude Brothers, 1968.

_____. "Zoroastre, Opéra, tragédie avec un prologue, par Cahusac, Musique de Rameau. 1749." *F-Po,* A.167^c.

Livrets

CASTOR / ET / POLLUX, / *TRAGEDIE* / *Représentée pour la prémiere fois,* / PAR L'ACADEMIE ROYALE / DE MUSIQUE; / *Le vingt-quatriéme jour d'Octobre* 1737. / DE L'IMPRIMERIE / De JEAN-BAPTISTE-CHRISTOPHE BALLARD, / Seul Imprimeur du Roy, & de l'Académie Royale de Musique / M. D CCXXXVII. / *AVEC PRIVILEGE DU ROY.*

CASTOR / ET / POLLUX, / TRAGÉDIE, / REPRÉSENTÉE / *POUR LA PREMIERE FOIS,* / PAR L'ACADÉMIE ROYALE / *DE MUSIQUE,* / *Le* 24 *Octobre* 1737. / Et Remise au Théâtre le huit Janvier 1754. / *PRIX XXX SOLS.* / *AUX DÉPENS DE L'ACADÉMIE.* / A PARIS,Chez la V. DELORMEL & FILS, Imprimeur de ladite / Académie, rue du Foin, à l'Image Ste. Geneviéve. / *On trouvera des Livres de Paroles à la Salle de l'Opéra.* / M. DCC. LIV. / *AVEC APPROBATION ET PRIVILEGE DU ROY.*

DARDANUS, / *TRAGEDIE* / REPRÉSENTÉE POUR LA PREMIERE FOIS, / PAR L'ACADEMIE ROYALE / DE MUSIQUE, / *Le Jeudy dix-neuf Novembre* 1739. / DE L'IMPRIMERIE / De JEAN-BAPTISTE-CHRISTOPHE BALLARD, / Seul Imprimeur du Roy, et de l'Academie Royale de Musique. / A Paris, au Mont-Parnasse, rüe Saint-Jean-de-Beauvais. / M. D CCXXXIX. / *AVEC PRIVILEGE DU ROY.* / LE PRIX EST DE XXX. SOLS.

DARDANUS, / *TRAGEDIE* / REPRÉSENTÉE POUR LA PREMIERE FOIS, / PAR L'ACADEMIE ROYALE / DE MUSIQUE, / *Le Jeudy dix-neuf No-*

vembre 1739. / NOUVELLE EDITION, / *Remise au théâtre, le mardi* 21 *Avril* 1744. / DE L'IMPRIMERIE / De Jean-Baptiste-Christophe Ballard, / Doyen des imprimeurs du Roy, seul pour la musique, / et pour l'Academie royale de musique. / A Paris, au Mont-Parnasse, ruë saint-Jean-de-Beauvais. / M. DCC XLIV. / *AVEC PRIVILEGE DU ROY.* / LE PRIX EST DE XXX SOLS.

HIPPOLYTE / ET / ARICIE, / *TRAGEDIE,* / REPRÉSENTÉE POUR LA PREMIERE FOIS, / PAR L'ACADEMIE ROYALE / DE MUSIQUE; / *Le Jeudy premier Octobre* 1733. / DE L'IMPRIMERIE / De Jean-Baptiste-Christophe Ballard, / Seul Imprimeur du Roy, & de l'Académie Royale de Musique. / M. D CCXXXIII. / *AVEC PRIVILEGE DU ROY.* / LE PRIX EST DE XXX. SOLS.

HIPPOLYTE / ET / ARICIE, / *TRAGEDIE,* / REPRÉSENTÉE / PAR L'A-CADEMIE ROYALE / DE MUSIQUE; / Pour la premiere fois, le jeudi premier octobre 1733. / *Remise au théâtre le mardy 11 septembre* 1742. / DE L'IMPRIMERIE / DE J-B-CHRISTOPHE BALLARD, seul imprimeur / du Roi, et de l'académie royale de musique; / Paris, au Mont-Parnasse, rue saint Jean-de-Beauvais. / M. DCC. XLII. / *Avec Privilége de Sa Majesté.* / LE PRIX EST DE XXX. SOLS.

Recueil general des opera representez par l'Académie royale de musique, depuis son etablissement. 16 vols. Paris: Ballard, 1703–1746. Facsimile ed. in 3 vols., Geneva: Slatkine, 1971.

ZOROASTRE, / TRAGEDIE. / *REPRESENTÉE* / PAR L'ACADEMIE ROY-ALE / *DE MUSIQUE,* / POUR LA PREMIERE FOIS, / *Le Vendredy cinq Décembre* 1749. / *PRIX XXX SOLS.* / *AUX DEPENS DE L'ACADEMIE.* / On trouvera les Livres de Paroles à la Salle de l'Opera & à l'Academie Royale / de Musique, rue S. Nicaise. / M. D.C.C. XLIX. / *AVEC APPROBATION ET PRIVILEGE DU ROY.*

ZOROASTRE, / *OPÉRA,* / REPRÉSENTÉ / *POUR LA PREMIERE FOIS* / PAR L'ACADÉMIE ROYALE / *DE MUSIQUE,* / Le 5. Décembre 1749. / ET REMIS AU THÉATRE / *Le Mardi 20 Janvier* 1756. / *PRIX XXX SOLS.* / *AUX DÉPENS DE L'ACADÉMIE.* / A PARIS, Chez la V. Delormel & Fils, Imprimeur de / ladite Académie, rue du Foin à l'Image St. Geneviéve. / *On trouvera des Livres de Paroles à la Salle de l'Opéra.* / M. DCC. LVI. / *AVEC APPROBATION ET PRIVILEGE DU ROI.*

Sources Originating before 1800

Alembert, Jean le Rond d'. *Elemens de musique, theorique et pratique, suivant les principes de M. Rameau.* Paris: David l'ainé, Le Breton, Durand, 1752. Reprint, Monuments of Music and Music Literature in Facsimile. 2 / 19. New York: Broude Brothers, 1966.

André, Yves-Marie. *Essai sur le beau.* Rev. ed. Paris: Ferra ainé, 1818.

Argenson, René-Louis de Voyer de Paulmy, Marquis d'. *Journal et mémoires du marquis d'Argenson.* Edited by E. J. B. Rathery. 9 vols. Paris: Madame veuve Jules Renouard, 1859–1867.

_____. "Notices sur les Oeuvres de théâtre." Edited by H. Lagrave. 2 vols. *Studies on Voltaire and the Eighteenth Century* 42–43 (1966).

Aristotle. *Generation of Animals.* Translated by A. L. Peck. The Loeb Classical Library. Cambridge: Harvard University Press, 1953.

[Batteux, Charles.] *Les Beaux arts reduits a un même principe.* Paris: Durand, 1747. Facsimile, N.p.: Johnson Reprint, 1970.

Boileau-Despréaux, Nicolas. *Oeuvres.* Edited by Georges Mongrédien. Paris: Garnier frères, 1961.

[Boindin, Nicolas.] *Lettres historiques sur tous les spectacles de Paris.* 2 vols. Paris: Pierre Prault, 1719.

Brossard, Sebastien de. *Dictionaire de musique, contenant une explication des termes grecs, latins, italiens, & françois, les plus usitez dans la musique.* 2d ed. Paris: Christophe Ballard, 1705. Reprint, edited by Harald Heckmann. Hilversum: Frits Knuf, 1965.

Cahusac, Louis de. *La Danse ancienne et moderne ou Traité historique de la danse.* 3 vols. The Hague: Jean Neaulme, 1754.

Chabanon, Michel-Paul-Guy de. "Chabanon's Éloge de M. Rameau." Translated by Edward R. Reilly. *Studies in Music from the University of Western Ontario* 8 (1983), 1–24.

"Chansonnier Maurepas." *F-Pn.* Français 12616–12659.

[Chateau-Lyon, Pierre-Louis d'Aquin de.] *Siecle litteraire de Louis XV ou Lettres sur les hommes celebres.* 2d ed. 2 vols. Amsterdam: Duchesne, 1754.

[Clément, Jean-Marie-Bernard.] *Anecdotes dramatiques.* 3 vols. Paris: La veuve Duchesne, 1775.

Collé, Charles. *Journal et mémoires de Charles Collé sur les hommes de lettres, les ouvrages dramatiques et les événements le plus mémorables du règne de Louis XV (1748–1772).* Edited by Honoré Bonhomme. Rev. ed. 3 vols. Paris: Firmin Didot frères, 1868.

Crousaz, Jean-Pierre de. *Traité du beau.* Amsterdam: François l'Honoré, 1715.

Desfontaines, Pierre-François-Guyot. *Observations sur les écrits modernes.* Reprint, 34 vols. in 4. Geneva: Slatkine, 1967.

Le Dictionnaire de l'Académie françoise. 2 vols. Paris: Jean-Baptiste Coignard, 1694.

Diderot, Denis. "Denis Diderot: Écrits inconnus de jeunesse." Edited by J. T. de Booy. 2 vols. *Studies on Voltaire and the Eighteenth Century* 119–20 (1974).

"Dissertation sur la musique italienne & françoise." *Mercure de France* (November 1713): 3–62.

Dubos, Jean-Baptiste. *Réflexions critiques sur la poësie et sur la peinture.* 7th ed. 3 vols. Paris: Pissot, 1770. Facsimile, Geneva: Slatkine, 1967.

Dubuisson, Simon-Henri. *Lettres du Commissaire Dubuisson au Marquis de Caumont, 1735–1741.* Edited by Albert Rouxel. Paris: P. Arnould, 1882.

Encyclopédie, ou Dictionnaire raisonné des sciences, des arts et des métiers. Edited by Denis Diderot and Jean le Rond d'Alembert. 28 vols. Paris: various publishers, 1751–1772. Facsimile in 5 vols. New York: Pergamon Press, 1969.

"Essai d'eloge historique de feu M. Rameau." *Mercure de France* (October 1764).

Fénelon, François de la Mothe. *Lettre a l'académie.* Edited by Ernesta Caldarini. Geneva: Droz, 1970.

Fontenelle, Bernard Le Bovier de. *Réflexions sur la poétique* [1742], *Oeuvres complètes,* 3. Paris, 1818. Facsimile, Geneva: Slatkine, 1968.

Grand dictionnaire universel du xixe siècle. Edited by Pierre Larousse. 17 vols. Paris: Administration du grand dictionnaire universel, 1866–1879. Facsimile, Geneva: Slatkine, 1982.

Grimm, Friedrich Melchior. *Correspondance littéraire, philosophique et critique par Grimm, Diderot, Raynal, Meister, etc.* Edited by Maurice Tourneux. 16 vols. Paris: Garnier frères, 1877–1882.

———. *Lettre de M. Grimm sur Omphale*. 1752.

Horace. *Horace on the Art of Poetry*. Edited by Edward Henry Blakeney. Freeport: Books for Libraries Press, 1928.

Jugemens sur quelques ouvrages nouveaux. 1744–1746.

[Laborde, Jean-Benjamin de.] *Essai sur la musique ancienne et moderne*. 4 vols. Paris: Ph.-D. Pierres, 1780. Facsimile, New York: AMS Press, 1978.

[Laugier, Marc-Antoine.] *Sentiment d'un harmoniphile sur différents ouvrages de musique*. Edited by A. J. Labbet and A. Léris. Amsterdam: Jombert, Duchesne, Lambert, 1756. Facsimile, Geneva: Minkoff, 1972.

[La Vallière, Louis-César-François de La Baume Le Blanc.] *Ballets, opera, et autres ouvrages lyriques, par ordre chronologique depuis leur origine; avec une table alphabetique des ouvrages et des auteurs*. Paris: Cl.-J. Baptiste Bauche, 1760. Facsimile, London: H. Baron, 1967.

[Mably, Gabriel Bonnot de.] *Lettres a madame la marquise de P . . . sur l'opera*. Paris: Didot, 1741. Facsimile, New York: AMS Press, 1978.

Masson, Charles. *Nouveau traité des regles pour la composition de la musique*. 2d ed. Paris, 1699. Facsimile, New York: Da Capo, 1967.

Mercure de France. 1672–1832.

Montdorge, Antoine-Gautier de. *Réflexions d'un peintre sur l'opéra*. The Hague: Pierre Gosse, 1743.

Parfaict, François and Claude. "Histoire de l'Académie royale de musique depuis son établissement jusqu'à présent." 2 vols. *F-Pn*. Nouvelles acquisitions françaises 6532.

[Pellegrin, Simon-Joseph.] "Dissertation sur la tragede de Médée." *Mercure de France* (January 1729): 152–73.

[Pluche, Noël-Antoine.] *Le Spectacle de la nature, ou Entretiens sur les particularités de l'histoire naturelle*. Rev. ed. 9 vols. Paris: Frères Estienne, 1755.

Prévost, Antoine-François, et al. *Le Pour et contre*. 1733–1746.

———. "*Le Pour et contre* (nos. 1–60)." Edited by Steve Larkin. 2 vols. *Studies on Voltaire and the Eighteenth Century* 309–310 (1993–1994).

Rameau, Jean-Philippe. *Code de musique pratique*. Paris: De l'Imprimerie royale, 1760.

———. *Complete Theoretical Writings*. 6 vols. Edited by Erwin R. Jacobi. N.p.: American Institute of Musicology, 1967–1972.

———. *Démonstration du principe de l'harmonie*. Paris: Durand, Pissot, 1750.

———. *Erreurs sur la musique dans l'Encyclopédie*. Paris: Sebastien Jorry, 1755.

———. *Nouveau système de musique theorique, où l'on découvre le principe de toutes les regles necessaires à la pratique*. Paris: Jean-Baptiste-Christophe Ballard, 1726.

———. *Observations sur notre instinct pour la musique, et son principe*. Paris: Prault fils, Lambert, Duchesne, 1754.

_____. *Treatise on Harmony.* Translated by Philip Gossett. New York: Dover, 1971.

[Rapin, René.] *Reflexions sur la poetique de ce temps, et sur les ouvrages des poètes anciens & modernes.* Edited by E. T. Dubois. Paris: F. Muguet, 1675. Reprint, Geneva: Droz, 1970.

Recueil general des opera representez par l'Académie royale de musique, depuis son etablissement. 16 vols. Paris: Ballard, 1703–1746. Facsimile in 3 vols. Geneva: Slatkine, 1971.

Richelet, Pierre. *Dictionnaire françois, contenant les mots et les choses, plusieurs nouvelles remarques sur la langue françoise: ses expressions propres, figurées & burlesques, la prononciation des mots les plus difficiles, le genre des noms, le regime des verbes: avec les termes les plus connus des arts et des sciences.* 2 vols. Geneva: Jean Herman Widerhold, 1685.

Rousseau, Jean-Baptiste. *Correspondance de Jean-Baptiste Rousseau et de Brossette.* Edited by Paul Bonnefon. 2 vols. Paris: Société nouvelle de librairie et d'édition, 1910–1911.

Rousseau, Jean-Jacques. *Lettre sur la musique françoise.* 1753.

Saint-Évremond, Charles de Saint-Denis, Seigneur de. "Sur les opéras." *Oeuvres en prose.* Edited by René Ternois. 11 vols. Paris: Marcel Didier, 1966.

[Saint-Mard, Toussaint Rémond de.] *Reflexions sur l'opera.* The Hague: Jean Neaulme, 1741. Facsimile, Geneva: Minkoff, 1972.

[Serré de Rieux, Jean de.] *Les Dons des enfans de Latone: La Musique et la Chasse du cerf, poëmes dédiés au roy.* Paris: Pierre Prault, Jean Desaint, Jacques Guerin, 1734.

Titon du Tillet, Évrard. *Description du parnasse françois, exécuté en bronze, suivie d'une liste alphabetique des poëtes, & des musiciens rassemblés sur ce monument.* Paris: La veuve Ribou, Pierre Prault, La veuve Pissot, 1727.

Viéville, Jean-Laurent Le Cerf de la. *Comparaison de la musique italienne et de la musique françoise.* 2d ed. 3 vols. Brussels: François Foppens, 1705. Facsimile, Geneva: Minkoff, 1972.

[Villiers, Pierre de.] "Epitre III. A un Homme qui estimoit de mauvais ouvrages, & sur tout les tragédies de l'opera." *Poesies de D* V***.* Rev. ed. Paris: Jacques Collombat, 1728.

Voltaire [François-Marie Arouet]. *The Complete Works of Voltaire.* Edited by Theodore Besterman et al. 135 vols. Oxford: The Voltaire Foundation, 1968– .

_____. *Oeuvres complètes de Voltaire.* 52 vols. Edited by Louis Moland. Paris: Garnier Frères, 1883–1885.

Sources Originating after 1800

Abbate, Carolyn. "Analysis." *The New Grove Dictionary of Opera.* Edited by Stanley Sadie. 4 vols. London: Macmillan, 1992.

_____. *Unsung Voices: Opera and Musical Narrative in the Nineteenth Century.* Princeton: Princeton University Press, 1991.

Abbate, Carolyn, and Roger Parker. "Dismembering Mozart." *Cambridge Opera Journal* 2 (July 1990): 187–95.

Adler, Guido. *Der Stil in der Musik.* Leipzig: Breitkopf und Härtel, 1929. Reprint, Wiesbaden: Dr. Martin Sändig oHG, 1973.

_____. "Style-Criticism." Translated by Oliver Strunk. *The Musical Quarterly* 20 (1934): 172–76.

Alpers, Svetlana. "Is Art History?" *Daedalus* 106 (Summer 1977): 1–13.

Anthony, James R. *French Baroque Music from Beaujoyeulx to Rameau.* Rev. ed. New York: W. W. Norton, 1978.

_____. "The French Opera-Ballet in the Early 18th Century: Problems of Definition and Classification." *Journal of the American Musicological Society* 18 (1965): 197–206.

Banducci, Antonia Louise. "'Tancrède' by Antoine Danchet and André Campra: Performance History and Reception (1702–1764)." Ph.D. diss., Washington University, 1990.

Barthes, Roland. "The Death of the Author." In *Image Music Text,* translated by Stephen Heath, 142–48. New York: Hill and Wang, 1977.

_____. "Rhetoric of the Image." In *The Responsibility of Forms: Critical Essays on Music, Art, and Representation,* translated by Richard Howard, 27–30. New York: Hill and Wang, 1985.

_____. *S / Z.* Translated by Richard Miller. New York: Hill and Wang, 1974.

Bloom, Harold. *A Map of Misreading.* New York: Oxford University Press, 1975.

Borrel, Eugène. *L'Interprétation de la musique française (de Lully à la révolution).* Paris: Félix Alcan, 1934.

_____. *Jean-Baptiste Lully.* Euterpe, no. 7. Paris: La Colombe, 1949.

Bouissou, Sylvie. In brochure notes for *Les Indes galantes,* by Jean-Philippe Rameau. Harmonia mundi France 901367.69.

_____. *Jean-Philippe Rameau: Les Boréades ou la tragédie oubliée.* Paris: Méridiens Klincksieck, 1992.

Brown, Bruce Alan. *Gluck and the French Theatre in Vienna.* New York: Oxford University Press, 1991.

Brown, Leslie Ellen. "Departures from Lullian Convention in the *Tragédie lyrique* of the *Préramiste* Era." *"Recherches" sur la musique française classique* 22 (1984): 59–78.

Burnham, Scott. "How Music Matters: Poetic Content Revisited." Unpublished paper.

_____. "Musical and Intellectual Values: Interpreting the History of Tonal Theory." *Current Musicology* 53 (1993): 76–88.

Cannone, Belinda. *Philosophies de la musique, 1752–1789.* Théorie et critique à l'âge classique, no. 4. Paris: Klincksieck, 1990.

Christensen, Thomas. *Rameau and Musical Thought in the Enlightenment.* Cambridge Studies in Music Theory and Analysis, no. 4. Cambridge: Cambridge University Press, 1993.

Christie, William, director. *Atys,* by Jean-Baptiste Lully. Harmonia mundi France 901257.59.

Corliss, Richard. "Opera for the Inoperative: Catchy Tunes and Deep Passions Highlight the *Aria* Anthology." *Time* 131 (May 2, 1988): 79.

Cowart, Georgia. *The Origins of Modern Musical Criticism: French and Italian Music 1600–1750.* Studies in Musicology, no. 38. Ann Arbor: UMI Research Press, 1981.

Culler, Jonathan. *Ferdinand de Saussure*. Rev. ed. Ithaca: Cornell University Press, 1976.

Dacier, Émile. "L'Opéra au xviiiᵉ siècle. Les Premières représentations du 'Dardanus' de Rameau (novembre-décembre 1739)." *La Revue musicale* 3 (April 1903): 163–73.

Dahlhaus, Carl. *Foundations of Music History*. Translated by J. B. Robinson. Cambridge: Cambridge University Press, 1983.

Dill, Charles. "Creative Process in Rameau's *Castor et Pollux*." In *The Creative Process*. Studies in the History of Music, no. 3. New York: Broude Brothers, 1992.

————. "Music, Beauty, and the Paradox of Rationalism." In *French Musical Thought, 1600–1800*, edited by Georgia Cowart. Studies in Music, no. 105. Ann Arbor: UMI Research Press, 1989.

————. "Rameau Reading Lully: Meaning and System in Rameau's Recitative Tradition." *Cambridge Opera Journal* 6 (March 1994): 1–17.

————. "The Reception of Rameau's *Castor et Pollux* in 1737 and 1754." Ph.D. diss., Princeton University, 1989.

Duron, Jean. "Pellegrin, Abbé Simon-Joseph." *The New Grove Dictionary of Opera*. Edited by Stanley Sadie. 4 vols. London: Macmillan, 1992. 3: 939–40.

Einzeldrucke vor 1800. 12 vols. Répertoire international des sources musicales, A / 1. Kassel: Bärenreiter, 1971–1992.

Fajon, Robert. *L'Opéra à Paris du roi soleil à Louis le Bien-aimé*. Geneva: Slatkine, 1984.

Farrar, Carol Reglin. "Seven String Instrument Treatises of Michel Corette: Translation with Commentary." Ph.D. diss., University of North Texas, 1978.

Flaherty, Gloria. *Opera in the Development of German Critical Thought*. Princeton: Princeton University Press, 1978.

Foucault, Michel. *The Order of Things: An Archaeology of the Human Sciences*. New York: Vintage Books, 1973.

————. "What Is an Author?" translated Josué V. Harari. In *The Foucault Reader*, edited by Paul Rabinow, 101–20. New York: Pantheon, 1984.

Freud, Sigmund. "The Unconscious." *The Standard Edition of the Complete Psychological Works of Sigmund Freud*. Edited by James Strachey. 24 vols. London: Hogarth Press and the Institute of Psycho-Analysis, 1953–1975.

Girdlestone, Cuthbert. *Jean-Philippe Rameau: His Life and Work*. Rev. ed. New York: Dover, 1969.

————. *La Tragédie en musique (1673–1750) considérée comme genre littéraire*. Geneva: Droz, 1972.

————. "Voltaire, Rameau et Samson." *"Recherches" sur la musique française classique* 6 (1966): 133–43.

Girdlestone, Cuthbert, Albert Cohen, and Mary Cyr. "Rameau, Jean-Philippe." *The New Grove Dictionary of Music and Musicians*. Edited by Stanley Sadie. 6th ed. 20 vols. New York: Macmillan, 1980. 15: 559–73.

Godfrey, Sima, ed. Preface to *The Anxiety of Anticipation*. Yale French Studies, no. 66. New Haven: Yale University Press, 1984.

————, ed. "The Anxiety of Anticipation: Ulterior Motives in French Poetry." In

The Anxiety of Anticipation. Yale French Studies, no. 66. New Haven: Yale University Press, 1984.

Green, Thomas R. "Early Rameau Sources: Studies in the Origins and Dating of the Operas and Other Musical Works." 3 vols. Ph.D. diss., Brandeis University, 1992.

———. "Les Fragments d'opéras dans la partition autographe de *Zéphyre.*" In *JPR,* 266–68.

Hosler, Bellamy. *Changing Aesthetic Views of Instrumental Music in 18th-Century Germany.* Studies in Musicology, no. 42. Ann Arbor: UMI Research Press, 1981.

Kallberg, Jeffrey. "The Rhetoric of Genre: Chopin's Nocturne in G Minor." *Nineteenth Century Music* 11 (Spring 1988): 238–61.

Keiler, Allan R. "Music as Metalanguage: Rameau's Fundamental Bass." In *Music Theory: Special Topics,* 83–100. Edited by Richmond Browne. New York: Academic Press, 1981.

Kintzler, Catherine. *Jean-Philippe Rameau. Splendeur et naufrage de l'esthétique du plaisir à l'âge classique.* Paris: Le Sycomore, 1983.

———. *Poétique de l'opéra français de Corneille à Rousseau.* N.p.: Minerve, 1991.

Kintzler, Catherine, and Jean-Claude Malgoire, eds. *Jean-Philippe Rameau. Musique raisonée.* N.p.: Stock, 1980.

Kramer, Lawrence. *Music as Cultural Practice, 1800–1900.* Berkeley: University of California Press, 1990.

Kuijken, Sigiswald. In brochure notes for *Zoroastre,* by Jean-Philippe Rameau. Harmonia mundi 1C 157.

Lacan, Jacques. "The Mirror Stage as Formative of the Function of the I as Revealed in Psychoanalytic Experience." In *Écrits: A Selection,* translated by Alan Sheridan. New York: W. W. Norton, 1977.

La Gorce, Jérôme de, ed. *Jean-Philippe Rameau. Colloque international organisé par la société Rameau. Dijon—21–24 septembre 1983.* Paris: Champion and Geneva: Slatkine, 1987.

———. *L'Opéra à Paris au temps de Louis XIV. Histoire d'un théâtre.* Paris: Éditions Desjonquères, 1992.

La Laurencie, Lionel de. *Rameau.* Paris: Librairie Renouard, 1926.

Laloy, Louis. *Rameau.* 3d ed. Paris: Félix Alcan, 1919.

Launay, Denise, ed. *La Querelle des bouffons.* 3 vols. Geneva: Minkoff, 1973.

Lewin, David. "Music Theory, Phenomenology, and Modes of Perception." *Music Perception* 3 (Summer 1986): 327–92.

Maniates, Maria Rika. "'Sonate, que me veux-tu?' The Enigma of French Musical Aesthetics in the 18th Century." *Current Musicology* 9 (1969): 117–40.

Margolin, Michael. "Our Critics Abroad: Ann Arbor." *Opera* 34 (March 1983): 298–99.

Masson, Paul-Marie. "Le 'Ballet héroïque.'" *La Revue musicale* 9 (1928), 132–54.

———. "Les Deux versions du 'Dardanus' de Rameau." *Acta musicologica* 26 (1954): 36–48.

———. "Lullistes et Ramistes, 1733–1752." *L'Année musicale* 1 (1911): 187–213.

———. "La Musique italienne en France pendant le premier tiers du xviiie siècle."

In *Mélanges de philologie, d'histoire et de littérature offerts à Henri Hauvette,* 353–65. Paris: Les Presses françaises, 1934. Reprint, Geneva: Slatkine, 1972.

———. "L'Opéra au xviiiᵉ siècle. Les premières représentations du 'Dardanus' de Rameau (novembre-décembre 1739)." *La Revue musicale* 2 (April 1903): 167–73.

———. *L'Opéra de Rameau.* Paris: Henri Laurens, 1930.

———. "Musique italienne et musique française. La première querelle." *Rivista musicale italiana* 19 (1912): 519–45.

Mitchell, W. J. T., ed. *Against Theory: Literary Studies and the New Pragmatism.* Chicago: University of Chicago Press, 1985.

Morel, Jacques. "*Hippolyte et Aricie* de Rameau et Pellegrin dans l'histoire du mythe de Phèdre." In *JPR,* 89–99.

Nehamas, Alexander. "Writer, Text, Work, Author." In *Literature and the Question of Philosophy,* edited by Anthony J. Cascardi, 265–91. Baltimore: Johns Hopkins University Press, 1987.

Neubauer, John. *The Emancipation of Music from Language: Departure from Mimesis in Eighteenth-Century Aesthetics.* New Haven: Yale University Press, 1986.

Pitt, Charles. "Our Critics Abroad: Lille." *Opera* 37 (August 1986): 940–41.

Poizat, Michel. *The Angel's Cry: Beyond the Pleasure Principle in Opera.* Translated by Arthur Denner. Ithaca: Cornell University Press, 1992.

Powers, Harold S. "Language Models and Musical Analysis." *Ethnomusicology* 24 (1980): 1–60.

Reckow, Fritz. "'Cacher l'Art par l'Art même.' Jean-Baptiste Lullys 'Armide'- Monolog und die 'Kunst des Verbergens.'" In *Analysen. Beiträge zu einer Problemgeschichte des Komponierens. Festschrift für Hans Heinrich Eggebrecht zum 65. Geburtstag.* Beiheft zum Archiv für Musikwissenschaft, no. 23. Stuttgart: F. Steiner, 1984.

Robrieux, Jean-Jacques. "Jean-Philippe Rameau et l'opinion philosophique en France au dix-huitième siècle." *Studies on Voltaire and the Eighteenth Century* 238 (1985).

Rosow, Lois. "Lully's *Armide* at the Paris Opéra: A Performance History: 1686–1766." Ph.D. diss., Brandeis University, 1981.

Russell, Trusten Wheeler. *Voltaire, Dryden, and Heroic Tragedy.* New York: Columbia University Press, 1946.

Russo, Paolo. "Les Incertitudes de la tragédie lyrique: *Zoroastre* de Louis de Cahusac." *Revue de musicologie* 75 (1989): 47–64.

Sadler, Graham. In brochure notes to *Castor et Pollux,* by Jean-Philippe Rameau. Erato 4509–95311-2.

———. "La Bruère, Charles-Antoine Le Clerc de." *The New Grove Dictionary of Opera.* Edited by Stanley Sadie. 4 vols. London: Macmillan, 1992. 2: 1071–72.

———. "Patrons and Pasquinades: Rameau in the 1730s." *Journal of the Royal Musical Association* 113 (1988): 314–37.

———. "Rameau, Pellegrin and the Opéra: The Revisions of 'Hippolyte et Aricie' during Its First Season." *The Musical Times* 124 (September 1983): 533–37.

———. "Rameau's Last Opera: *Abaris, ou Les Boréades.*" *The Musical Times* 116 (April 1975): 327–29.

_____. "Rameau's 'Zoroastre': The 1756 Reworking." *The Musical Times* 120 (April 1979): 301–3.

_____. "A Re-Examination of Rameau's Self-Borrowings." In *Jean-Baptiste Lully and the Music of the French Baroque: Essays in Honor of James R. Anthony*, edited by John Hajdu Heyer, 259–89. Cambridge: Cambridge University Press, 1989.

Sadler, Graham, and Albert Cohen. "Jean-Philippe Rameau." In *The New Grove French Baroque Masters: Lully, Charpentier, Lalande, Couperin, Rameau*, 205–308. New York: W. W. Norton, 1986.

Saussure, Ferdinand de. *Course in General Linguistics*. Edited by Charles Bally and Albert Sechehaye. Translated by Roy Harris. London: Duckworth, 1983.

Schneider, Herbert. *Die Rezeption der Opern Lullys im Frankreich des Ancien régime*. Mainzer Studien zur Musikwissenschaft, no. 16. Tutzing: Hans Schneider, 1982.

Sclippa, Norbert. *La Loi du père et les droits du coeur: Essai sur les tragédies de Voltaire*. Histoire des idées et critique littéraire, no. 326. Geneva: Droz, 1993.

Snyders, Georges. *Le Goût musical en France aux xviie et xviiie siècles*. Études de psychologie et de philosophie, no. 18. Paris: J. Vrin, 1968.

Stafford, Barbara Maria. *Body Criticism: Imaging the Unseen in Enlightenment Art and Medicine*. Cambridge: The MIT Press, 1991.

Tessier, André. "Correspondance d'André Cardinal des Touches et du Prince Antoine 1er de Monaco (suite)." *La Revue musicale* 8 (February 1927): 104–17.

Tiersot, Julien. "Lettres inédites de Rameau." *La Revue musicale* 16 (1935), 15–21.

Verba, E. Cynthia. "The Development of Rameau's Thoughts on Modulation and Chromatics." *Journal of the American Musicological Society* 26 (1973): 69–91.

_____. "Rameau's Views on Modulation and Their Background in French Theory." *Journal of the American Musicological Society* 31 (1978): 467–79.

Walsh, Michael. "Sound Track: 'Aria' Operatunities." *Film Comment* 24 (June 1988): 76–77.

Webster, James. "Mozart's Operas and the Myth of Musical Unity." *Cambridge Opera Journal* 2 (July 1990): 197–218.

Index

Page references in italics refer to music examples.

About the Author

CHARLES DILL is Associate Professor of Music History
at the University of Wisconsin–Madison.